JUST AMERICAN WARS

This book examines the moral choices faced by U.S. political and military leaders in deciding when and how to employ force, from the American Revolution to the present day.

Specifically, the book looks at discrete ethical dilemmas in various American conflicts from a just war perspective. For example, was the *casus belli* of the American Revolution just, and more specifically, was the Continental Congress a "legitimate" political authority? Was it just for Truman to drop the atomic bomb on Japan? How much of a role did the egos of Kennedy, Johnson, and Nixon play in prolonging the Vietnam War? Often there are trade-offs that civilian and military leaders must take into account, such as General Scott's 1847 decision to bombard the city of Veracruz in order to quickly move his troops off the malarial Mexican coast. The book also considers the moral significance and policy practicalities of different motives and courses of action. The case studies provided highlight the nuances and even limits of just war principles, such as just cause, right intention, legitimate authority, last resort, likelihood of success, discrimination, and proportionality, and principles for ending war such as order, justice, and conciliation.

This book will be of interest for students of just war theory, ethics, philosophy, American history, and military history more generally.

Eric Patterson is Dean of the School of Government at Regent University and a Research Fellow at Georgetown University's Berkley Center for Religion, Peace, and World Affairs, U.S.A. He is the author or editor of over a dozen books, including *Ending Wars Well* (2012) and *Philosophers on War* (2017).

War, Conflict and Ethics

Ethical judgments are relevant to all phases of protracted violent conflict and inter-state war. Before, during, and after the tumult, martial forces are guided, in part, by their sense of morality for assessing whether an action is (morally) right or wrong, an event has good and/or bad consequences, and an individual (or group) is inherently virtuous or evil. This new book series focuses on the morality of decisions by military and political leaders to engage in violence and the normative underpinnings of military strategy and tactics in the prosecution of the war.

Series Editors:

Michael L. Gross
University of Haifa
and
James Pattison
University of Manchester

Chinese Just War Ethics

Origin, development, and dissent
Edited by Ping-cheung Lo and Sumner B. Twiss

Utilitarianism and the Ethics of War

William H. Shaw

Privatizing War

A moral theory
William Brand Feldman

Just War Thinkers

From Cicero to the 21st Century
Edited by Daniel R. Brunstetter and Cian O'Driscoll

Contemporary Just War

Theory and Practice
Tamar Meisels

Just American Wars

Ethical Dilemmas in U.S. Military History
Eric Patterson

For more information about this series, please visit: https://www.routledge.com/War-Conflict-and-Ethics/book-series/WCE

JUST AMERICAN WARS

Ethical Dilemmas in U.S. Military History

Eric Patterson

Routledge
Taylor & Francis Group

LONDON AND NEW YORK

First published 2019
by Routledge
2 Park Square, Milton Park, Abingdon, Oxon OX14 4RN

and by Routledge
711 Third Avenue, New York, NY 10017

Routledge is an imprint of the Taylor & Francis Group, an informa business

British Library Cataloguing-in-Publication Data
A catalogue record for this book is available from the British Library

Library of Congress Cataloging-in-Publication Data
Names: Patterson, Eric, 1971– author.
Title: Just American wars : ethical dilemmas in U.S.
military history / Eric Patterson.
Other titles: Ethical dilemmas in U.S. military history
Description: Milton Park, Abingdon ; New York, NY : Routledge, [2019] |
Series: War, conflict and ethics | Includes index.
Identifiers: LCCN 2018021617 | ISBN 9781138313989 (hardback) |
ISBN 9781138314016 (pbk.) | ISBN 9780429457302 (e-book)
Subjects: LCSH: United States–History, Military–Case studies. | Military
ethics–United States. | War–Moral and ethical aspects. | Just war doctrine.
Classification: LCC E181 .P388 2019 | DDC 355.00973–dc23
LC record available at https://lccn.loc.gov/2018021617

ISBN: 978-1-138-31398-9 (hbk)
ISBN: 978-1-138-31401-6 (pbk)
ISBN: 978-0-429-45730-2 (ebk)

Typeset in Bembo
by Out of House Publishing

With gratitude to my teachers, especially Mrs. Elizabeth Pierce, who ignited a love of learning in me and a generation of their pupils.

CONTENTS

ACKNOWLEDGMENTS

This book grew out of a challenge: "Was the American Revolution a just war?" That challenge, and what became Chapter 2, was presented on a conference panel at the 2013 annual meeting of the American Political Science Association (APSA). Of course, the American "Revolution" was not really revolution, in the strictest sense of the word, because it did not burn down the old regime and implant a radical, revolutionary one in its place as did the French, Chinese, and Russian revolutions. Instead, the colonists argued for decades that they were simply Englishmen who wanted to have the same rights as Englishmen living on the British Isles. As Professor Emeritus Joseph Kickasola remarked to me in 2013, what was self-defensive in 1775 became the American War for Independence by 1776.

That APSA experience surprised me because several panelists and many in the audience were skeptical of the justness of the American cause in the 1770s. Indeed, from time to time one hears a phrase that is simply incomprehensible to me: "One man's terrorist is another man's freedom fighter," thus equating George Washington with scoundrels, criminals, and terrorists such as Che Guevara and Osama bin Laden. This demonstrates a lack of moral clarity in contemporary thinking that cannot, as Jean Bethke Elshtain observed, "make right distinctions." Such distinctions include the difference between George Washington wearing a uniform and building a modern army under the civilian control of the Continental Congress and Osama bin Laden, an international criminal on the run even from his own homeland, launching civilian jet liners at civilian office buildings in New York City. Such distinctions include the difference between Washington, Adams, and Jefferson on the one hand, and Lenin, Trotsky, and Stalin on the other. It is the counterfactual difference between the U.S. getting the atomic bomb in 1945 rather than the Soviet Union. And, I believe, we would find similar differences between our closest allies (e.g. the United Kingdom, Canada, Australia, and some others) if we were to make similar comparisons.

One can quickly see the genesis of this book. I do not think that the U.S. was always or is always just, but as many scholars from Niebuhr to Elshtain have noted, the U.S. has been unique in attempting to marry its democratic idealism with its pursuit of the national interest. The approach of this writing is indebted also, in part, to an author whom I have never met: Michael Burleigh, whose careful analysis of the ethical, moral, and religious underpinnings of political decisions in World War II is a model that I wanted to emulate.

A book of this nature is aided by many individuals, from Mark David Hall, who sponsored that first APSA panel, to many fellow scholars who read individual chapters or the entire manuscript. This includes Marc LiVecche, Keith Pavlischek, James Turner Johnson, Cian O'Driscoll, Mark Tooley, at least three anonymous reviewers, and certainly some friends that I have mistakenly neglected. I have also been aided by excellent research assistance by my graduate students at Regent University, including Nathan Gill (who co-authored a parallel essay with me for *Journal of Military Ethics*), Brian Ballas, Jacob Stephens, Linda Waits-Kamau, Alise Krapane, and Peter Purcell.

Finally, this book is dedicated to my teachers. I am confident that I can speak for most scholars that we can point to many individuals from our childhood as well as our maturing years who cultivated a love of learning and forced the honing of our academic skills. I am indebted to those individuals, and many of my classmates from Fallbrook, California, will recognize these names as individuals who motivated and shaped us: Mrs. Okey, Mr. Howell, Mrs. Crain, Mrs. Stillman, Mrs. Burton, Mr. Burton, Mrs. McCarthy, Mrs. Howard, Mrs. Cathers, Mr. Graves, Ms. Cafferel, Mr. Jones, Mr. Kettering, Mrs. Hartford (who later hired me to teach high school), Mr. Allison, Mr. Walker, Ms. Bradley, Mrs. Critchley, Mr. Carpenter, Mr. Berglund, Mr. Fleming, Mr. Farrimond, Ms. Esbensen, Mrs. O'Connor, and others.

But in a league of her own, is my second and third grade teacher, Mrs. Elizabeth "Libby" Pierce in Room 5½. She made learning a matter of science, magic, and song not only for me, but for many others. Indeed, last Christmas she and her husband Mike ensured that my children practiced archery and axe throwing in her back yard before reading Christmas stories to them over tea and cake, and then she presented them with their very own copies of Strunk and White. Libby, thank you for inspiring us!

1

JUST AMERICAN WARS?

From Lieber's Code to the Cold War and beyond

On November 13, 1862, a Columbia College professor wrote the following letter to Union General-in-Chief Henry Halleck:

> My dear General,
>   Ever since the beginning of the present War, it has appeared clearer and clearer to me that the President ought to issue a set of rules and definitions providing for the most urgent issues occurring under the Law and usages of War, and on which our Articles of War are silent … My idea—I give it as a suggestion to you—that the President as Commander in Chief, through the Secretary of War, ought to appoint a committee, say of three, to draw up a code … in which certain acts and offences (under the Law of war) ought to be defined and, where necessary, the punishment be stated.
>   I do not know that any such thing as I design exists in any other country … I should propose that you, both as General-in-Chief and as a prominent writer on the Law of Nations, ought to be chairman …

Halleck, buried under administrative and political details of being recently promoted to General-in-Chief, did not dismiss the offer. After all, Halleck authored a tome on international law and he had previously asked Professor Lieber's views on the problem of guerrilla warfare. Nonetheless, at first Halleck simply could not add one more thing to his burdened shoulders, writing back two days later, "I have no time at present to consider the subject." Lieber, however, was not to be denied and wrote again on November 20, persuading General Halleck that it was in the best interests of the United States to formalize a better code for military conduct and expectations than what currently existed. What neither Lieber nor Halleck could have expected at the time was that Lieber's Code was a turning point in applied just war thinking and international law, adopted by Great Britain, France, and Prussia just after the U.S. Civil War and the foundation for the subsequent Hague, Geneva, and other conventions restraining the resort to war and how war is fought.[1]

The American way of war and Lieber's Code

For at least the last half-century it has been said that there is an "American way of war" characterized by the massive mobilization of manpower, financial resources, and technology. Investment in technology leads to successive "next generations of warfare" and/or the next "revolution in military affairs." In the concluding chapter, I will look further at these issues, agreeing that there is an American way of war.[2] However, I disagree that the best way to understand the "American way of war" is in terms of technology and material resources.

What makes the U.S. distinct, and characterizes the American way of war all the way back to colonial times, is *ideas*: the widespread discussion and debate about the morality of war among citizens and experts. Just war experts realize that this is true, but those discussions are largely left to the footnotes of American history. In fact, during every U.S. conflict there has been robust public debate about whether or not to go to war in the first place, and after the decision has been made, debate continues on the ethics of how the war is fought. Moreover, the U.S. is unique in the fact that even when it's victorious, it prosecutes some of its own military personnel who have violated the laws of armed conflict. This simply was not the case in most polities over the past thousands of years.

Thus, a major dimension of an American way of war, and the chief focus of this book, is a concern with the intersection of politics, military force, and morality. This book, rooted in the just war tradition, takes a twofold approach: it tells stories and does so to illuminate ethical challenges in those situations. More precisely, this book will look at specific American wars and tease out the ethical challenges, controversies, and possibilities faced by real people in conditions of stress, uncertainty, and combat. An indispensable pivot point in U.S. history is the contribution of Lieber's Code to national and international law.

Francis J. Lieber was born in Berlin and fought at the Battle of Waterloo during the Napoleonic Wars. He also fought in the Greek War of Independence, in the meantime earning a doctorate in philosophy from the University of Jena in 1820. He immigrated to Boston in 1827 and subsequently found work as a university professor at South Carolina College, where he resided and raised a family for two decades. During this time Lieber was horrified by Southern slavery, and for years he tried to find academic employment elsewhere, but was consistently disappointed. In 1857 he finally was able to leave his post at South Carolina College and took a position at Columbia College (now Columbia University) in New York City.

Lieber taught and wrote about the law of armed conflict, which was largely based in customs that have developed slowly over the centuries and founded upon just war principles, such as legitimate authority and just cause, as well as pragmatic guidelines, such as the unwritten injunction that heads of state should not assassinate other heads of state. Lieber corresponded with many individuals, on both sides of the Atlantic, interested in these issues at the start of the U.S. Civil War. He had reason to care: two of his sons fought for the Union and a third fought for the Confederacy. One of Lieber's many correspondents was an American businessman and warrior, General Henry Halleck. Halleck was a graduate of West Point who fought in the Mexican–American War. He was subsequently assigned to California, considered a post of no return, and ultimately left the U.S. Army (although holding rank in the California militia) and became a successful lawyer and businessman in mining and other fields. Halleck collected laws and policies, publishing a number of books including *Report on the Means of National Defense* and *Elements of Military Art and Science*, as well as translating Jomini's *Life of Napoleon* and *A Collection of Mining Laws of Spain and Mexico*. By far the most important of Halleck's works was his 970-page volume on international law published in 1861, *International Law; or, Rules Regulating the Intercourse of States in Peace and War,* which had large sections cataloging customary law on issues of war and peace.

While serving as the senior Union commander over the western theater, General Halleck began to correspond with Lieber after becoming aware of Lieber's public talks in New York on international law and its application to the U.S. Civil War. These talks achieved some notoriety due to the many grey areas in the war. For instance, the Confederate States of America argued that it was a sovereign state seceding from a volitional compact; the Union saw the Confederacy as an illegal rebellion. Did Lincoln's blockade of Southern ports constitute an act of war? Some said yes (if the South was an independent country); others said no (if the South was simply a criminal rebellion). The list of controversies and legal technicalities went on and on, compounded in the national press by wider moral discussions about a "crusade to end slavery" and the revolting behavior of bushwhackers and other partisans. Lieber's lectures (October 1861–February 1862), many of which were reprinted in newspapers and distributed across the country, dealt with some of these issues and it was one such issue that caught the attention of General Halleck. That issue was guerrilla warfare.

On August 6, 1862, Halleck wrote to Lieber "particularly request[ing] his views on 'the usages and customs of war' regarding guerrilla warfare."[3] Lieber complied with a document that continues to this day to offer sophisticated analysis of the nuances of guerrilla warfare. Most importantly, Lieber distinguished between "partisan" fighters (e.g. Mosby's Raiders) who could be considered to be formally connected, but detached, from a regular army and "guerrilla" fighters who were not formally connected and operated detached from the regular army (e.g. Quantrill's bushwhackers). In his guerrilla pamphlet, of which thousands of copies were printed and distributed, Lieber defined a host of irregular forces, including marauders, freebooters, partisans, guerrillas, brigands, spies, "arming of peasants," and the like, emphasizing that nearly all of them are illegitimate and deserving of the full extent of martial law.

It was this engagement between Lieber and Halleck that caused Lieber to write to Halleck in November 1862 about a code for the armies. What resulted, in very short order, was the establishment of a commission of three individuals to draft that code. Lieber did nearly all of the writing and it was completed within just a few months. Because there was a concern that making it an official part of U.S. code would require lengthy involvement with the U.S. Congress, President Lincoln used his executive authority to make this General Order No. 100 applicable to all Union troops on April 24, 1863. As it was disseminated widely, it quickly became known by Confederate forces as well, who typically followed much of "Lieber's Code."

Historian Richard Shelly Hartigan writes,

> the Code was the first instance in Western history in which the government of a sovereign nation established formal guidelines for its army's conduct toward its enemies … never before had a government set down in clear, explicit, formal terms not only the rights and obligations of its own army, but of its enemy's army and civil population as well.[4]

As mentioned previously, the document was quickly translated and spread across Europe. The intelligence, sophistication, and yet simplicity of Lieber's Code made it applicable across the Western world and it acted synergistically with another turning point of 1863: the establishment of the International Committee for Relief to the Wounded (later International Committee of the Red Cross) by Henri Dunant and four of his friends. These two developments were crucial, alongside the horrors of modern warfare witnessed in the Crimea and on U.S. Civil War battlefields, for the establishment of formal laws of armed conflict over the next few decades, such as the 1868 Petersburg Declaration and the later Hague and Geneva Conventions. Moreover, Lieber's work has continued to provide a backbone for subsequent U.S. Army manuals to this day.

Military ethics, foreign policy, and just war thinking

The purist might say that military ethics and the law of armed conflict, particularly as elaborated in Lieber's Code, are narrowly defined rules for battlefield behavior. Soldiers either follow the rules or they do not and that is all there is to it. Francis Lieber would disagree. The fifteenth article of his Code states, "Men who take up arms against one another in public war do not cease on this account to be moral beings, responsible to one another and to God." This comports with U.S. history. As a democracy with intellectual and moral roots in classical and Judeo-Christian thought, the American public and its institutions have long engaged in contentious deliberation about the morality of warfare.

This book utilizes just war thinking as the lens for considering the morality of the policies, achievements, and failures of past U.S. wars. The just war tradition is a Western philosophical school of thought with roots in the Greco-Roman world (e.g. Cicero) and early Christianity (e.g. Romans 13, Augustine). The classical just war framework provides the foundation for individual behavior, customary international law, and the formal laws of armed conflict, in addition to ethical reflection on issues of war and peace.[5] It is the foundation from which numerous Western political principles, such as *sovereignty*, *political legitimacy*, and *just cause* in war, are derived, with all of these being firmly rooted today both in international conventions and foreign policy practice. Just war thinking begins with three deontological criteria for the just decision (*jus ad bellum*) to use military force: *legitimate authority* acting on a *just cause* with *right intent*. Practical—or better, prudential[6]—secondary *jus ad bellum* considerations include: *likelihood of success*, *proportionality of ends*, and *last resort*. Just war thinking also has criteria regarding how war is conducted (*jus in bello*): using means and tactics proportionate (*proportionality*) to battlefield objectives and which limit harm to civilians, other non-combatants, and property (*discrimination*).

More specifically, political actors should carefully examine the following principles when considering the implementation of military force:

Jus ad Bellum
- Legitimate authority: Supreme political authorities are morally responsible for the security of their constituents, and therefore are obligated to make decisions about war and peace.
- *Just cause*: Self-defense of citizens' lives, livelihoods, and way of life are typically just causes; more generally speaking, the cause is likely just if it rights a past wrong, punishes wrongdoers, or prevents further wrongful acts.[7]
- *Right intent*: Political motivations are subject to ethical scrutiny; violence intended for the purpose of order, justice, and ultimate conciliation is just, whereas violence for the sake of hatred, revenge, and destruction is not just.
- *Likelihood of success*: Political leaders should consider whether or not their action will make a difference in real-world outcomes. This principle is subject to context and judgment, because it may be appropriate to act despite a low likelihood of success (e.g. against local genocide). Conversely, it may be inappropriate to act due to low efficacy despite the compelling nature of the case.
- *Proportionality of ends*: Does the preferred outcome justify, in terms of the cost in lives and material resources, this course of action?
- *Last resort*: Have traditional diplomatic and other efforts been reasonably employed in order to avoid outright bloodshed?

Jus in Bello
- *Proportionality*: Are the battlefield tools and tactics employed proportionate to battlefield objectives?
- *Discrimination*: Has care been taken to reasonably protect the lives and property of legitimate non-combatants?

It is noteworthy that military doctrine recognizes a third prudential criterion called *military necessity*, which is the idea that battlefield commanders may take actions on the battlefield that meet battlefield objectives—even if there is some harm to civilians or private property—if those actions do not otherwise violate the laws of war. Military necessity is not *carte blanche*, yet it is an important principle both for winning within the confines of a specific battlefield and especially for protecting one's own troops.[8] Obvious recent cases come from Iraq where insurgents utilized mosques, hospitals, and other sites as emplacements for snipers and artillery. To protect their own troops, commanders had to thoughtfully evaluate the threats, risks, and alternatives to "winning" that objective (e.g. go around, attack at night, sniper assault, etc.), including the secondary effects of turning the civilian population against you. Most books on just war theory do not have a lot to say about military necessity, but it is a key applied military doctrine alongside proportionality and distinction and part of the training of every U.S. military member. Military officers must keep military necessity in mind and thus it is part of the environment for how war is planned for and fought; it will raise its head from time to time throughout the book, such as in the decisions made at Veracruz during the Mexican–American War (Chapter 5).

Although classical just war thinkers, such as Cicero and Augustine, have long held that the end of a just war is peace, there has not been a discrete *jus post bellum* literature until recently. In recent years, in the wake of endless wars in the developing world and post-conflict shambles in the Balkans, Rwanda, and elsewhere, some scholars such as Brian Orend, Eric Patterson, Mark Evans, and others have fleshed out a *jus post bellum* to give ethical and policy direction to this affirmation.[9] At the same time, Western governments began articulating strategies of post-conflict "reconstruction and stabilization," "stability operations," post-conflict justice (e.g. transitional justice, truth and reconciliation commissions), and the "responsibility to protect and rebuild." Considering *jus post bellum* as its own category links it to the reality that most wars are cyclical in nature, starting and restarting because the settlement sets the stage for the next war (e.g. Rwanda). A robust *jus post bellum* also aligns with contemporary military doctrine, which sees multiple phases of war, from the pre-conflict phase through hot war to the post-conflict phase, all of which involve the U.S. military. In earlier books,[10] I articulated three principles of *jus post bellum*:

- *Order*: Beginning with existential security, a sovereign government extends its roots through the maturation of government capacity in the military (traditional security), governance (domestic politics), and international security dimensions.
- *Justice*: Getting one's "just deserts," including consideration of individual punishment for those who violated the law of armed conflict and restitution policies for victims when appropriate.
- *Conciliation*: Coming to terms with the past so that parties can imagine and move forward toward a shared future.

Excellent volumes have been written on the history of just war thinking, making a full presentation here redundant.[11] What this book will do is tease out the challenge of meeting specific just war principles in the case of a particular war, such as the ethics of presidential war aims during the Vietnam War or competing interests in the post-conflict settlement we know as the Versailles Treaty (1918). The reader will quickly see that there are often moral claims and counter-claims, various limits, and a palette of shades of grey, such as in cases where actions were restrained and just but motivations may not have been as praiseworthy. The goal is not so much to illuminate every feature of a specific war, but rather to focus on just war principles through real-world historical cases.

Including morality in the American way of war

Americans have a lot to be proud of when it comes to the ethics of war. From George Washington through Francis Lieber to Michael Walzer, American thinking about morality in foreign and national security policy has had a profound impact, not only on America's wars, but on the global law and practice of conflict as well.

General George Washington set the tone from the beginning by submitting himself to elected authorities and emphasizing the development of a "regular" army that was professional in training, equipment, and expectations. He was explicit in instructing his troops on behavior and heavy-handed in punishing his own soldiers for theft, murder, and rape.[12] In 1846, U.S. General Zachary Taylor begged the War Department, without success, to provide greater instructions and authority to prosecute his own soldiers who violated customary and criminal law.[13] Taylor's colleague, General Winfield Scott, refused to let the ambiguity of the 1806 Articles of War let violators off the hook in Mexico by elaborating "martial law" in General Order No. 20, which governed the behavior of his own troops as well as the occupied civilian population.[14] Scott asserted, in General Order No. 20:

> This unwritten code is *Martial* Law ... it is an unwritten code that all armies are obligated to follow in enemy countries, not only for their own safety, but also to protect the inoffensive inhabitants and their properties within the theater of military operations, from offenses committed against the laws of war.

Moreover, throughout the nineteenth century there were vociferous debates across the country, from churches to public houses to legislatures, about the prudence, expense, and morality of going to war, whether it be against France, Spain, Great Britain, Mexico, the Barbary pirates, or American Indians.

It is well-known that at the end of the U.S. Civil War, General Robert E. Lee refused the immoral order of Confederate President (and former U.S. Secretary of War) Jefferson Davis to continue the fight via guerrilla warfare. Lee's open letter to the Confederacy called for surrender and reconciliation. At the same time, President Lincoln told his generals that after decisively beating the South, his policy was to "let them up easy" in pursuit of national conciliation. The U.S. followed policies of restorative justice and reconciliation, from the military courtesy shown by Grant to Lee at Appomattox through general amnesties—even for Jefferson

Davis—between 1865 and 1868.[15] Perhaps the longest-lasting effect on military ethics was the role played, as noted above, by a college professor named Francis Lieber and his "code" that was adopted not just by the U.S. but also by France, Prussia, and the United Kingdom within just a few years and which became a foundation for the subsequent Hague Conventions (1899 and 1907) and later for the Geneva Conventions after World War II.

The twentieth century too has many stories of limits, morality, and restraint which can only be briefly nodded to here. The U.S. court-martialed a number of military personnel, including a Brigadier General[16] who responded to Moro terrorists with atrocities-in-kind at the end of the Spanish–American War, prior to the benevolent and industrious Philippines Governor Generalship of William Howard Taft and unusual outreach methods of General John J. "Black Jack" Pershing (see Chapter 7). During World War II the U.S. government provided troops fighting in North Africa with booklets directing appropriate, culturally sensitive behavior in relation to the indigenous Muslim population.[17] At war's end, it was the U.S. that indispensably led the establishment of the Nuremberg and Tokyo war crimes tribunals, which deepened and extended the expectations of moral behavior in war. The U.S. was also a critical player in establishing other aspirational documents that limited and refined war, including the Pact of Paris (also known as the Kellogg–Briand Pact, 1928), the United Nations (UN) Charter, the Genocide Convention, and the 1949 Geneva Conventions. Perhaps even more important was the synergy between justice at Nuremberg and the Marshall Plan and other restorative policies, which demonstrated that a victor's justice could be just, provide order, and establish the conditions for almost inconceivable international conciliation.

One could go on and on listing examples of the constructive role of the U.S., including the role that diplomats play in balancing military necessity and political savvy with ethics in negotiating covenants such as the Nuclear Non-Proliferation Treaty and the Convention on Certain Conventional Weapons, to the science fiction-level of restraint in U.S. precision weapons, matched by a sincere commitment to protect non-combatants and private property.

Moreover, one way that the U.S. has departed from the path of most of its historical antecedents is that it attempts to hold itself accountable. The week that this chapter was edited in the summer of 2017, the British Broadcasting Service (BBC) reported that only the U.S.—out of a coalition of seventeen governments—was willing to publicly report and take responsibility for collateral damage in bombing campaigns against Islamic State (ISIS) in Syria. All others claimed that airstrikes had caused zero collateral damage.[18] This emphasis on right conduct and transparency, however imperfect, is rooted in the wider context of democratic debate that is constantly ongoing in the U.S. on the ethics of war. This is inherent to the U.S. system of government, such as the separation of powers between Congress, which pays for and organizes the military, and the President, with his executive role as Commander in Chief. Just as important is the nature of a free society where citizens, clergy, journalists, academics, and others openly debate the morality of

U.S. foreign and national security policies. It is not only elites who get to participate in these debates: mothers and fathers and other family members are taxpayers
and voters and thus have direct leverage, usually in a limiting fashion, on U.S. war-
making. It is not that the U.S. is perfect, nor that its soldiers do not make mistakes
or act poorly, but the U.S. is different from many past governments in indicting
and trying many of its own military personnel for crimes. My Lai and Abu Ghraib
remind us, shockingly, that moral and legal violations occur and that we must hold
individuals accountable.

What is less appreciated, at least outside of academia, is the role that American
just war theorists have played and continue to play in arguments about the ethics
of going to war and war-fighting. Francis Lieber was not the last college professor to exercise influence on how the U.S. national security establishment thinks
about war. Lieber's intellectual descendants include authors, theologians, ethicists,
and social scientists carefully evaluating the morality of warfare, including Reinhold
Niebuhr, Paul Ramsey, Michael Walzer, Jean Bethke Elshtain, and James Turner
Johnson, which does not in any way diminish the superb contributions by allies
such as the Canadian Brian Orend and British thinkers such as Oliver O'Donovan
and Nigel Biggar.[19]

In sum, this book illuminates the depth and nuance of specific just war criteria in the context of America's wars. It does so by isolating one or two discrete
principles, such as proportionality and discrimination, in the context of a single war.
For example, one chapter looks at the War of 1812, carefully considering President
Madison's enumerated grievances (just cause, right intention), such as the impressment of American citizens and the decision to go to war, but does not evaluate how
the war was fought.

My hope is that the reader will be intrigued by learning more about unique
elements of America's wars, as well as developing greater appreciation for the dif-
ficulty of applying just war criteria in the real world of politics and the fog of war.
This is not an apology in any sense of the word for all or any of America's wars.
I am not in the camp that argues that all that the U.S. has done is right, but nor
am I in the camp that constantly denigrates U.S. actions and motives. Someone
interested in such Manichean views will not find them hard to find elsewhere. My
own perspective is that the U.S. has been unique in history in trying to live up to
its moral vision while dealing with the realities of power and security. Yet, at times,
U.S. personnel have failed badly, such as in broken promises to American Indians
and at No Gun Ri, My Lai, and Abu Ghraib. Consequently, the reader will see the
good and the bad of U.S. policies, ranging from the deplorable behavior of some
"volunteers" in the Mexican–American War to post-war investment made under
Governor General Taft in the Philippines.

Due to space, I simply could not delve into every facet of every armed conflict and all the detail might be historically overwhelming while simultaneously
obscuring a discussion about just war ethics. Nevertheless, the choice of cases and
the focus on the morality of intentions and behavior are novel and I hope it will
cause the reader to think critically and enjoy the process while doing so.

Overview of the book

This book is structured in three parts based on the three areas of just war thinking: the ethics of going to and continuing war (*jus ad bellum*), the ethics of how war is fought (*jus in bello*), and the ethics of war's end (*jus post bellum*). Chapter 2 deals with the ethics of the American War for Independence. The just war tradition begins with the idea that a just war proceeds from a legitimate political authority acting on a just cause with right intentions. The question, when it comes to the War for Independence, was whether or not the United Colonies met these criteria. For instance was there a legitimate political authority or was this an illegitimate rebellion? How could this be a just cause if its purpose was to establish a new country after causing a civil war? Was independence the early goal of the English colonists? Should we agree with some revisionist scholars who say that this was really a craven class war promoted by financiers and elite white men, rather than truly a war for justice and the rule of law?

When it comes to the American War for Independence, many who read traditional military history do not often encounter these types of critiques; instead, the literature focuses on the noble debates at the Continental Congresses and the long-suffering campaigns of Washington and his soldiers. However, allegations questioning the very legitimacy of this war are very common in U.S. universities—indeed it was studying this controversy that led me to write this book in the first place. Consequently, this chapter will examine what the colonists were saying about their situation, motivations, and grievances, particularly in the critical year of 1775 to 1776. The timeline is noteworthy: many Americans think that the so-called "shots heard 'round the world," the attacks by British troops at Lexington and Concord, occurred shortly before the Declaration of Independence in July 1776. This is wrong. The British troops attacked in April of 1775, and the Declaration of Independence was not written for more than a year. Instead, in July 1775 the colonists sent a "declaration of rights and grievances" to London, the latest in a series of documents protesting British behavior toward the colonies. This July 1775 document declared that the colonists did not want to fight and were not seeking independence, but after being assaulted in multiple ways, they would exercise their legitimate right of self-defense. This chapter will evaluate whether the colonial governments were *legitimate authorities* and whether taking up arms met just war criteria of *just cause* and *right intentions* because the goal, following Concord and Lexington, was self-defense.

The War of 1812 is poorly known today, remembered vaguely for trivia quiz novelties such as the burning of the White House by British troops (and Dollie Madison saving Washington's portrait) and the fact that the Battle of New Orleans—which Andrew Jackson and a motley force that included pirates won—occurred after peace had already been signed in Europe. But why did the United States go to war with Britain in the first place? This chapter looks at the *casus belli* that brought the small-government, anti-military Republican administrations of Thomas Jefferson and his successor James Madison to the point of war. Were the controversies of impressment, restricted trade, and "insults" to Washington enough to justify this war? More specifically, do they meet the secondary, prudential just war criteria of "last resort" and "likelihood of success?" We will look at the case made by President Madison in his famous war address, in which he argued that a state of war already existed in London's policies toward the U.S. Madison's evidence included thousands of American citizens impressed to work in British naval vessels and millions of dollars lost to various trade strictures. I conclude that after a decade of trying diplomacy and economic statecraft, the U.S. government had a just cause and right intentions and was at the point of reasonable "last resort," although it is clear that the U.S. was poorly prepared and the likelihood of success at the strategic level was uncertain at best.

Chapter 3 looks at the Vietnam War. Because just war thinking begins with the ethics of going to war, this chapter looks at the justifications given by U.S. presidents in going to and prolonging the Vietnam War. These are often called "presidential war aims." Although we typically think of presidential war aims, in a republic, as being tied to the democratic idea of elected officials having to justify war to the electorate bearing the war's cost, the idea of presidential war aims is also directly connected to just war thinking due to the emphasis on legitimate political authorities acting on just cause(s) with right intentions. During the Vietnam War President Eisenhower and his successors advanced war aims informed by a heuristic: the domino theory. The domino theory was the idea that if one country fell to communism, the contagion would spread across the neighborhood due to the ruthless, nefarious activities of communist insurgencies. This did not seem at all unrealistic to observers at the time who witnessed the loss of China to "the Reds" (1949), the Korean War, and communist insurgencies in Vietnam, Laos, Cambodia, Malaysia, and elsewhere.

The domino theory comprised three major justifications for considering the use of force in Vietnam and elsewhere: the doctrine of *containing communism*, the doctrine of spreading and/or *holding democracy* around the world, and the concept of *demonstrating credibility* in supporting one's allies. All three of these may be legitimate reasons for going to war or prolonging war in discrete cases. However, I argue that there are at least two more war aims, expressed explicitly or implicitly, by Presidents Kennedy, Johnson, and Nixon. One has to do with *national honor* and the other with *personal reputation*. When it comes to national honor, these presidents often made arguments that one might call sunk cost assertions, such as "we have to keep fighting so that those who died haven't died in vain." This chapter looks very carefully at the notion of national honor, which is not a just war principle, and what is "owed" to soldiers, veterans, families, the general citizenry, and survivors. When it comes to personal reputation, each of these presidents conveyed in their memoirs, in private conversation, and by their deeds that they were very concerned about their personal reputation for toughness in the international arena. Is one's ego a just reason to prolong a war? This chapter looks critically at the problem of waging or prolonging war for reasons of vanity.[20]

The second section of the book, on how war is fought, begins in Chapter 5 with the lesser-known Mexican–American War (1846–1848). Today's Americans grow up with a fait accompli: the U.S. bested the Mexican army of General Santa Anna and today controls the region known as the American Southwest; despite marching all the way to Mexico City, much larger parts of the country were not annexed. Furthermore, the conditions on the northern side of the border are often better than the conditions on the southern side of the border, so few people reflect on the dynamics that led to that conflict. Yet many revisionist historians criticize it as an unjust American war. They look to the writings of Henry David Thoreau (i.e. "Civil Disobedience"), Abraham Lincoln, and an out-of-context quote from General Ulysses S. Grant, who famously called it "a wicked war." When I read Grant's quote in its entirety, however, it made me re-evaluate the war. Grant thought that the war was unnecessary, but he reflected, "The troops behaved well in Mexico, and the government acted handsomely about the peace … Once in Mexico … the people, those who had property, were our friends."[21]

"The troops behaved well …" This chapter carefully asks, how did American troops behave in the war with Mexico? I scrutinize some of the issues about how the war was fought, including the difference between untrained "volunteer" troops (e.g. Texas Rangers, short-enlistment volunteers, militia) and the "regulars" or professional U.S. soldiers. The chapter also looks at the bombardment of the city of Veracruz and trade-offs that U.S. generals had to make between discrimination and proportionality on the one hand, and military necessity on the other. General Scott was particularly concerned with protecting his troops from tropical diseases such as yellow fever while his opponent was holed up in an urban fortress full of civilians. This chapter will look specifically at the policies and actions of General Zachary Taylor, General Winfield Scott, and others.

What about nuclear weapons? At the advent of their use, President Harry S. Truman famously said that he didn't lose a night's sleep over the decision to drop the atom bomb on Japan because he was able to save so many U.S. lives by not invading the Japanese mainland. It is possible that Truman also saved hundreds of thousands of Japanese lives by this approach as well. But critics from diverse backgrounds label the use of the atomic bomb on Japan to bring the Pacific war to an end as unjust. When we put ourselves in the position of American leaders at the time, what principles should guide the decision whether or not to use the atomic bomb? What is the responsibility of an elected leader to protect his own troops? The troops of his opponent? His opponent's civilian population and property? When reflecting on World War II, these issues demand cautious, sophisticated ethical reasoning. For instance, Japanese munitions factories were often located in civilian centers and the Japanese government was assiduously training women and children to attack and resist Allied troops. Were they not combatants, or at least potential combatants? At the same time, most American GIs had been civilians in December 1941. The pre-war U.S. Army was tiny. The infamous Japanese attack on Pearl Harbor forced a reluctant and unprepared United States into the war, so most of Truman's soldiers were not long-term, professional warriors. They were average citizens who had been bakers, doctors, lawyers, farmers, factory workers, and the like until their nation was attacked. What responsibility did President Truman have for bringing the war to the most rapid possible end and protecting these husbands, fathers, brothers, and sons? In sum, Chapter 6 takes a novel look at the intersection of the *jus ad bellum* principle of political authority, *jus in bello* criteria of proportionality and discrimination, and the leader's responsibility to create the conditions for war's end and enduring peace.

Another chapter, Chapter 7, deals with the aftermath of the Spanish–American War. More specifically, I look at the way the U.S. dealt with the annexation of the Philippines, with a focus on policies that we would today call "reconstruction and stabilization" operations. In a previous book I outlined a model for *jus post bellum* that begins with political *order*, attempts to advance *justice*, and ultimately seeks *conciliation*. The chapter examines U.S. policies, particularly under the leadership of Governor General William Howard Taft, which attempted to establish order in the Philippines and lay a foundation for economic and social development. Over time, efforts at political order, targeted justice, and amnesty made a high level of conciliation and security possible. The ultimate outcome was unusual amity and cooperation, lasting decades, between the majority of Filipinos and the American leadership. But this was only possible when a dramatic change in post-war policies was implemented. We will see how in the first months after the Spanish–American War, a Filipino insurgency broke out and a bloody war was perpetrated with atrocities on both sides. Fortunately, the U.S. changed course, including providing some amnesty to Filipinos and court-martialing some U.S. military personnel for their heavy-handedness in the field. At the same time, the U.S. invested heavily in trying to make the Philippines financially independent in the twentieth century by dredging harbors, enacting land reform, opening roads, laying railroads, and importing thousands of English-speaking teachers to prepare students. In the years that followed, whether in the field under the military leadership of the famous Black Jack Pershing or the Governor Generalship of William Howard Taft, efforts at partnership and development were made, demonstrating how post-conflict reconstruction and stabilization can occur, despite many challenges, in a very underdeveloped country.

How should war end? That was the question dominating national legislatures and then the Paris Peace Conference a century ago. Chapter 8, on World War I, looks at the dynamics in national capitals that led to Versailles and other treaties that brought an end to the war. Using the *jus post bellum* model of order, justice, and conciliation, we will see that the German High Command, fearful that disorder was leading to a communist take-over, advised Kaiser Wilhelm that he must accept the unconditional form of surrender demanded by the Entente (he quietly retired to the Netherlands). The chapter evaluates the negotiating positions of the Big Three who dominated the conference: France's Clemenceau, who demanded vengeance, German acknowledgment of war guilt, and reparations; David Lloyd George, who argued for limited justice without disordering European power politics, lest a new war break out; and Woodrow Wilson, who messianically believed that he could transform world politics by leaping beyond history. In retrospect, we know what happened in subsequent years, but at the time, were there seeds of a different kind of peace, one that would have endured?

Chapter 9 asks, "What is victory?" Although past generations understood the importance of victory, whether at Yorktown or Appomattox, today's Western governments and militaries often refrain from discussions of victory. Why is it that winning has lost its luster? Is there a moral component to winning? Strangely, it appears that Western victors feel guilty about winning for some reason, even if they are defeating repulsive regimes and terrorists. The chapter on victory is less a historical analysis than a contemporary examination of where the U.S. and its allies are today when considering the morality of winning. This chapter defines three notions of victory (defensive, offensive, moral), considers why victory has fallen out of vogue since World War II, discusses the linkage between war aims and winning, and argues that achieving victory can be a praiseworthy, necessary end such as in cases of self-defense, punishment of wrongdoing, restoration, and self-determination. All of these tie in to the holistic classical just war idea linking the ethics of going to war and how war is fought with war's ends: the object of war ought to be a better state of peace.

This book in your hands is about just war issues in American political and military history, so it has not dealt at length with the latest contemporary issues, particularly those at the forefront of national policy since the end of the Cold War and the age of terrorism associated with the events of 9/11 and the wars in Afghanistan and Iraq. It would take another complete book to do justice to the ethics of U.S. military involvement, and non-involvement, in cases of genocide, Responsibility to Protect (R2P), the Middle East and Central Asia, the employment of smart and stealth armaments, issues of "enhanced interrogation," torture, and claims to protect the citizenry, the erosion of national sovereignty, and the increasing role of supranational bodies (e.g. the United Nations, the International Criminal Court) in issues of security and justice, and the like. Nevertheless, the book will conclude with a short investigation of the unique challenges to just war thinking currently being raised and how they may be settled as weapons, law, and experience evolve. For now, it is time to turn our attention back to the beginning: the ethics of the American War for Independence.

Notes

1 Richard Shelly Hartigan, *Lieber's Code and the Law of War* (Chicago: Precedent Press, 1983), p. 1, pp. 79–81.
2 The author realizes that there may be some who object to using the term "American" as an adjective to describe the United States of America, somehow thus disenfranchising the rest of the governments of the Western hemisphere. However, it is the most precise way to describe the actor in question and it is doubtful that anyone will misinterpret the use of "American" to mean other "North Americans" such as the Canadians and Mexicans. Indeed, Ottawa and Mexico City, for reasons of justifiable national pride, prefer to be called Canadians and Mexicans rather than Americans.
3 Hartigan, p. 2.

4 Ibid., pp. 1–2.

5 The Greek concept of "morality" is usually translated as "character" (*ethos*) and the Roman term for customary behavior (morals) is *moralis*, so both words are used somewhat interchangeably in this book.

6 James Turner Johnson originated this wise description of the secondary *jus ad bellum* criteria and consistently uses it across numerous books and articles. In a famous *First Things* article he compared "several recently invented prudential criteria" to the original deontological trio of legitimate authority, just cause, and right intention (see his "Just War: As It Was, and Is" in *First Things*, January 2005). He says that the role of the prudential criteria, however important, is "secondary" in elucidating *jus ad bellum* in *The War to Oust Saddam Hussein: Just War and the New Face of Conflict* (Lanham, MD: Rowman & Littlefield, 2005).

7 This formulation derives directly from Augustine, as recorded in Aquinas' *Summa Theologica* (New York: Christian Classics, 1981), Question 40, Secunda Secundae.

8 Lieber's Code has three articles dealing with military necessity (Articles 14–16).

> **Article 14:** Military necessity, as understood by modern civilized nations, consists in the necessity of those measures which are indispensable for securing the ends of the war, and which are lawful according to the modern law and usages of war.
>
> **Article 15:** Military necessity admits of all direct destruction of life or limb of armed enemies, and of other persons whose destruction is incidentally unavoidable in the armed contests of the war; it allows of the capturing of every armed enemy, and every enemy of importance to the hostile government, or of peculiar danger to the captor; it allows of all destruction of property, and obstruction of the ways and channels of traffic, travel, or communication, and of all withholding of sustenance or means of life from the enemy; of the appropriation of whatever an enemy's country affords necessary for the subsistence and safety of the army, and of such deception as does not involve the breaking of good faith either positively pledged, regarding agreements entered into during the war, or supposed by the modern law of war to exist. Men who take up arms against one another in public war do not cease on this account to be moral beings, responsible to one another and to God.
>
> **Article 16:** Military necessity does not admit of cruelty—that is, the infliction of suffering for the sake of suffering or for revenge, nor of maiming or wounding except in fight, nor of torture to extort confessions. It does not admit of the use of poison in any way, nor of the wanton devastation of a district. It admits of deception, but disclaims acts of perfidy; and, in general, military necessity does not include any act of hostility which makes the return to peace unnecessarily difficult.

9 Brian Orend's 2002 article was a critical first step in this literature: "Justice after War," *Ethics and International Affairs*, vol. 16, no. 2 (2002), pp. 43–56. Also see Eric Patterson's edited volume (that includes Orend, Evans, Elshtain, Johnson, Walzer, and others), *Ethics beyond War's End* (Washington, DC: Georgetown University Press, 2012); Eric Patterson, *Ending Wars Well: Order, Justice, and Conciliation in Post-Conflict* (New Haven, CT: Yale University Press); Dan Caldwell and Robert E. Williams, Jr., *Seeking Security in an Insecure World*, (Oxford: Rowman & Littlefield, 2006); Doug McCready, "Ending the War Right: Jus Post Bellum and the Just War Tradition," *Journal of Military Ethics*, vol. 8, no. 1 (March 2009), pp. 66–78; Davida E. Kellogg, "Jus post Bellum: The Importance of War Crimes Trials," *Parameters*, vol. 32 (2002): pp. 87–99; Camilla Bosanquet, "Refining Jus post Bellum," paper for the annual meeting of the International Society for Military Ethics (formerly JSCOPE), (January 25–26, 2007); and Mark Evans, "Moral Responsibilities and Conflicting Demands of Jus Post Bellum," *Ethics and International Affairs*, vol. 23, no. 2 (2009), 159.

10 Patterson, *Ethics Beyond War's End*; *Ending Wars Well*.

11 Two of the best are Frederick H. Russell, *The Just War in the Middle Ages* (Cambridge: Cambridge University Press, 1975), and James Turner Johnson, *The Just War Tradition and the Restraint of War* (Princeton, NJ: Princeton University Press, 1981). A recent application is Nigel Biggar, *In Defence of War* (Oxford, Oxford University Press, 2014).

12 James Kirby Martin and Mark Edward Lender, *A Respectable Army: The Military Origins of the Republic, 1763–1789* (Wheeling, IL: Harlan Davidson, 1982); Don Higginbotham, *George Washington and the American Military Tradition* (Athens: University of Georgia Press, 1985).

13 John Frost, *Life of Major General Zachary Taylor; With Notices of the War in New Mexico, California and in Southern Mexico* (New York: D. Appleton & Co., 1847), pp. 104–106.

14 "General Headquarters of the Army, General Order #20," Rice University (last modified June 7, 2010), available at: https://scholarship.rice.edu/jsp/xml/1911/27562/3/aa00208tr.tei.html.

15 Jay Winik, *April 1865: The Month That Saved America* (New York: HarperCollins Publishers, Inc., 2001).

16 Brigadier General Jacob H. Smith was court-martialed, in part, for urging his troops to kill anyone over the age of ten and promoting a scorched-earth campaign. See Stuart Creighton Miller's *Benevolent Assimilation: The American Conquest of the Philippines, 1899–1903* (New Haven, CT: Yale University Press, 1981), p. 247.

17 Rick Atkinson, *An Army at Dawn* (New York: Holt Paperbacks; revised ed., 2007).

18 "Mosul Retaken," BBC *Newshour* (July 10, 2017), available at: www.bbc.co.uk/programmes/p057l39f.

19 The important books by all of these individuals are fully referenced in this book's bibliography.

20 Thomas Hobbes wrote that the causes of war are, "First, Competition; Secondly, Diffidence; Thirdly, Glory. The first, maketh men invade for Gain; the second, for Safety; and the Third, for Reputation"; *Leviathan*, ed. Edwin Curley (Indianapolis, IN: Hackett, 1994), ch. 13, par. 88. I am not arguing that Kennedy, Johnson, or Nixon had a Napoleonic instinct for glory in Vietnam, but rather that they feared being labeled as losers and wanted to be seen as tough. This does not seem to have been a personal issue for General of the Armies Dwight D. Eisenhower.

21 John Russell Young, *Around the World with General Grant: A Narrative of the Visit of General U.S. Grant, Ex-President of the United States, to Various Countries in Europe, Asia, and Africa in 1877, 1878, 1879; To Which Are Added Certain Conversations with General Grant on Questions Connected with American Politics and History*, vol. 2 (New York: The American News Co., 1800), pp. 447–448.

JUST WAR CRITERIA

Jus ad bellum

Legitimate authority: Supreme political authorities are morally responsible for the security of their constituents, and therefore are obligated to make decisions about war and peace.

Just cause: Self-defense of citizens' lives, livelihoods, and way of life are typically just causes; more generally speaking, the cause is likely just if it rights a past wrong, punishes wrongdoers, or prevents further wrong.

Right intent: Political motivations are subject to ethical scrutiny; violence intended for the purpose of order, justice, and ultimate conciliation is just, whereas violence for the sake of hatred, revenge, and destruction is not just.

Likelihood of success: Political leaders should consider whether or not their actions will make a difference in real-world outcomes. This principle is subject to context and judgment, because it may be appropriate to act despite a low likelihood of success (e.g. against local genocide). Conversely, it may be inappropriate to act due to low efficacy despite the compelling nature of the case.

Proportionality of ends: Does the preferred outcome justify, in terms of the cost in lives and material resources, this course of action?

Last resort: Have traditional diplomatic and other efforts been reasonably employed in order to avoid outright bloodshed?

Jus in bello

Proportionality: Are the battlefield tools and tactics employed proportionate to battlefield objectives?

Discrimination: Has care been taken to reasonably protect the lives and property of legitimate non-combatants?

Jus post bellum

Order: Beginning with existential security, a sovereign government extends its roots through the maturation of government capacity in the military (traditional security), governance (domestic politics), and international security dimensions.

Justice: Getting one's just deserts, including consideration of individual punishment for those who violated the law of armed conflict and restitution policies for victims when appropriate.

Conciliation: Coming to terms with the past so that parties can imagine and move forward toward a shared future.

PART I

The ethics of going to war

When is it just to go to war? In the real world, where political leaders must make decisions on the basis of imperfect information, how does the statesman consider the moral, strategic, and practical issues confronting the employment of deadly force? In the U.S. experience, how does an elected official do this amid the din of the opposition and media and the checks and balances of the American constitutional system, and with an eye on election cycles?

These realities are precisely why the just war tradition is so important. Just war thinking begins with three deontological criteria for going to war: *legitimate authority*, *just cause*, and *right intention*. To these are added a number of secondary, prudential criteria that demonstrate stewardship, including *likelihood of success*, *proportionality of ends*, and *last resort*.

The first section of this book looks very specifically at the morality of going to war in three cases. The first case is the American War for Independence. The chapter looks at the arguments made by colonial leaders through 1775 and the grievances enumerated in the July 1775 document titled, "The Declaration of Rights and Grievances of the United Colonies," which was written about two months after British troops fired on colonial citizens at Lexington and Concord, Massachusetts. The chapter specifically looks at the three deontological just war criteria with a focus on the following questions: was the Continental Congress and the provincial legislatures that it represented, a legitimate political authority? Were the self-defense claims of the colonists, such the quartering of troops in their homes and confiscation of property to admiralty courts, the basis for a self-defense response? What were the true intentions of the colonists: were they seeking revenge? The confiscation of Crown property? Destruction of the political system, as happened a decade later in the French Revolution?

Chapter 3 goes beyond the primary *jus ad bellum* criteria to look at issues of *last resort*, *proportionality of ends*, and *likelihood of success* in the War of 1812. When it started, this war was only a small battlefield in London's world war against Napoleon, but for Washington it was deeply personal due to the impressment of thousands of U.S. citizens into the British Navy as well as other issues left unresolved since 1783. The chapter concludes that the Madison administration, and its predecessors, demonstrated considerable patience with the British and that only war was likely to end the virtual slavery of U.S. personnel on British warships. However, Washington was over-optimistic about U.S. readiness for war and its weak strategy was demonstrated early in the war.

Chapter 4 fast-forwards a century and a half to the Vietnam War, a subcontinental cataclysm with roots in the Korean conflict and fall of China to communism at the end of World War II. Active U.S. involvement in support of the government of South Vietnam was the policy of the administrations of Presidents Eisenhower, Kennedy, Johnson, and Nixon. Too often the focus has been on how the U.S. fought the war, rather than on comparing how both sides fought the war. Such an analysis would demonstrate that despite many U.S. errors, the North Vietnamese and Viet Cong were simply diabolical in their use of terror, torture, and mass killing of their fellow Vietnamese people, not to mention the grotesque, sustained torture of their enemies. But, for our purposes, what has been even less studied is the justification for going to war and the rationale for prolonging the war. Consequently, this chapter looks carefully at the stated and unstated presidential war aims of four presidents, paying strict attention to whether or not those claims by *legitimate political authorities* met the criteria of *just cause* and *right intention*.

2

ARGUING THE AMERICAN REVOLUTION

Just cause, legitimate authority, and right intention

Was the American War for Independence just? This question seems like a novelty when tossed around today, but in the 1770s American colonists thought that the answer to it could very well determine the outcome of the war, and thus put much time and effort into making cases that it was just. Today's scholars, however, are divided on the question. This chapter contends that the war was not only just, but that the colonists themselves took great pains to make sure that it was ethical in a very particular sense: that of customary international law, which is rooted in historical just war thinking. In the July 1775 *Declaration of the United Colonies on the Causes and Necessity of Taking Up Arms* (hereafter referred to by its unofficial title, the "Declaration of the United Colonies" or simply "the Declaration"),[1] penned under the auspices of the Second Continental Congress, colonial statesmen left us a document that clearly articulates a classical just war approach.

The Declaration argues first and foremost that the colonists had this war forced on them: they were only fighting because their lives, their property, and the liberty guaranteed to them under British law were in danger of being destroyed if they did not. But although a war truly fought in self-defense is nearly always just, the document is careful to also make a thorough case that the conflict fit all the stipulations of classical just war theory. It asserts that, by virtue of their charters, the British constitution and the principles of natural law, the colonial assemblies had *legitimate authority* to resist Parliament's aggression; that they had a *just cause* since they were defending their birthright as Englishmen and human beings, and that they were taking up arms with *right intent*—at this juncture in 1775 they were, after all, only seeking a restoration of their rights under British law as it stood in the early 1760s, not independence or revolution.

In other words, a full year before the July 1776 Declaration of Independence, the Declaration of the United Colonies laid out a rationale for self-defense consistent with just war thinking. This chapter looks at the historical context and considers the paucity of scholarly consensus on the arguments made in the Declaration of the United Colonies, and then elucidates the just war arguments made in the document. I conclude that the arguments made in the Declaration are compelling and historically accurate—and that what ultimately became the American War for Independence was a just war.

The historical backdrop: 150 years of autonomy

Britain's colonies in America enjoyed significant autonomy–they were, after all, founded at the expense of private individuals rather than the British government.[2] In return for taming a wilderness for the glory and profit of a distant monarch, the Crown gave the colonists charters that promised them the right to govern themselves (agreeably to English law and in conjunction with Crown-appointed governors), and "all Liberties … and Immunities … as if they had been … born, within this our Realm of England."[3] Perhaps the chief of these rights of Englishmen was freedom from taxes levied without consent.[4]

Although not many generations passed before Britain tried to redefine her legal relationship with the colonies, the historical evidence indicates that, during the formative seventeenth century, Crown and Parliament (save for the later Stuarts) generally agreed with the colonial view of the charter privileges.[5] The charters, Americans held, granted perpetual immunity from British taxation and gave the colonial assemblies sovereignty over their internal affairs, while Parliament, in the interest of the empire, remained supreme over their external affairs (in other words, it could regulate commerce, grant navigation and fishing rights, etc.).

Charles I's attempt to make Virginia "dependent upon the Crown" illustrates this. After the king's actions provoked a legal maelstrom, he conceded that the colony would continue to enjoy its rights as its charter specified. Similarly, Parliament in the 1650s was obliged to acknowledge the House of Burgesses' exclusive right to levy taxes in Virginia.[6] When Parliament later took advantage of circumstances to try to gain power over the colonies, it was denounced by colonial governments in Rhode Island and Connecticut.[7] New York merchants, too, resisted the future James II's overbearing policies, insisting that "as Englishmen they could not be taxed except by their own representatives."[8] Even a Massachusetts governor declared that "the laws made by your Majesty and, your Parliament, obliged [the colonies] in nothing."[9]

In the mid-1680s, James—whose disregard for British laws and rights eventually got him dethroned—tried to unite all the New England colonies under the Crown so that his agents could rule them without interference.[10] The charters of New York and Massachusetts were thus denied legal status, and the colonists of New England were subjected to the "Absolute and Arbitrary" rule of the king's deputy, Edmund Andros.[11] Andros not only tried to levy taxes without the assemblies' consent, he went so far as to impose the Anglican Church on fiercely Puritan Massachusetts.[12] Up and down the East Coast, the colonists inveighed against this denial of their charter rights and rights as Englishmen.[13]

With the accession of William and Mary following the Glorious Revolution of 1688, there came a new era of government based on the peoples' consent. The colonists naturally assumed that their own struggles to "[tame] the royal governors … as Parliament tamed the King" and secure their English liberties were vindicated, too.[14] They were, after all, unrepresented in the Parliament that now declared Englishmen forever immune from taxation without representation. Charters in England were declared immune from forfeiture—and surely this principle applied to charters in the colonies as well.[15]

British citizens in North America were bitterly disappointed. Although subsequent ministries were not brazen enough to tax the colonies, ambiguous laws soon permitted British ships to impress colonists into their service, despite the fact that this violated charter privileges (a major cause of the War of 1812). Even rules such as the 1733 Molasses Act, ostensibly a trade regulation for the general good of the empire (and therefore, as the colonists admitted, binding on them), penalized American merchants to enrich Britain's interests elsewhere.[16] More ominously still, the White Pine Acts clearly overstepped the assemblies' jurisdictions and regulated how Americans used their own property.[17]

By the middle of the eighteenth century, the imperially minded Whig Party justified this intrusion into colonial affairs by an innovative theory of sovereignty which argued that since Parliament represented the collective will of the entire empire and its estates, its power was "final, unqualified and indivisible."[18] There could be no constitutional boundaries, then, around the will of the British people—not even rights promised to colonists "forever," "any statute … to the contrary notwithstanding."[19] As an editorial put it, when they cease to serve the "general good," "let me inform my fellow subjects of America, that … the British parliament can at any time set aside all the charters that have ever been granted."[20] Gone was the understanding that charters were "exemptions" from Parliament's regular jurisdiction.[21] They were now subject to the vicissitudes of the public weal. But, if that was so, why had the first settlers been so anxious to obtain them, and why had they struggled in defense of them? Moreover, could legislators confined to one small, distant island really presume to act for the "general good" of the whole empire?

When the Seven Years War with France came to an end in 1763, Britain and her colonies lapsed into a deep recession. Anxious to pay down its crushing debts, Parliament put its theory of sovereignty to the ultimate test by levying taxes on its American colonies for the first time.[22] Legislators preparing the Sugar, Currency, and Stamp Acts refused to read American petitions and did not adequately consult colonial agents.[23] The resulting Acts sacrificed colonial commerce to mercantile interests and laid taxes on many products necessary for families and governments. To the astonishment even of members of the British ministry,[24] it also undermined the right to trial by jury by giving admiralty courts power to summon suspects to trial far from their homes—a mammoth expense—where juries were likely to be hostile.[25] Most troubling of all, no legal arguments were presented: the administration merely asserted that the taxes were constitutional since Parliament "virtually" represented Americans.[26] Even some prominent Whigs in Parliament were unsettled by the administration's brazenness and tenuous justification for taxing the American colonies.[27]

The colonists were alarmed: though they had long opposed encroachments on their rights, their patriotism was unimpeachable.[28] They had fought alongside English soldiers and emptied their coffers to fund Britain's conquest of Canada, yet now their property—that bulwark of life and livelihood for the eighteenth-century family—was under assault by an arbitrary legislature.[29] Their initial response to these threats was measured and conciliatory.[30] The "Stamp Act Congress" proposed a boycott of British goods, and sent a declaration and petitions to Britain. These documents proclaimed subordination to Britain, and maintained that Parliament had authority over their external affairs; but they also insisted that the colonists were Englishmen and thus could not be tried in foreign courts or taxed by Parliament unless actually represented.[31] Influential pamphlets of the time similarly insisted only on a return to the way things had been before 1763, and that it was Parliament's theoretical notions of sovereignty and "virtual" representation— the fallacies of which they capably destroyed—that were dividing the empire, not the colonies' defense of their laws.[32] Clergymen's sermons, too, enjoined loyalty to the laws, while displaying marked reluctance to make America's cause a "holy" one.[33] Although some isolated violence occurred, this was rare and widely condemned by colonial leaders and newspapers.[34] Generally speaking, the colonists' protests and civil disobedience were remarkably orderly and peaceful.[35]

By 1766, thanks to the complaints of British merchants, the administration repealed the stamp tax, deeming it "detrimental to the commercial interests of the kingdom."[36] Parliament ignored the Congress' petitions,[37] however, and issued the Declaratory Act, which asserted their right to "make laws ... to bind the colonies ... in all cases whatsoever."[38] Even in the face of a brash statement like this, and with their trade and rights suffering under other Acts, the colonists were still placated by the repeal and determined to believe the best. In fact, the celebrations of the king's birthday that year were the grandest yet seen in the colonies.[39]

Things quickly got worse when Parliament decided that levying high import duties on its virtual constituents in the colonies would make easing taxes on its actual constituents in Britain possible. These "Townshend Acts" augmented the number of Crown officials in America and stipulated that they be paid by London, ensuring their absolute loyalty. Dismayed by this unprovoked renewal of hostilities, the colonists responded as before, meeting taxation with boycott, and speculation with legal precedent. This time John Dickinson gave voice to the colonists' old case that Parliament could regulate the colonies' trade, but could not tax them directly because of their charter and English rights.[40]

The new customs officers proved to be, in Edmund S. Morgan's words, "a rapacious band of bureaucrats." They "exploit[ed] [the law] ... to the utmost." and "used ... technicalities in a deliberately capricious manner to trap colonial merchants." The officers could haul the accused into juryless courts on little evidence, frequently costing the merchant as much as a new ship in court fees, whether he was convicted or not. Worse, practically upon arrival, the officers requested troops from Britain to protect them even though they had not yet experienced any threats—this in an era when Englishmen everywhere viewed standing armies as the surest sign of nascent tyranny. When the requested troops arrived in 1768, however, they were met with perfect tranquility, making "the whole policy ... seem as ridiculous as it was odious."[41]

Over the next year, "such an embarrassing calm prevailed that no ... use could be found for the troops at all" and half of them departed for Halifax. That half remained, however, only increased suspicions that their presence had a more insidious purpose than keeping the peace. As if to confirm these fears, British soldiers in March 1770 responded to a bombardment of snowballs and ice with a volley of bullets, killing three Bostonians and wounding eight others.[42] And yet—astonishingly, given the hysteria that followed—patriot leaders, in a testimony to their devotion to justice, ensured that the soldiers received a fair trial. Future U.S. President John Adams successfully represented the British soldiers.[43]

In April 1770 Parliament once again bowed to economic pressure and repealed the Townshend Acts. The boycott promptly fell apart and there followed three years of relative peace, even though Parliament maintained its claims of absolute sovereignty, and the customs officers remained behind.[44] The colonists, for the most part, accepted the remaining taxes, despite principled disagreement. They were glad to have won "a partial victory or even a stalemate. They were still proud to be part of the British Empire. Reasonable men did not wish to tempt fate by demanding more or to meet conciliation with doctrinaire rigidity."[45]

Once again, the peace ended because of Parliament's exceptional penchant for taxation, this time taxing the colonies to save the nearly bankrupt East India Company. The 1773 Tea Act, "an extreme case of shortsighted discrimination against ... Americans," allowed the company to easily edge out colonial merchants. Even worse was the gravity of the precedent that might be set if the tea were landed and the tax put into effect, namely, that the colonists yielded the charter their ancestors had worked and died for to the total control of Parliament.[46] In Boston, the only city where the government refused to yield to popular pressure, the "Tea Party" was the only possible response that preserved colonial rights in the corner that Britain's policies had backed them into. It was a defensive, limited act of civil disobedience. Participants destroyed only the offending tea and nothing else, though anger with Britain flared higher than it had in many years.[47]

Parliament's response was swift and disproportionate in a way that shocked not only the colonials but some in London as well. The Coercive Acts of 1774 shut down Boston's harbor, revoked Massachusetts' charter, prohibited town meetings, gave the governor near-dictatorial powers, allowed him to commandeer vacant buildings for the purpose of quartering troops, and gave America's western lands to the autocratic Canadian government.[48] Yet even at this juncture the colonists refused to take up arms or actively move toward independence. Instead, they once more spared no pains to conciliate Britain, as the proceedings of the First Continental Congress show.

Although the idea of independence was now cautiously floated as a last resort to utter subjection, the delegates did little more than the Stamp Act Congress had done ten years before: they outlined objections to Britain's actions, proposed a boycott, addressed the British people and petitioned the king for a redress of grievances.[49] These documents said little that was new. Although they used the language of natural law to demand the repeal of British usurpations of colonial rights, they were, remarkably, content to insist on the mere restoration of their charter rights—including the Crown's right to veto colonial legislation—and Parliament's ability to legislate on their external affairs.[50] All this was despite their knowledge that Parliament had previously abused even this power.

These efforts at brokering peace, like those of the previous congress, were rejected without consideration.[51] After over a decade of entreaties from the colonists, the British government still refused to answer the American legal position with arguments of its own, short of touting the long-discredited notion of virtual representation. In truth, there was nothing else they could fall back on, save the Declaratory Act, "in which members of Parliament assured themselves that they had the authority by announcing that they had it."[52]

A conciliatory offer from Britain did arrive in 1775, but because it merely expressed Parliament's ultimate right to tax the colonies in a different manner, it was roundly rejected.[53] It was at this impasse that war finally erupted following General Gage's attempt to seize colonial munitions in the Massachusetts countryside. Rather than using the exigencies of warfare as an opportunity to further its own designs, the Second Continental Congress soberly provided for a defensive army and, in a display of "glorious moderation," issued two documents in a last-ditch attempt at brokering peace.[54]

The *Declaration of the Causes and Necessities of Taking Up Arms*, penned primarily by conservative John Dickinson, was essentially Congress' declaration of self-defense. It laid out a detailed history of British oppression, made a legal case distinguishing colonial from parliamentary sovereignty, and contended that the colonists were fighting at British provocation, "not for glory or for conquest," but "in defence of the freedom that is our birthright" and "for the protection of our property." Moreover, it promised that the colonists would lay down their arms as soon as aggression ceased.[55]

By showing how earnest the colonies were to defend their rights to the last extremity, the Declaration was intended to provide even more incentive for the king to take the second document, the *Olive Branch Petition* (also by written by Dickinson), seriously.[56] It was a noble, but futile, attempt. Although the Petition was full of effusive declarations of loyalty to Britain and the Crown, its pleading for intervention on the colonies' behalf, like every petition from the colonies since 1764, was ignored.[57] After more than a decade of defending their Charter rights from the incitements of an avaricious British legislature, the colonists had exhausted all peaceful solutions. The following year, a reluctant Congress would issue a new declaration that embraced the only alternative to absolute submission. As Carl L. Becker put it, American independence was not the result of desire, but of practical difficulties.[58]

Just war thinking

As noted in Chapter 1, classical just war theory considers two things: under what conditions it is moral to go to war (*jus ad bellum*) and how violence can be employed and restrained during war in ways that comport with just war principles (*jus in bello*). Just war theory begins with three deontological criteria for the just decision (*jus ad bellum*) to use military force: *legitimate authority* acting on a *just cause* with *right intent*. Practical, secondary *jus ad bellum* considerations include: *likelihood of success, proportionality of ends,* and *last resort.* This chapter focuses on those primary criteria: did the colonists have a legitimate political entity representing them and did they act in ways that comport with just cause and right intentions? In 1775, the colonists made such arguments rooted in self-defense, but many scholars have overlooked or disregarded the colonists' arguments. Before we look at the arguments made by the colonists themselves, it is worthwhile to briefly consider some of the revisionist views popular among contemporary scholars.

Considering that the July 1775 *Declaration of the Causes and Necessities of Taking Up Arms* was the first and most comprehensive defense of the war that the colonies made, and that it so succinctly fit their reasoning into a just war framework, it is remarkable how seldom it is mentioned by scholars of the war, whether just war theorists or historians. Why has it been so overlooked and undervalued? There are several possible reasons for this. One may be that the Declaration was soon overshadowed by another document penned a year later that was destined to become more famous: the Declaration of Independence of July 1776. It also seems that many contemporary scholars are inordinately distrustful of official declarations, assuming from the outset that they are mere rhetorical gloss over baser motives.

Whatever the reasoning, this lack of attention to the Declaration of the United Colonies has had consequences for how scholars judge the justness of the colonists' cause. Although relatively little has been written specifically analyzing the American War for Independence in the light of classical just war theory, what has been written often displays misunderstandings that could be corrected by carefully considering the Declaration's arguments. John Keown and George M. Marsden are among a small group of contemporary scholars who have directly confronted the question this chapter addresses about the justness of the war. For example, in "America's War for Independence: Just or Unjust?" Keown makes a case that the war was not just in light of the 1776 Declaration of Independence's claims.[59] However, Keown fails to place that document in the context of the 1775 Declaration of the United Colonies and its arguments—so critical from the colonies' point of view—that the war began in self-defense with the attacks in Massachusetts in April 1775. In effect, he advances the Declaration of Independence, instead of the Declaration of the United Colonies, as the colonists' attempt to justify the war, giving the false impression that independence was the majority of colonists' goal from the very beginning.[60]

Marsden's assessment of the war suffers from a similar tendency to conflate the colonists' justification of independence and their defense of taking up arms. Neglecting to mention the earlier declaration at all, Marsden, like Keown, concludes that the Declaration of Independence was not only a statement of the colonists' independence, but "an attempt to justify ... an already existing war."[61] This mistaken inference leads him to express no small amount of surprise that, when given the chance to defend their actions, the colonists "directed their efforts not toward providing their rationale for a just war ... but toward rationalizing a just revolt against a king." The "revolutionaries," he continues, seem to have been "far more concerned to justify ... revolution [than] warfare"[62] and did not display "any need to provide an elaborate rationale for resorting to violence and killing."[63] How could such people possibly have a "just cause" or "right intent"? While Marsden spends a few pages examining the Declaration of Independence's claims about British tyranny, he nowhere considers the Declaration of the United Colonies' argument that the colonists had taken up arms in defense, not rebellion. Perhaps if he had used this as a starting point, their rationale would not have seemed so "puzzling."[64]

There are a handful of scholars who take the 1775 Declaration, written on the heels of Lexington and Concord, seriously, including Reginald C. Stuart[65] and Carl L. Becker.[66] Other scholars recognize the importance that the clergy's arguments about the justice of going to war had on the colonial citizenry. For instance, James P. Byrd, Melvin B. Endy, Jr., and Mark Valeri have found records of U.S. clergy speaking about the morality of the war, using the term "holy war,"[67] although what was meant was justified war, not an unlimited crusade. More specifically, when the "black-robed regiment" spoke of "holy war" they were talking about war justified by religious impulses, including protection of that most precious of individual liberties: freedom of religion. They were also describing, often in Old Testament terms, the obligations free men had to defend their neighbors and promote justice. Thus, religious language was indeed present in sermons and pamphlets; the patriots "saw the conflict as a just war, fully defensible on those grounds, but ... fought it with religious resolve."[68] As Endy notes, "[the clergy's] understanding of legitimate authority for the war, its justifying causes ... more often fit the just war tradition ... than the interpretation of the Revolution as a holy war."[69] Because clergymen were so influential in forming the beliefs of the common man, these writings, too, are important for assessing the justice and intent of the war. However, they can only be supplementary to a comprehensive approach that uses congressional documents such as the Declaration as well. Consequently, we must turn our attention to the claims the colonists made for themselves, with a focus on the document signed by the Continental Congress in July 1775: the Declaration of the United Colonies.

Just war theory and the *Declaration on the Causes and Necessities of Taking Up Arms*

Penned primarily by Pennsylvania's John Dickinson—a man of Quaker sympathies who later abstained from voting on the 1776 Declaration of Independence, the

1775 *Declaration of the United Colonies on the Causes and Necessities of Taking Up Arms* laid out a rationale for self-defense that completely aligns with just war thinking. Indeed, the colonists beseech London to not provoke "the calamities of civil war"; there is no talk of independence.

The Declaration begins with a question about *legitimate authority*: does God grant to government "unbounded power … never rightfully resistible, however severe and oppressive" or is it "instituted to promote the welfare of mankind"? This is a critical question, because it harks back to the very foundations of the just war tradition. Christian just war thinking—that associated with Ambrose, Augustine, Aquinas, and others—always goes back to the New Testament, or more specifically, Romans 13. This passage argues that political order is a divinely instituted social institution: "For he [the government official] is the minister of God to thee for good." Because of this, temporal authorities have the responsibility to "bear the sword" to "execute wrath upon him that doeth evil."

The colonists were deeply embedded in a Christian worldview, regardless of the unorthodoxy of the faith of some prominent individuals such as Thomas Jefferson and Benjamin Franklin. They took this and other Biblical passages about the ethics of political authority very seriously, as can be seen in the Mayflower Compact and other documents. Their argument is simple: political authority is a divinely ordained good. Thus, when political leaders become tyrants, and when there are alternative forms of political authority that will preserve the lives, livelihoods, and way of life of citizens, then it is perfectly acceptable to act in self-defense. Indeed, there was a strong theological argument made at the time, and that had been made for centuries, that oppressive regimes lose their legitimacy when they harm their own citizens, and so it is appropriate for the citizenry to act on behalf of the principles of law and righteousness.

This is a critical issue because it harks back to the very foundations of the just war tradition. Indeed, it begs the question, "What is the purpose of political order in the first place?" This was a question that had been hotly debated in Great Britain over the past century, as King James and others had argued for a divine right of kings that gave government *carte blanche* based on its supreme authority. By the late eighteenth century, some Parliamentarians were making a similar claim: London could do as it pleased. The Declaration makes this point: "By one statute it is declared, that parliament can 'of right make laws to bind us in all cases whatsoever …' What is to defend us against so enormous, so unlimited a power? … We saw the misery to which such despotism would reduce us."

The colonists, in contrast, are arguing that London lost its authority to govern when it violated its basic responsibility to protect the well-being of citizens within the commonwealth. This includes a variety of threats to their security, both passive and active, that are discussed below.[70]

The Declaration goes on to suggest that governing charters, constitutional rights, and colonial legislatures represent a richer understanding of the political arrangement providing political order in the colonies: "Our forefathers … left their native land, to seek on these shores a residence for civil and religious freedom." The writers note that at little cost to the Crown, over a period of nearly 150 years British colonists had, through their own blood, sweat, and fortunes, settled the "distant and unhospitable wilds of America." They were largely self-governing with royal charters; the relationship was so "mutual[ly] beneficial" as to "excite astonishment."

The Declaration transitions from a discussion of *legitimate authority* to one of *just cause*:

> Parliament ... in the course of eleven years, [has]:
> - undertaken to give and grant our money without our consent, though we have ever exercised an exclusive right to dispose of our own property;
> - statutes have been passed for extending the jurisdiction of courts of admiralty and vice-admiralty beyond their ancient limits;
> - for depriving us of the accustomed and inestimable privilege of trial by jury, in cases affecting both life and property;
> - for suspending the legislature of one of the colonies;
> - for interdicting all commerce to the capital of another;
> - and for altering fundamentally the form of government established by charter, and secured by acts of its own legislature solemnly confirmed by the crown;
> - for exempting the "*murderers*" of colonists from legal trial, and in effect, from punishment;
> - for erecting in a neighbouring province, acquired by the joint arms of Great-Britain and America, a despotism dangerous to our very existence;
> - and for quartering soldiers upon the colonists in time of profound peace.
> - It has also been resolved in parliament, that colonists charged with committing certain offences, shall be transported to England to be tried.

The Declaration enumerates trampled liberties, and it is a damning list. Running throughout it all is a series of taxes ("acts") that have been imposed upon the colonies one after the other for the previous eleven years, many with the explicit purpose not only of raising revenue but of demonstrating the political primacy of the British Empire. These taxes were buttressed by a naval blockade and various anti-smuggling initiatives designed to choke American trade, and thus the livelihood of thousands of colonials. This is a direct assault on the notions of individual liberty and private property—including risk of penury and starvation—that the colonists faced in their first century on the North American continent.

The Declaration describes the motivation for this economic warfare: "These devoted colonies were judged to be in such a state, as to present victories without bloodshed, and all the easy emoluments of statuteable plunder." And now, the king and Parliament had called the self-defensive actions of the colonists "a rebellion" and promised to take "measures to inforce due obedience."

A second set of "just cause" arguments revolves around the legal rights of citizens within the understood constitutional framework of the British Empire. The colonists were accustomed to trial by jury of their peers, but London had revoked this in numerous instances, setting up an alternative juridical system. Admiralty courts were empowered to deal with many cases, meaning that what had formerly been a civil case (e.g. contraband found among legitimate cargo) now could be tried under Admiralty law, with no jury or appeal, including the confiscation of the entirety of one's property and imprisonment.

More concerning, however, was that the colonists had every reason to fear being transported to Canada or even London for trial before a most inhospitable audience, without recourse to local witnesses and evidence. Additionally, the armies quartered on North American soil, which no longer were focused on fighting the French and which increasingly were in league with American Indians—who at times terrorized the borders of the colonies—all suggested a malign plot to force the colonies into virtual slavery.

Revisionist historians sometimes call these arguments hype, but consider the text and context of the Declaration. The document reports that on April 19, 1775, a "large detachment" of General Gage's army, which "had taken possession of the town of Boston," "made an unprovoked assault on the inhabitants of" Lexington and Concord. Gage extended the battle: "Hostilities, thus commenced by the British troops, have been since prosecuted by them without regard to faith or reputation." One might argue that Gage and the colonial militia were simply opposing armies on the battlefield, but the colonists justifiably saw this differently. Gage was garrisoned in the city of Boston. His was a war against civilians, because he had promised that the civilians could freely leave Boston "with their effects" if they gave up their weapons (which many did). However, "they accordingly delivered up their arms, but in open violation of honour, in defiance of the obligation of treaties," the weapons were "seized by a body of soldiers" who then "detained the greatest part of the inhabitants in the town, and compelled the few who were permitted to retire, to leave their most valuable effects behind."

Indeed, Gage went on to brand them all as rebels and traitors. The Declaration cites General Gage's June 12, 1775, order to "declare them all ... to be rebels and traitors, to supersede the course of the common law, and to ... exercise of the law martial." "His troops have butchered our countrymen [at Lexington and Concord] ... and he is exerting his utmost power to spread destruction and devastation around him." Not only this, but "General Carleton, the governor of Canada, is instigating the people of that province and the Indians to fall upon us."

It was not only Massachusetts that was threatened by armed might. On April 20, 1775, one day after the Lexington and Concord assaults, Virginia Governor Lord Dunmore ordered the clandestine emptying of the Williamsburg arsenal, which was countered by Virginia militia led by Patrick Henry. The Battle of Great Bridge, near Norfolk, Virginia, ensued just a few months later on December 9, 1775.

In short, the colonists made a classic *legitimate authority* proposition, arguing that London had neglected its responsibilities to the commonwealth, choosing a tyrannical course of action to gravely limit the basic rights of the colonists. And, the colonists made a *just cause* argument that their actions were legitimate self-defense.

They went on to emphasize their *right intent*. Their purpose was not to plunder their neighbors or establish a new kingdom. There was no imperial design here, nor were acts of self-defense intended to promote anarchy:

> Lest this declaration should disquiet the minds of our friends and fellow-subjects in any part of the empire, we assure them that we mean not to dissolve that union which has so long and so happily subsisted between us ... We have not raised armies with ambitious designs of separating from Great-Britain, and establishing independent states. We fight not for glory or for conquest ... [but] in our native land, in defence of the freedom that is our birthright ... for the protection of our property ... against violence actually offered, we have taken up arms.

The colonists counted the cost, and they reminded London that there was a strong likelihood of success if the colonies had to defend themselves. Despite the powerful British navy, the colonists could turn internally for all of the basic resources of life. The North American continent was rich in resources and space, and the colonies had a robust population. The colonies spread over a wide geography that would not be easy for London to tame, particularly if the colonists could achieve some sort of alliance with foreign powers. Such an alliance would not be surprising and would have been seen as clearly threatening by Great Britain: there was little doubt that France, Spain, and others could have become involved in a global war like the Seven Years War (French and Indian War). Furthermore, if some in London believed that they could split off rebellious Massachusetts from "loyal" New York or the southern colonies, the signers of this Declaration insisted on the unity of the colonies.

The colonists summarized this strategic milieu:

> Our cause is just. Our union is perfect. Our internal resources are great, and, if necessary, foreign assistance is undoubtedly attainable. We gratefully acknowledge, as signal instances of the Divine favour towards us, that his Providence would not permit us to be called into this severe controversy, until we were grown up to our present strength, had been previously exercised in warlike operation, and possessed of the means of defending ourselves.

In conclusion, the colonists reminded London of their many previous petitions, making claims about *last resort* and *proportionality of ends*. Since 1765, individual colonies had sent various petitions and appeals to London, nearly all of which were met with hostility. American representatives, such as Benjamin Franklin, crossed the Atlantic to make their case, but were typically not given audience in official settings. They had seen their freedoms reduced, their options limited, and their livelihoods, across all sectors of the economy, challenged. More specifically, the 1774 Coercive ("Intolerable") Acts were essentially acts of war: Boston Harbor was closed, the Charter of Massachusetts was revoked, the Administration of Justice Act remitted criminal cases to be tried in Britain, the Quartering Act allowed troops to be housed in private homes (not only inns and public houses), and the territory of Canada was extended to deny colonists access to western lands (it also granted a larger measure of autonomy to Roman Catholics). What was next, the imposition of English bishops? Banishment of dissenters? Mercenary troops sent to conquer the civilian populace?

> We are reduced to the alternative of chusing an unconditional submission to tyranny … or resistance by force … We have counted the cost of this contest and find nothing so dreadful as voluntary slavery.

Conclusion

The American War for Independence was not a revolution: it was a just war. After 150 years in North America, the colonists had to make a choice in the 1770s about whether or not they would continue to allow their fundamental rights to be trampled upon. Of course, contemporary sophists may quibble over the issue of *last resort* over cups of cappuccino, but small-business owners and parents can easily imagine what it would have been like to have been a merchant in Boston or New York in the 1770s, with revenues drying up and redcoats taking over your home and stables for their use, with little financial compensation, not to mention concern for one's teenage daughters.

It is often these practical matters of life and livelihood that are forgotten in academic discussions of just war. But the colonists understood them well, articulating a document—the Declaration of the United Colonies—which was a last-ditch effort to forestall war. The Declaration was written after the British attacks at Lexington and Concord, yet a full year before the 1776 Declaration of Independence. Its focus on self-defense and justice makes it the first great just war document in U.S. history.

Notes

1 The Declaration is available at: http://avalon.law.yale.edu/18th_century/arms.asp.
2 Edmund S. Morgan, *The Birth of the Republic: 1763–1789* (Chicago, IL: University of Chicago Press, 1992), p. 9.
3 "The First Charter of Virginia," Yale Law School Lillian Goldman Law Library, available at: http://avalon.law.yale.edu/17th_century/va01.asp (accessed July 27, 2013).
4 Archibald Freeman and Arthur Leonard, eds., *Conciliation with the Colonies: The Speech by Edmund Burke* (Cambridge, MA: Houghton Mifflin Co., 1915), pp. 59–60; Carl L. Becker, *The Declaration of Independence: A Study in the History of Political Ideas* (New York: Random House, Inc., 1970), p. 86.
5 Donald S. Lutz, ed., *Colonial Origins of the American Constitution: A Documentary History* (Indianapolis, IN: Liberty Fund, Inc., 1998), p. xxxiii.
6 Richard Bland, "An Inquiry into the Rights of the British Colonies," in *American Political Writing During the Founding Era: 1760–1785*, vol. I, ed. Charles S. Hyneman and Donald S. Lutz (Indianapolis, IN: Liberty Fund, Inc., 1983), pp. 77–79.
7 Max Savelle and Darold D. Wax, *A History of Colonial America* (Hinsdale, IL: Dryden Press, 1973), p. 224.

8 Ibid., p. 250.

9 Quoted in S. Adams, J. Hancock, et al., "Answer of the House of Representatives to the Speech of the Governor," in *Classics of American Political and Constitutional Thought: Origins through the Civil War, Vol. 1*, ed. Scott J. Hammond, Kevin R. Hardwick, and Howard Leslie Lubert (Indianapolis, IN: Hackett Publishing Company Inc., 2007), p. 242.

10 For a comprehensive summary of the Crown's late-seventeenth-century interactions with the colonial charters, see Philip S. Haffenden, "The Crown and the Colonial Charters, 1675–1688: Part I," *The William and Mary Quarterly*, vol. 15, no. 3 (1958), pp. 297–311.

11 "The Boston Declaration of Grievances," in *The American Republic: Primary Sources*, ed. Bruce Frohnen (Indianapolis, IN: Liberty Fund, Inc., 2002), p. 103.

12 Savelle and Wax, p. 291.

13 Ibid., pp. 251–252.

14 Morgan, p. 13.

15 John Adams, "Novanglus, No. VIII," in *John Adams: Revolutionary Writings, 1755–1775*, ed. Gordon S. Wood (New York: Literary Classics of the United States, Inc., 2011), p. 542.

16 Savelle and Wax, p. 477.

17 Pauline Maier, *From Resistance to Revolution: Colonial Radicals and the Development of American Opposition to Britain, 1765–1776* (New York: W.W. Norton and Company, 1991), pp. 20–21.

18 An excellent and detailed discussion of the evolution of this theory of sovereignty and the colonists' challenge to it can be found in Bernard Bailyn, *The Ideological Origins of the American Revolution* (Cambridge, MA: Harvard University Press, 1982), pp. 198–229.

19 Maier, pp. 186–187; The "Charter of Carolina," (March 24, 1663), Yale Law School Lillian Goldman Law Library, available at: http://avalon.law.yale.edu/17th_century/nc01.asp (accessed July 27, 2013).

20 William Pym, "Letter to the London General Evening Post and the Newport Mercury," in Hammond, et al., p. 176.

21 Lutz, p. xxxiii.

22 Edmund Burke, *Edmund Burke, Esq. on American Taxation, April 19, 1774* (London: J. Dodsley, 1775), pp. 51–52; James P. Byrd, *Sacred Scripture, Sacred War* (New York, NY: Oxford University Press, 2013), p. 28; Morgan, pp. 16–17; Friedrich von Gentz, *The Origin and Principles of the American Revolution Compared with the Origin and Principles of the French Revolution* (Indianapolis, IN: Liberty Fund, Inc., 2010), pp. 17–18.

23 Savelle and Wax, p. 637; Burke, p. 55; Stephen Hopkins, "The Rights of Colonies Examined," in Hyneman and Lutz, pp. 52–53.

24 Maier, p. 231.

25 Morgan, p. 20; Savelle and Wax, pp. 629–634, especially 631–632; John Adams, "Braintree Instructions," 1765, in Frohnen, pp. 115–116; Hopkins, p. 54.

26 Thomas Whately, "The Regulations Lately Made," 1765, in Hammond et al., pp. 166–170.

27 Robert Middlekauff, *The Glorious Cause: The American Revolution, 1763–1789* (New York: Oxford University Press, 2007), pp. 115–117; Edmund Burke, *Observations on a Late State of the Nation* (London: J. Dodsley, 1782), pp. 1–149.

28 Becker, pp. 80–81; Letter of Governor Bernard to a member of the British ministry, quoted in Burke, p. 54; Hopkins, pp. 58–59, 61; Morgan, p. 12–13; James Otis, "Rights of the British Colonies Asserted and Proved," 1764, in Hammond et al., p. 154.

29 Morgan, pp. 8, 17.

30 Maier, pp. 52–53; Morgan, p. 18.

31 "Resolutions of the Stamp Act Congress," in Hammond et al, p. 175; Gentz, p. 54; Morgan, pp. 26–27.

32 Hopkins, pp. 45–61; Bland, pp. 67–87; Daniel Dulany, "Considerations on the Propriety of Imposing Taxes on the British Colonies," in Hammond, et al, pp. 177–182; Becker, p. 89; Morgan, p. 25.

33 Byrd, pp. 30–31; Melvin B. Endy, Jr., "Just War, Holy War, and Millennialism in Revolutionary America," *The William and Mary Quarterly*, vol. 42, no. 1 (1985), pp. 16–17.

34 Gentz, p. 54; Maier, pp. 63–75, 114.

35 For a striking account of the colonial leadership's insistence on "ordered resistance," see the account of the demonstrations in Boston (supposedly the hub of violent mob activity) on the day the Stamp Act was thought to go into effect, and surrounding the "*Liberty* affair," in Maier, pp. 67, 69, 123–124.

36 "The Act Repealing the Stamp Act," in Frohnen, p. 135.

37 Clinton Alfred Weslager, *The Stamp Act Congress: with an Exact Copy of the Complete Journal* (Newark: University of Delaware Press, 1970), pp. 238–239.

38 "The Declaratory Act," in Frohnen, p. 135.

39 Gentz, pp. 54–55; Maier, p. 145; Savelle and Wax, p. 638.

40 John Dickinson, "Letters from a Farmer in Pennsylvania," nos. II, IV, VI, VII, XI, and XII, in Hammond et al., pp. 200–213; Morgan, p. 34–36; Savelle and Wax, 638–642.

41 Morgan, pp. 37–40. See also the details of "customs racketeering" given in Maier, pp. 14–16, and Savelle and Wax, p. 640. On Whig beliefs about standing armies, and the pervasiveness of this thinking in the colonies, see Bailyn, pp. 61–63; Morgan, p. 46.

42 Morgan, pp. 47–48.

43 Hiller Zobel, *The Boston Massacre* (New York: W.W. Norton and Company, 1970), pp. 285–298.

44 Morgan, p. 50; Savelle and Wax, p. 665.

45 Morgan, pp. 52–53.

46 Becker, p. 113; Savelle and Wax, p. 667; Morgan, pp. 58–59.

47 John Adams, diary entry, December 17, 1773, in Wood, pp. 286–287; Gentz, p. 56.

48 Savelle and Wax, pp. 668–669.

49 Gentz, p. 58.

50 Morgan, pp. 64–66.

51 Gentz, p. 58.

52 Morgan, p. 62.

53 Savelle and Wax, p. 677.

54 Gentz, p. 60.

55 Ibid., p. 680; Julian P. Boyd, "The Disputed Authorship of the Declaration on the Causes and Necessities of Taking Up Arms, 1775," *The Pennsylvania Magazine of History and Biography*, vol. 74, no. 1 (1950), pp. 51–73; "A Declaration by the Representatives of the United Colonies of North-America, Now Met in Congress at Philadelphia, Setting Forth the Causes and Necessity of Their Taking Up Arms," Yale Law School Lillian Goldman Law Library, available at: http://avalon.law.yale.edu/18th_century/arms.asp (accessed August 2, 2013).

56 Boyd, pp. 70–72.

57 Savelle and Wax, pp. 680–682.

58 Becker, p. 128.

59 John Keown, "America's War for Independence: Just or Unjust?," *Journal of Catholic Social Thought*, vol. 6, no. 2 (2009), p. 283.

60 Ibid., p. 304.

61 George M. Marsden, "The American Revolution," in *The Wars of America: Eight Christian Views*, ed. Ronald A. Wells (Macon, GA: Mercer University Press, 1991), p. 15.

62 Ibid., p. 15.

63 Ibid., p. 14.

64 Histories of the conflict have also been colored by either failing to include, or failing to take seriously, the claims the Continental Congress made in the Declaration of the United Colonies. For example, the "Progressive" school of thought, as exemplified by Arthur Meier Schlesinger, Sr., *The Colonial Merchants and the American Revolution, 1763-1776, Vol. 78* (New York: Columbia University, 1918) and Charles A. Beard, *Economic Interpretation of the Constitution of the United States* (New York: The Macmillan Co., 1952), read the colonists' official justifications of the war as a kind of gloss over crass, material motives. In their view, it was the commercial interests of the colonial merchant class—largely based in New England ports—that drove the Revolution. However, this does not take into account that the economic warfare London exercised hit every stratum of American society: western farmers could not move their goods across the Atlantic; western lands were sealed off from further exploration and settlement; the colonies were no longer allowed to print paper money; and taxes such as the Stamp Act affected everyone. Economic motivations are not crass when they are a question of the survival of one's family, and when the loss of private property and opportunity is paralleled by other restrictions, such as on freedom of speech, press, assembly, and movement.

65 Reginald C. Stuart, "The American View of War: the Revolutionary Perspective," *Historical Papers*, vol. 11, no. 1 (1976), p. 37.

66 Ibid., p. 128.

67 Byrd, p. 52.

68 Ibid., p. 167.

69 Endy, p. 4.

70 It is noteworthy that whereas some Loyalist clergy argued that the colonials should be ever respectful of king and Parliament, an influential group provided a different reading of Romans 13, the New Testament basis for citizens submitting to government authority. For instance, Jonathan Mayhew, Samuel West, John Tucker, and other influential ministers interpreted Scriptural passages like Romans 13 to both emphasize obedience to authority and support the right of resistance. A typical example of this is Samuel West's claim that "'the same principles which oblige us to submit to government do equally oblige us to resist tyranny." Some of the writing referred to at the time included Peter Martyr Vermigli (who advocated resistance), John Ponet's *A Short Treatise on Political Power* (he supported tyrannicide), John Knox, and others, who argued that resistance was justified—even morally required in some cases—if the national political authority became corrupt and tyrannical. The appropriate body to take such action, it was generally argued, was intermediate political authorities (e.g. chartered colonial governments) acting within the rule of law to preserve the security, rights, and freedom of the citizens. The most famous American making these claims was Jonathan Mayhew in his 1750 "Discourse Concerning the Unlimited Submission and Non-Resistance to Higher Authorities." This sermon was printed and reprinted numerous times in the colonies and in London; John Adams famously said that everyone had read it in the colonies. For more on this line of thinking, see Mayhew's sermon at www.founding.com/founders_library/pageID.2299/default.asp# (accessed March 1, 2015) and Steven M. Dworetz's *The Unvarnished Doctrine: Locke, Liberalism and the American Revolution* (Durham, NC: Duke University Press, 1990).

3

WHEN IS ENOUGH *ENOUGH?*

Last resort and likelihood of success in the War of 1812

Samuel Dalton was an American seaman working on a British merchant ship, docked in Barbados, when he was impressed into the British Navy in 1803. Despite the fact that Dalton had a document from the U.S. government (a "protection") that verified his U.S. citizenship and thus was supposed to protect him from the press gang, his remonstrances fell on deaf ears. He spent the next decade serving as a seaman in the British Navy, living under the harsh conditions of a country involved in a world war against Napoleon. Corporal punishment and austerity were the norm aboard ship. In 1809 Dalton wrote a letter to his brother in Massachusetts, and later that year he received additional documents proving his American identity: a copy of his baptismal certificate and a copy of his parents' marriage license from Salem, Massachusetts. But, as Dalton wrote in a letter, "the Captain got my protection and kept it and kept promising me my Discharge Every Day ... at last he swore that I had as good a right to serve his Majesty as he had & so I have been in the service ever since." In 1812, at the outbreak of war between the United States and Great Britain he was imprisoned as an enemy, only to be released in 1814. In a letter to his mother written before his imprisonment, Dalton wrote, "I am but a wanderer in the world ... If you only knew the anguish of my mind you would pity me."[1]

The War of 1812 is often called the Second War of American Independence because it was fought, in part, to deal with unresolved issues stemming from the United States' first break with Britain and because its aftermath was characterized by the successful resolution of those issues. The U.S. went to war with a strong sense of grievance and impugned national honor on issues ranging from impressment and trade restrictions to British support of an Indian alliance that was terrorizing settlers along the frontier. The issue of impressment of U.S. citizens, such as the case of Samuel Dalton, was particularly galling for Americans. From the U.S. perspective, the issues were local and intensely personal. From the British perspective,

North America was a tiny front in its major effort to break Napoleon's stranglehold on Europe.

The purpose of this chapter is not to evaluate the conduct of the war or its aftermath, although these are important in themselves. This chapter begins with a short discussion of the contours of the conflict to remind the reader of the elements of this almost forgotten war: such an analysis will show that the U.S. enjoyed some luck or good fortune when one considers how woefully unprepared the nation was for war. We then turn our attention to decisions made in Washington that led to war in the first place, evaluating them from a *jus ad bellum* perspective. More specifically, did the decision by President James Madison to go to war meet the prudential just war criteria of *last resort* and *likelihood of success*? A careful look at the security and economic situation of the U.S. in the run-up to the war (1807–1812) suggests that Madison correctly claimed that he and his predecessor, Thomas Jefferson, had tried "every experiment short of the last resort of injured nations"[2] in dealing with critical issues of national sovereignty and security and thus were legitimate political authorities acting on a just cause with right intentions. However, it is also clear that the Madison administration was poorly prepared for war and vastly overestimated the "likelihood of success."

Remembering the War of 1812

The War of 1812 was not just a narrow war between Great Britain and America. The British monarch, the same King George III still sitting on the throne twenty-five years after the American War for Independence, ruled colonial dominions from southwest Asia to the Pacific. Most importantly, however, for the United Kingdom of Great Britain and Ireland was the fact that it had been at war with France (and France's conquered vassals) off and on since 1792. The British had a global perspective, both in terms of trade and in terms of military alliances: they wanted British merchants to have the upper hand on global markets and at the same time wanted to deny the French access to resources and allies from the Western hemisphere. From the U.S. perspective, George Washington's missive to avoid foreign entanglements kept the U.S. out of the drama of Continental politics, but at the same time the U.S. relied heavily on European markets for exports. Nevertheless, to the U.S. the most important factor was the ongoing uncertainty and insecurity caused by British policies on the Atlantic and on U.S. land borders to the north and west.

The naval war

The United Kingdom had the world's largest navy and largest merchant marine. Its captains had dominated the Dutch, Spanish, French, and all other navies for a century. According to the meticulous records of His Majesty's Navy, the British fleet had 152 ships of the line (battleships) and 183 cruisers (e.g. frigates). In contrast, the U.S. Navy had no ships of the line, making large-scale naval battles impossible and allowing the British to partially blockade the American coastline. The

U.S. Navy only had about 5,000 sailors and 1,000 marines, as compared with the British Navy's 140,000 personnel. This overwhelming force was most effective at blocking trade: U.S. exports dropped from $45 million to $7 million between 1811 and 1814.[3]

Because the policy of the Jefferson administration (1801–1808) had been to reduce the size of America's fledgling military, many of the naval ships built under the previous Federalists had intentionally been left to rot. The U.S. began the war with no battleships (ships of the line), six frigates, three sloops of war, seven brigs, and a number of the infamous Jeffersonian "gunboats" that were too small and weak to leave the immediate coast.[4] The frigates, however, were heavy frigates made with advanced techniques and considerably more sturdy and powerful than their British counterparts. Thus, in the early part of the war—before a British blockade more or less shut down all U.S. ports—the American Navy had a number of victories that shocked the British public and enhanced U.S. morale: the USS *Constitution* over the HMS *Guerriere*, the USS *Wasp* over the HMS *Frolic*, the USS *Hornet* over the HMS *Peacock*, the USS *Constitution* over the HMS *Java*, and the surrender and capture of HMS *Macedonia* by the USS *United States*. Moreover, in the first year of the war American privateers took 450 British merchant vessels, although this was to dramatically slow in 1813 as the British blockaded the U.S. eastern seaboard.

However, the U.S. also had some strategic success on the Great Lakes, most notably the victory of Oliver Hazard Perry on Lake Erie (1813) and later Thomas Macdonough at Lake Champlain (1814). The latter set up a major American military victory at Plattsburgh. These naval battles were important primarily because they were auxiliaries to the land contest between the U.S. on one side and the British, Canadians, and Indian forces on the other. With the U.S. ultimately winning these battles for the Great Lakes, the British land forces retreated fully back into Canada, abandoning the vision of a defensible, independent Indian state on America's north-west border.

The war on land

One might claim that the War of 1812 actually started on November 7, 1811, with the Battle of Tippecanoe. Indiana Territorial Governor, and future U.S. President, William Henry Harrison defeated an Indian force at Tippecanoe (near today's Lafayette, Indiana). This victory emboldened Americans fighting Indians, especially in the South and West, and convinced the Indians that they must obtain significant British support in order to successfully ward off the pressures from ever-encroaching settlers (the Indians had moved to this area from further east under an agreement with Washington). The British had long sought a robust buffer between Canada and the U.S. and one of London's war aims was the establishment, or re-establishment, of a clearly defined Indian state with security guarantees from the U.S.

In addition to the frontier situation, the U.S. was dealing with more than a decade's worth of grievances, including impressment, confiscation, and a naval blockade. President James Madison sent a message to Congress on June 1, 1812, apprising them of the deteriorating situation with Britain. Within a few days, the House of Representatives voted 79–49 in favor of a declaration of war, with the Senate following suit (19–13). War was formally declared on June 18, 1812.

It is hard for the contemporary reader to grasp how different communication and travel were in 1812. A declaration of war could be handed off to the British Ambassador in Washington, DC, but then must also travel by ship to Canada and England (the latter a journey of at least three weeks). During this period, news that the British Orders in Council had been replaced with a somewhat less onerous set of restrictions was traveling from London to Washington via sail, but did not make it to Washington prior to the declaration of war.[5]

The U.S. was poorly prepared for war and it had a singular strategy: beat the British forces in Canada and force the British to sue for peace. Two invasions of Canada were launched in 1812, the first just a month after the declaration of war. However, in August U.S. forces surrendered to an inferior force at Detroit, losing most of the Michigan territory to a force made up of British troops, Canadian militia, and Indians. In October 1812, the second invasion of Canada suffered defeat at the Battle of Queenstown Heights. A year later, a third attempt to "liberate" Canada resulted in a U.S. retreat after failing to take Montreal.

Fortunately for the U.S., in October 1813 William Henry Harrison defeated an Anglo-Indian force at the strategic Battle of the Thames. This resulted in the U.S. effectively taking control of sparsely populated Western Ontario and ending

---

BOX 3.1 AN ACT DECLARING WAR BETWEEN THE UNITED KINGDOM OF GREAT BRITAIN AND IRELAND AND THE DEPENDENCIES THEREOF AND THE UNITED STATES OF AMERICA AND THEIR TERRITORIES

Be it enacted by the Senate and House of Representatives of the United States of America in Congress assembled, That war be and the same is hereby declared to exist between the United Kingdom of Great Britain and Ireland and the dependencies thereof, and the United States of America and their territories; and that the President of the United States is hereby authorized to use the whole land and naval force of the United States to carry the same into effect, and to issue to private armed vessels of the United States commissions or letters of marque and general reprisal, in such form as he shall think proper, and under the seal of the United States, against the vessels, goods, and effects of the government of the said United Kingdom of Great Britain and Ireland, and the subjects thereof.

APPROVED, June 18, 1812

Source: http://avalon.law.yale.edu/19th_century/1812-01.asp

the era of the British supplying Indian forces with weapons and coordinating efforts in the western theater. Ultimately, this victory signaled that one of America's chief war aims had been met, although this was not entirely clear at the time.

In short, by the winter of 1813 the war had been going on for eighteen months but with numerous setbacks for the ground forces of the U.S. military. Britain remained in command of the seas and the U.S. economy was beginning to suffer. One of the first pieces of news in the spring campaigning season was that Napoleon abdicated on April 6, 1814, and a major peace treaty settling Europe's affairs was in the offing. The Treaty of Paris was signed on May 30, 1814, allowing the British to turn their full attention to defeating the U.S. The U.S. economy was in serious decline due to inflation, the naval blockade, poor institutions, uncertainty, weak federal coffers, and the lack of support of Anglophone Federalists in New England.

Indeed, the American situation in mid-1814 in many ways looked perilous. The British attacked the major seaport of Baltimore and burned the national capital, Washington, DC, to the ground in August. It appeared that there was little to stop a British advance through the middle of the country. Nevertheless, even during this period, it is clear that the British did not have a strategy of actually crushing the U.S. and reabsorbing it as a colony. Rather, like most traditional wars, this was a war of positioning for the strategic upper hand in eventual peace negotiations.

In fact, the British could control parts of the seas and hurt the U.S., but they could not conquer such a vast land mass, nor did they have the appetite for more war. The clamor in London was for peace. The British had been at war with France for almost twenty years (1793–1815) at this point, with only a brief respite during the short-lived Peace of Amiens (1802–1803) a decade earlier. The focus of attention was on settling affairs in Europe now that Napoleon was exiled to Elba, and the general public was tired of the heavy taxation required to support the war effort. Merchant interests wanted trade to North America reopened immediately. Perhaps most importantly, with the end of the war against France, the major *casus belli*—trade restrictions and impressment—were no longer issues.

Hence, at the same time that Washington was burning, American and British negotiators began to meet in Ghent (in today's Belgium). The U.S. side was represented by major luminaries, including diplomat and future President John Quincy Adams, Speaker of the House Henry Clay, Treasury Secretary Albert Gallatin, diplomat and future Congressman John Russell, and U.S. Senator James A. Bayard. The British sent minor diplomats, but these could be in direct contact with London for direction.

In August 1814, there was uncertainty on both sides, but the British had recently launched four ground invasions: one of the middle states (Maryland), one in Maine, one in New York, and finally one toward New Orleans. Although they were successful at Bladensburg and Washington, the siege of Baltimore was unsuccessful, with the British pulling out after the death of the commanding officer. Although the invasion of Maine had minor successes, it was not a strategic victory that would alter the course of the war. In September, the British defeat at the

Battle of Plattsburgh (also known as the Battle of Lake Champlain) had strategic consequences, forcing the British back to Canada and earning the U.S. control of the Great Lakes. The Battle of New Orleans was not to take place until the war was officially over.

During the autumn of 1814, while British opinion was divided over the war, American resolve hardened. This was, in part, due to battlefield victories, particularly at Plattsburgh. Moreover, when the initial position of the British war negotiators was made public, there was an outcry in the U.S., even in anti-Madison (Federalist) New England. The British were demanding an Indian buffer state in the Northwest Territory (modern-day Ohio and beyond), naval rights on the Great Lakes, commercial access along the entirety of the Mississippi River, and other trade concessions. Ultimately, more realistic voices prevailed. For instance, Lord Wellington, victor over Napoleon in Europe, advised the Prime Minister,

> I think you have no right, from the state of war, to demand any concession of territory from America ... You have not been able to carry it into the enemy's territory, notwithstanding your military success, and now undoubted military superiority, and have not even cleared your own territory on the point of attack. You cannot on any principle of equality in negotiation claim a cession of territory except in exchange for other advantages which you have in your power ... You can get no territory: indeed, the state of your military operations, however creditable, does not entitle you to demand any.[6]

Shortly thereafter, the Prime Minister informed the Foreign Minister, "I think we have determined, if all other points can be satisfactorily settled, not to continue the war for the purpose of obtaining, or securing any acquisition of territory."[7]

Negotiations were completed on Christmas Eve 1814, with the British Parliament approving the Treaty of Ghent shortly thereafter. The Battle of New Orleans, a victory for General Andrew Jackson and the American military, was fought on January 8, 1815, before either side knew of the peace treaty. The treaty was ratified by the U.S. Senate in February, officially terminating the war.

The Treaty of Ghent restored property to both sides and reinforced the existing boundaries of the U.S. with respect to Spanish Florida and Canada. Trade was opened and impressment ended, although such items were not fully explicated in the Treaty. One outstanding issue was the loss of "property" in the form of approximately 3,000 escaped slaves. Ultimately, an indemnity of approximately $1.2 million was paid to the U.S. At war's end, the British had lost approximately 1,600 killed in action, 3,679 wounded, and another 3,321 to disease. The U.S. had 2,260 killed in action and 4,505 wounded. Historians suggest that in total, due to civilian deaths and disease, between 10,000 and 15,000 Americans died during the war. Economists estimate that the war cost each side approximately $105 million.[8] With all of this mind, did this war meet the just war criteria of last resort and likelihood of success?

Last resort and likelihood of success

Last resort and the War of 1812

When considering the ethics of going to war—any war—one must start with the cardinal just war principles of legitimate authority, just cause, and right intention. As noted in Chapter 1, it is widely agreed that these principles are deontological in nature, meaning that they have primacy because they are rooted in first-order moral obligations. The moral purpose of the state's existence is the security of its people. These principles are explicit in classical just war writing, in contrast to last resort or likelihood of success. It is after these fundamental criteria are met that government officials begin to consider the secondary, prudential criteria that flow from them. It is inappropriate, and disingenuous, therefore, for the notion of *last resort* to be used as the principle criterion for critiquing the justness of going to war, despite the fact that many facile arguments purporting to be "just war theory" do so. The place to begin is the responsibility that political leaders have to act on behalf of the security of their fellow citizens.

In 1812, was the American situation in accord with these principles? Were American grievances aligned with just war tenets? More specifically, was the war to be waged led by a legitimate political authority acting on just cause with right intentions? When one looks at President Madison's 1812 message to Congress and subsequent congressional findings that resulted in the declaration of war, it is clear that the U.S. government (legitimate authority) was acting to defend and secure the lives, livelihoods, and way of life of its citizens (just cause) without baser intentions or motivations such as burning London or wrecking the British Empire.

What is last resort? Chapter 1 defines last resort as political leaders, who have a just cause and right intention, answering the following question: have traditional diplomatic and other efforts been reasonably employed in order to avoid outright bloodshed? The Catholic bishops' letter defines last resort as "force may be used only after all peaceful alternatives have been seriously tried and exhausted." Demy and Charles write, "Have all reasonable efforts to utilize normal (e.g. diplomatic, economic, political) alternatives been exhausted? The operative word here is 'reasonable' since those who oppose all war in principle will never see diplomatic possibilities as having been exhausted."[9]

This issue—that of making last resort a fig leaf for stopping war altogether—has been discussed by James Turner Johnson and Michael Walzer. Johnson writes, "the criterion does not mean always postponing the use of military force until every possible means short of force has been tried." That is because postponing action can make things worse: "the gradualist way might simply postpone what is necessary until still later, perhaps making the situation worse and requiring a more robust, costly, and dangerous intervention when force is finally brought in."[10] Michael Walzer similarly criticizes the use of last resort to stop all deliberation about going to war. Critics of war "never reach lastness, for we can never know that we have reached it."[11] This makes last resort a tool for those who want to use it as a barrier to any and all use of military force.

Last resort is smart stewardship. It means having considered the options. It does not mean waiting so long to use military force that one violates one's responsibility to defend the country. It does not mean one has to wait until the enemy has every advantage. It is not a fig leaf for dithering, weakness, cowardice, or poor strategy. Last resort does not mean waiting until it is too late.

Historians estimate that as many as 15,000 Americans had been impressed by the British Navy by 1812. With a population, according to the 1810 census, of 7.2 million people, that 15,000 was a very large number that touched hundreds of thousands of families and neighbors. To put that number in perspective, if the Chinese or Russians were impressing U.S. citizens today at the same rate, something like 729,000 Americans would have been seized and put to work on foreign warships. This would clearly be a *casus belli*. Furthermore, this situation was heightened by the official and unofficial periods of British embargo of U.S. goods. The British Orders in Council (1807–1812) specifically forbade trade to French ports, including by neutrals:

> it is hereby ordered, that no vessel shall be permitted to trade from one port to another, both which ports shall belong to, or be in the possession of France or her allies, or shall be so far under their control as that British vessels may not freely trade thereat; and the commanders of his majesty's ships of war and privateers shall be, and are hereby instructed to warn every neutral vessel coming from any such port, and destined to another such port, to discontinue her voyage, and not to proceed to any such port; and any vessel, after being so warned, or any vessel coming from any such port after a reasonable time shall have been afforded for receiving information of this his majesty's orders which shall be found proceeding to another such port, shall be captured and brought in, and together with her cargo, shall be condemned as lawful prize.[12]

What had the U.S. done to stop the maritime depredations of Britain? President Thomas Jefferson (1801–1809), whose Secretary of State was James Madison, opposed the expansion of the U.S. military for ideological reasons and, for more practical reasons, was unwilling to use force against either Britain or France (both blocked U.S. merchants from their ports). Jefferson's response was economic sanctions: the Embargo Act made it illegal for U.S. ships to trade with either France or Britain. The effect of the Embargo Act was to destroy American trade with far less adverse effects on the European economies, because France could provide itself with supplies from Europe under the Continental System and Britain turned to Spanish colonies and smuggling via Canada. In Paris, the U.S. Ambassador famously stated, "Here it is not felt, and in England … it is forgotten." Between 1807 and 1808, exports from the U.S. to Europe dropped from $108 million to $22 million.[13] The unpopular Embargo Act did little to curtail impressment or relieve American grievances and ultimately was replaced by a less onerous series of non-importation Acts. Again, American remonstrances, diplomatic initiatives, and economic sanctions did little to check British policy on the high seas, nor did it check British weapons flowing to American Indians on the frontier.

President Madison's war address

President James Madison had been in office for nearly four years when, on June 1, 1812, he presented Congress with a document describing the despoliations of the British on the U.S. Madison leveled a number of charges against Great Britain in this speech, which resulted in a few days of debate in both chambers of Congress and a formal declaration of war on June 12.

Madison began by arguing that "the conduct of her [Great Britain's] government presents a series of acts hostile to the United States as an independent and neutral nation."[14] The first of these "hostile acts" was the violation of American neutrality and commercial rights. The U.S. merchant fleet consisted of neutral vessels, and there was no right under international law for these vessels to be stopped on the high seas by the British Navy:

> British cruisers have been in the continued practice of violating the American flag on the great highway of nations, and of seizing and carrying off persons sailing under it, not in the exercise of a belligerent right founded on the law of nations against an enemy, but of a municipal prerogative over British subjects.

In other words, the British Navy had stopped American vessels claiming an interest in repatriating deserters to the British Navy, without a formal declaration of war against the U.S. Madison rightly noted that if the U.S. were to behave similarly, the British would declare it to be an act of war or piracy. More to the point, however, Madison recognized that international law, as well as British common law, demanded "a regular investigation before a competent tribunal" and "the fairest trial where the sacred rights of persons were at issue," but instead "these rights are subjected to the will of every petty commander." In other words, none of the individuals who were being seized from American ships, whether that individual was a former British seaman, a British deserter, a foreigner, or an American citizen, was given a lawful trial by jury or competent magistrate. Their "sacred rights" were being violated unlawfully and extrajudicially.

In addition to the violation of American neutrality, British naval vessels were kidnapping and enslaving American citizens: "under the pretext of searching for these, thousands of American citizens, under the safeguard of public law and of their national flag, have been torn from their country and from everything dear to them." Anyone who has studied this era of the British Navy and the conditions aboard a ship of war at the time knows that Madison was not exaggerating when he wrote that these Americans were:

> dragged on board ships of war of a foreign nation and exposed, under the severities of their discipline, to be exiled to the most distant and deadly climes,

to risk their lives in the battles of their oppressors, and to be the melancholy instruments of taking away those of their own brethren.

Madison had probably received hundreds if not thousands of letters from families of those impressed into the Royal Navy.

Despite repeated efforts at diplomacy, these activities continued. Madison goes on to expose the illegal blockade of American ports. This blockade was both informal and formal:

> Under pretended blockades, without the presence of an adequate force and sometimes without the practicability of applying one, our commerce has been plundered in every sea, the great staples of our country have been cut off from their legitimate markets, and a destructive blow aimed at our agricultural and maritime interests.

So not only were British warships waiting just off the coast but they were also stopping American vessels from reaching European ports.

Madison goes on to publicly explain some of the motives for the blockade. Its purpose was not only to deny the French Empire American goods, but also to stifle competition for British interests. Moreover, British naval commanders had a huge incentive to attack American vessels because one of their chief sources of revenue, if a prize court affirmed, was contraband taken from such "prizes." Madison writes,

> The cabinet of Britain resorted at length to the sweeping system of blockades, under the name of Orders in Council, which has been molded and managed as might best suit its political views, its commercial jealousies, or the avidity of British cruisers.

These acts by the British led directly to Madison's fourth justification for action, the massive loss of American money and property:

> It has become, indeed, sufficiently certain that the commerce of the United States is to be sacrificed, not as interfering with the belligerent rights of Great Britain; not as supplying the wants of her enemies, which she herself supplies; but as interfering with the monopoly which she covets for her own commerce and navigation. She carries on a war against the lawful commerce of a friend.

Again, Madison reports on the actions that the U.S. had taken to this point to protect its interests: "the United States have withheld from Great Britain, under successive modifications, the benefits of a free intercourse with their market." He calls the years of diplomacy and economic sanctions "every experiment short of the last resort of injured nations."

Madison goes on to record the changing nature of British policy, which can only be understood as devious.

There was a period when a favorable change in the policy of the British cabinet was justly considered as established. The minister plenipotentiary of His Britannic Majesty here proposed an adjustment of the differences more immediately endangering the harmony of the two countries. The proposition was accepted with the promptitude and cordiality corresponding with the invariable professions of this government. A foundation appeared to be laid for a sincere and lasting reconciliation. The prospect, however, quickly vanished. The whole proceeding was disavowed by the British government without any explanations which could at that time repress the belief that the disavowal proceeded from a spirit of hostility to the commercial rights and prosperity of the United States; and it has since come into proof that at the very moment when the public minister was holding the language of friendship and inspiring confidence in the sincerity of the negotiation with which he was charged, a secret agent of his government was employed in intrigues having for their object a subversion of our government and a dismemberment of our happy union.

British policy, even when it provided some slight accommodation to American grievances, tended to revert—either by design or circumstance—to its former unlawful and destabilizing behavior.

Finally, Madison raises a security issue that had long haunted the American frontier. As the U.S. population grew and settled westward, it came into conflict with American Indians. The long history of this struggle is well documented elsewhere, but in 1812 the problem facing the Madison administration was that British agents were actively arming Indians as allies to contain the U.S. British policy was to create an Indian buffer state between the U.S. and Canada, but one can imagine the rage American citizens felt when it was a British gun or knife that was used to scalp and kill an American woman. Madison remonstrates,

> In reviewing the conduct of Great Britain toward the United States our attention is necessarily drawn to the warfare just renewed by the savages on one of our extensive frontiers, a warfare which is known to spare neither age nor sex and to be distinguished by features peculiarly shocking to humanity. It is difficult to account for the activity and combinations which have for some time been developing themselves among tribes in constant intercourse with British traders and garrisons without connecting their hostility with that influence and without recollecting the authenticated examples of such interpositions heretofore furnished by the officers and agents of that government.

Madison provides a stirring conclusion about the trampled rights of Americans, but he also succinctly puts the matter into its baldest possible formulation: "We behold, in fine, on the side of Great Britain, a state of war against the United States, and on the side of the United States a state of peace toward Great Britain."

In sum, President Madison cataloged a list of intrigues and depredations that violated the sovereignty of the U.S., destroyed or looted private property, and transgressed the rights of individual U.S. citizens. These outrages had been occurring since 1793 but had become increasingly serious for a decade, and U.S. efforts at diplomacy and economic sanctions had been batted aside. America's last resort was war.

Canada: A U.S. war aim?

There is considerable scholarly debate about what the intentions of the U.S. were toward Canada at the outset of the war. Did President Madison intend to conquer and annex Canada? From a just war perspective, a war of liberation or conquest is not the same as a war of self-defense, righting past wrongs, and preventing future wrongs. Certainly there were those like Andrew Jackson who felt that the British presence in North America (Canada, Oregon) was a long-term threat. Old Hickory opined,

> The hour of national vengeance has arrived ... [we are fighting for] our national character ... the protection of our maritime citizens impressed on British ships of war ... to seek some indemnity for past injuries, some security against future aggression by the conquest of all the British dominions upon the continent of North America.[15]

Others wrongfully believed that many Canadians, whether French Quebecois or Anglo-Canadians, were ripe to be liberated from the British crown. This hubris was to be severely tested from the outset, as it was already clear that a Canadian identity was developing, based in large part on the citizens' identity as Loyalists during the American War for Independence. However, the most realistic reading of the Madison administration's position on Canada was not that Canada would be conquered, but that an attack on Canada could yield a knock-out blow at the outset of the war. The U.S. could not beat the British on the seas, but with London absorbed by Napoleon in Europe, an American army—despite the fact that it was primarily militia—should be able to beat the thin British military presence in Canada, putting the U.S. into a strong negotiating position and perhaps securing some additional territory. Of course, this is not what occurred.

Likelihood of success

What is "likelihood" or "probability" of success? It is the prudential weighing of alternatives by the statesman. When it comes to issues of war and security, the political leaders must take into account the past situation and the most likely outcome of going to war or not going to war. The leader calculates, with imperfect knowledge, how the tools and stratagems at his disposal make the achievement of the objectives likely. Likelihood of success takes into account what is to be gained and what is potentially to be lost when choosing whether or not to go to war.

Likelihood of success, however, is not one of the cardinal *jus ad bellum* criteria. That is not because forecasting the likelihood of success is an imperfect science (although it is). The reason that it is a secondary criterion is because it can be trumped by legitimate authority and just cause. For instance, an overwhelming power may make battlefield victory seem impossible, but to concede defeat in some cases means slavery or extinction. For instance, should the Jews have "surrendered" to the Nazis? Should Tutsis, or Kurds, or Bosnians, or any other minority have surrendered to their antagonists when genocide was the likely outcome? Of course not.[16]

But, in normal times of war, if there is such a thing, likelihood of success does have some practical dimensions. The leader must ask: what do we mean by success? What is the goal? Can we achieve the goal? Is it likely that the security situation will be better, or worse, than before? What is the cost/benefit ratio? In some cases, the cost/benefit ratio may not be promising but there is nevertheless a compelling interest in going to war. Evaluating the likelihood of success is particularly important in such cases. It is the leader's critical responsibility, as a steward of the public's resources including the lives of military personnel, to honestly count the cost.

Perhaps the greatest recent example of this was Winston Churchill. When he took over as Prime Minister in 1940, his appetite for statistics and data about the war effort was insatiable: tanks, jeeps, guns, ordnance, fuel, etc. He wanted to know how much, where, when, cost, improvements, and the like. Part of this stemmed from his own experience as a soldier and as First Lord of the Admiralty, but it also seems to be an essential part of his natural strategic sense. Churchill demonstrates that analyzing likelihood of success is about commitment. It sees war as more than just a life-sized version of chess. It recognizes the destructive potential of war and as such forces the wise leader to match a resource commitment to provide the finances, manpower, and materiel necessary to win the war effort. Likelihood of success considers, as Churchill did, that intangible factors such as troop morale, public support, and institutional vitality must complement the material factors of war.

Did President Madison consider likelihood of success? Did the hawkish Republican Congress that was seated in November 1811 consider likelihood of success? On the one hand it appears that the strategic climate that the U.S was living in seemed to be deleterious and that there was no way other than war to protect the rights of U.S. citizens and businesses. Although twelve years of Democratic-Republican administrations had seriously weakened the diminutive U.S. military, nonetheless, the 1811 Congress did pass a series of measures in the autumn of 1811 that began to strengthen the U.S. military. These initiatives included growing the size of the army, providing funding for weapons and military supplies, and building new ships. But it was far too little and it was far too late for these elements to have a major effect against British military power.

Americans were counting on at least two strategic factors, both of which proved elusive. The first factor was the belief in some quarters, as noted above, that American audacity could strike a blow against Canada that would, at the least, force Britain to the negotiating table, perhaps even resulting in territorial acquisition. The second was that London would be so fixated on dealing with Napoleon on the Continent that it could little afford another war in the Western hemisphere. When it comes to the former, as discussed above, untested American land forces were poorly prepared, poorly led, and repeatedly repulsed on the Canadian front.

When it comes to the war in Europe, the Americans could not have known that just two weeks after they declared war, Napoleon would launch his ill-fated attack on Russia. Napoleon invaded Russia with his Grande Armée of 500,000 men in June 1812, but by October they were in disarray. Six weeks later, with 400,000 lost, the tattered remains of that army crawled out of the frozen, burnt wastes of Russia. Within the year it was clear that the British could focus far more attention on the Atlantic theater.

Although these strategic presuppositions were presumptuous, many American leaders did recognize that there were factors in their favor, such as the size of the North American continent and the fact that the British could not completely conquer, on land, the U.S. A military strategy like that of the first War of Independence, that focused on attrition and scoring victories that caused damage to the enemy, could ultimately be successful in achieving some war aims, such as dealing with the threat of Indians on the frontier and causing pain to British merchant ships (450 of which were captured by American privateers in the first year of the war).

Conclusion

The land and sea battles of the War of 1812 were part of a larger global landscape that included twenty years of Napoleonic warfare in Europe, Africa, and Asia. The War of 1812 was caused by festering resentment in the U.S. at real injustices perpetrated by the British, including the impressment of thousands of U.S. citizens into the squalid, brutal conditions of the Royal Navy and the loss of millions of dollars in trade, especially from the period following the January 7, 1807, Orders in Council, which opened up neutral shipping to condemnation for trading in French-controlled ports and subsequent seizure by the Royal Navy. American citizens on the frontier were also deeply concerned about Indian raids and demanded action by their representatives in Washington.

American leadership in Washington met the basic just war criteria of *legitimate political authority* having *just cause* and *right intentions* by seeking to defend the lives, livelihoods, and way of life of its people. But did President James Madison and the U.S. Congress act as a *last resort* with some *likelihood of success*? Madison clearly believed so, explicitly stating in his 1812 war address that a state of war already existed vis-à-vis London and Washington, and that the U.S. was simply responding in kind as "the last resort of injured nations." The historical record suggests that no one at the time could reasonably imagine a change in the U.S. position without a dramatic change in the conditions of the relationship. War was clearly "politics by other means" and morally defensible. At the same time, President Madison and his political allies may have poorly understood their strategic weakness as compared with British might, or at least dramatically overestimated U.S. power to deliver a knock-out blow on the Canadian front that would result in London quickly suing for peace. In other words, this appears to be a case where the essential *jus ad bellum* criteria were met, but where the president and his compatriots lacked a realistic discernment of what it would take to succeed. In any event, it is a happy accident of history that 1815 can be counted as a victory for both sides, with Britain beating Napoleon a second time and ultimately ending his role in global affairs, and the upstart U.S. feeling victorious in its confrontation with the United Kingdom. Indeed, in the years to come these two former adversaries would draw increasingly closer in what would ultimately become a uniquely "special relationship."

Notes

1 Denver Brunsman, "Subjects vs. Citizens: Impressment and Identity in the Anglo-American Atlantic," *Journal of the Early Republic*, vol. 30, no. 4 (December 2010).

2 James Madison, "Special Message" (June 1, 1812), Gerhard Peters and John T. Woolley, The American Presidency Project, available at: www.presidency.ucsb.edu/ws/index.php?pid=65936.

3 Jeremy Black, "A British View of the Naval War of 1812," *Naval History Magazine*, vol. 22, no. 4 (August 2008).

4 There is some confusion as to the actual number of U.S. frigates, and this appears to be due to their being two "Adams" vessels: the USS *Adams* and the USS *John Adams*, both launched in 1799. The former was scuttled in 1814 to prevent capture by the British; the latter served through the U.S. Civil War and was sold off in 1867. What makes this even more confusing is that the USS *John Adams* was built as a frigate, trimmed down to a corvette in 1809 (and thus considered a corvette during the War of 1812), and rebuilt as a frigate in 1830. The other U.S. frigates included *Essex*, *Boston*, and *New York*, plus the famous six heavy frigates: *Constitution*, *United States*, *Chesapeake*, *President*, *Congress*, and *Constitution* (popularly known as "Old Ironsides" and still in service in Boston Harbor).

5 There are historians who suggest that had Madison known of the rescission of the Orders in Council (the trade blockade), the War of 1812 would never have happened. It is hard to know whether or not this is accurate because there had been so many years of mistrust built up. Indeed, Madison explicitly claims in his war message that London is devious and changes its policies, suggesting it cannot be trusted.

6 Quoted in George C. Daghan, *1812: The Navy's War* (New York: Basic Books, 2013), p. 201.

7 Ibid., p. 202.

8 15,000 impressed (www.pbs.org/opb/historydetectives/feature/british-navy-impressment/); U.S. population at the time 7.2 million (www.census.gov/history/www/through_the_decades/fast_facts/1810_fast_facts.html). This is the equivalent of roughly 729,000 Americans being impressed today.

9 J. Daryl Charles and Timothy J. Demy, *War, Peace, and Christianity: Questions and Answers from a Just War Perspective* (Wheaton, IL: Crossway, 2010), p. 171.

10 Quoted in Charles and Demy, p. 172.

11 Quoted in Charles and Demy, p. 170.

12 William S. Dudley, ed., *The Naval War of 1812: A Documentary History*, vol. II (Washington, DC: Naval Historical Center, 1992), p. 15.

13 See Faye Margaret Kert, "The Fortunes of War: Commercial Warfare and Maritime Risk in the War of 1812," *Northern Mariner*, vol. 8 (Oct. 1998), pp. 1–16; and Dudley, p. 15.

14 This and subsequent quotes are from Madison's message to Congress of June 1, 1812 (see note 2 above).

15 Miriam Greenblatt, *War of 1812*, updated ed. (New York: Facts on File, Inc., 2003), p. 63, in the "America at War" series, general editor John Stewart Bowman.

16 There are arguments made that suggest the alternative point of view. See David Rodin, *War and Self-Defense* (Oxford and New York: Oxford University Press, 2003) and David Rodin and Henry Shue, eds., *Just and Unjust Warriors: The Moral and Legal Status of Soldiers* (Oxford: Oxford University Press, 2008).

4

DOMINOS, EGO, AND NATIONAL HONOR

The ethics of going to, and prolonging, the Vietnam War

Reflecting on the French debacle at Dien Bien Phu in 1954, U.S. President Dwight D. Eisenhower observed, "You have a row of dominoes set up. You knock over the first one, and what will happen to the last one is the certainty that it will go over very quickly."[1] Eisenhower had not only Indochina in mind, but the recent war in Korea and "loss" of China to Mao Zedong's Communists. Sixteen years later, Eisenhower's former Vice President was President and he affirmed the "domino theory" at a press conference:

> Now I know there are those who say the domino theory is obsolete. They haven't talked to the dominoes. They should talk to the Thais, to the Malaysians, to the Singaporeans, to the Indonesians, to the Filipinos, to the Japanese, and the rest. And if the United States leaves Vietnam in a way that we are humiliated or defeated, not simply speaking in what is called jingoistic terms, but in very practical terms, this will be immensely discouraging to the 300 million people from Japan clear around to Thailand in free Asia; and even more important it will be ominously encouraging to the leaders of Communist China and the Soviet Union who are supporting the North Vietnamese. It will encourage them in their expansionist policies in other areas.[2]

President Kennedy told a 1963 press conference that he believed in the domino theory; in his inaugural address he warned "our security may be lost piece by piece, country by country."[3] President Johnson was characteristically raw when he opined, "If you let a bully come into your front yard one day, the next day he'll be up on your porch and the day after that he'll rape your wife in your own bed."[4]

The presidents of America's Vietnam era, as well as their advisors, utilized similar language. The domino theory was informed by all of these men's experiences during World War II and a shared understanding among their generation that the appeasement at Munich had emboldened Hitler and his allies and that the dominos had fallen: Austria, Czechoslovakia, Poland. The domino theory is really shorthand, or a heuristic, for a larger set of assumptions that informed U.S. war aims with regard to Vietnam and its neighborhood from the 1950s through the 1970s.

"War aims" are the desired outcomes of a political-military strategy, or what political and military leaders desire and intend to achieve in the context of war. War aims are thus statements of policy and have explicit moral content, not just because they are political objectives but also because they demand stewardship of human life, military materiel, and the national treasury. Because war aims are the purview, at least in the U.S., of the President as Commander in Chief, it is appropriate to consider both the ethical context and content of stated and unstated war aims. When it comes to Vietnam, that means considering the strategic environment in which the domino theory developed as well as the explicit and implicit justifications for going to war and continuing to fight in Vietnam.

Just war thinking provides clear ethical guidelines for going to war, most notably the three principles of *sovereign political authority*, *just cause*, and *right intention*. Each of these moral presuppositions can help us examine and analyze the war aims of U.S. presidents during the Vietnam War. A later chapter in this book deals with the morality of victory and specifically considers how legitimate, ethical war aims are an obvious component of *jus ad bellum*, both in theory and in practice. For the purposes of this chapter, however, the focus will be specifically on the stated, and unstated, war aims of U.S. presidents regarding Vietnam and its neighbors from the administrations of Dwight D. Eisenhower (1952–1960) through Richard M. Nixon (1969–1974).[5] Were the war aims of Eisenhower, Kennedy, Johnson, and Nixon commensurate with *jus ad bellum* principles? What were the actual war aims that derived from the domino theory? Did the war aims change over time? This chapter identifies and analyzes five presidential war aims, arguing that war aims focused on defense of one's allies and keeping treaty commitments in a dangerous, bipolar world may have met the *jus ad bellum* criteria, but that there were other war aims that developed over time, including the sanctity of national "honor" and presidential ego, that are not in keeping with the essential just war criteria for going to, and prolonging, war.

The domino theory and presidential war aims

In 1956 Senator John F. Kennedy claimed that Vietnam was "the cornerstone of the Free World in Southeast Asia, the keystone in the arch, the finger in the dike, and should the red tide of Communism pour into it … much of Asia would be threatened."[6] General Maxwell Taylor, World War II hero and later civilian Ambassador to Vietnam (1964–1965), said this about the domino theory:

> I personally do not believe in such a theory if it means belief in a law of nature which requires the collapse of each neighboring state in an inevitable sequence, following a Communist victory in Vietnam. However I am deeply

impressed with the probable effects world-wide, not necessarily in areas contiguous to South Vietnam, if the "war of liberation" scores a significant victory there.[7]

In 1966 social psychologist Ralph White called Taylor's the "sophisticated version of the domino theory." White elaborated the assumptions of the sophisticated domino theory as follows:

It seems entirely consistent with the psychological evidence to suppose: (1) that complete withdrawal by the United States would encourage the Communist to attempt seizures of power in various other developing countries, including some in which they would not have the degree of popular support that they have had in Vietnam; (2) that the degree of cruelty and ruthlessness on both sides is now such that the complete withdrawal by us would leave our anti-Communist friends exposed to some very rough treatment, which would tend to discourage anti-Communists in other countries who might otherwise have the courage to resist terror and threats of assassination; and (3) the complete withdrawal would in Communist eyes seem to confirm the Chinese Communist philosophy of village-centered warfare against the infrastructure of non-Communist societies.

Each of these processes could operate especially in countries near the borders of South Vietnam (Laos, Cambodia, Thailand, Malaysia) ... but each could presumably operate also in any country in the world where conditions are ripe for violence and men have images of the physical and psychological strength of Communism and anti-Communism ... If Communists gained a decisive victory in Vietnam, Communists elsewhere would tend to be confirmed in their belief that Communism is the wave of the future, anti-Communists would tend to be disheartened by the same thought, and many Communists, presumably, would decide that Mao's strategy for dissolving the power of anti-Communist governments is a strategy that pays off in the long run.

Doubts about this more complex and sophisticated version of the domino theory do not center around the probable fact of such a tendency; they center around its probable importance in the overall scheme of things.[8]

The domino theory provided a heuristic that was more complicated than a simple child's game. It included a number of assumptions about the adversary's intentions, the responsibility of the U.S., and the nature of international affairs in a dangerous, bipolar world. The domino theory demanded active national security and foreign policies from successive presidential administrations. What were the grand strategic war aims, as located within global policy objectives, for which the U.S. was fighting? A careful study of the statements and policies of four presidential administrations demonstrates a high level of continuity on war aims and the rationale for pursuing them. There were at least five major war aims, most of which are associated with the domino theory, which were used to justify supporting the South Vietnamese government and continuing to fight the Vietnam War:

1. Contain communism.
2. Spread democracy, or at least hold it in places where it already existed.
3. Demonstrate resolve to various foreign audiences.
4. Vindicate national honor.
5. Protect the personal reputation and credibility of the President.

The first U.S. war aim was to contain communism. In the early years of the Cold War the United States had to decide what its policy would be for dealing with the apparently insatiable, ubiquitous assault of the Soviet Union and global communism. Some argued that the U.S. should return to its pre-war isolationist policy and not attempt to mind other people's business. Even if more European governments fell to Stalin's Soviet Union, nonetheless the U.S. was largely safe in North America. Others who took the "mind our own business" position believed that the advent of nuclear weapons simply made any sort of confrontation with the Soviets too dangerous for humanity. Some Americans were concerned about the "Red Menace" but felt that the costs of the Great Depression and then a world war were so great that it was time for Americans to care for their own and enjoy a peace dividend. At the other end of the spectrum were those who felt that, in one way or another, the U.S. should not only stand up to this latest aggressor but even consider pushing back on the Soviet Union if it was going to play hardball. John Foster Dulles famously called for the "rollback" of communist advances.[9]

The U.S. ended up taking a middle road that became known as "containment." The idea of containment is associated with State Department official George Kennan and his "X Article," published in *Foreign Affairs* in 1947. Kennan wrote,

> The main element of any United States policy toward the Soviet Union must be that of a long-term, patient but firm and vigilant containment of Russian expansive tendencies … Soviet pressure against the free institutions of the Western world [should be countered] through the adroit and vigilant application of counter-force at a series of constantly shifting geographical and political points, corresponding to the shifts and maneuvers of Soviet policy … [to] promote tendencies which must eventually find their outlet in either the break-up or the gradual mellowing of Soviet power.[10]

A strategy to contain "Russian expansive tendencies" through "counter-force" is precisely what many Americans thought was occurring in the early years of the Vietnam War. After Kennan left the position of Director of Policy Planning at the State Department, his successor, Paul Nitze, fleshed out the idea of containment as a politico-military strategy in National Security Council Directive 68 (NSC-68), which envisioned a more muscular, military containment than Kennan later claimed that he had meant. NSC-68 observed, "In the context of the present polarization of power a defeat of free institutions anywhere is a defeat everywhere."[11] As containment developed as an idea, policies such as the Truman Doctrine (to support democracies everywhere) and institutions such as NATO (North Atlantic Treaty Organisation) and its Southeast Asian sibling, SEATO (Southeast Asia Treaty Organization), were being developed. In sum, U.S. foreign policy responded in the Truman presidency with a coherent, adaptive grand strategy called "containment" that was the foundation of U.S. policy for the next half-century. U.S. leaders saw the defense of a quasi-democratic, Western-oriented South Vietnam (and neutral Laos and Cambodia) as consistent with a global policy of containment. Indeed, if the U.S. did not "contain" communism in Indochina, then, as Eisenhower argued after Dien Bien Phu, the dominos might start to fall.

President Eisenhower embraced the Truman administration's doctrine of containment and its application to Far Eastern "dominos:"

> If the capture of the offshore islands [Quemoy and Matsu] should, in fact, lead to the loss of Formosa, the future security of Japan, the Philippines, Thailand, Vietnam, and even Okinawa would be placed in jeopardy and United States vital interest would suffer severely. Such a chain of disaster would not be wrought instantaneously, perhaps, but assuming success in the initial blow, disintegration would follow, we thought, within the course of several years.[12]

In a 1959 speech President Eisenhower said, "The loss of South Vietnam would set in motion a crumbling process that could, as it progressed, have grave consequences for us and for freedom."[13]

The last foreign policy crisis of the Eisenhower administration, and the one he briefed John F. Kennedy on the day before Kennedy's inauguration, was Laos. Kennedy had to deal with communist destabilization of both Laos and Vietnam from his first days in office, including a March 1961 press conference calling out (with maps and charts) communist activity in Laos.[14] Shortly thereafter, President Kennedy's National Security Action Memorandum 52 (NSAM-52, May 11, 1961) succinctly laid out a policy of containment with regard to Vietnam:

> The U.S. objective and concept of operations stated in the report are approved: to prevent Communist domination of South Vietnam; to create in that country a viable and increasingly democratic society, and to initiate, on an accelerated basis, a series of mutually supporting actions of a military, political, economic, psychological and covert character designed to achieve this objective ...
>
> Additional actions ... are authorized, with the objective of meeting the increased security threat resulting from the new situation along the frontier between Laos and Vietnam. In particular, the President directs an assessment of the military utility of a further increase in GVN forces from 170,000 to 200,000, together with an assessment of the parallel political and fiscal implications.

At times, President Lyndon Johnson directly quoted Kennedy's language about Vietnam: "mutually supporting actions of a military, political, economic … character." Within days of taking office Johnson signed a National Security Action Memorandum (NSAM-288) which outlined action items from the recent Honolulu Conference (for SEATO allies) on Vietnam.[15] NSAM-288 begins with containment language: "It remains the central object of the United States in South Vietnam to assist the people and Government of that country to win their contest against the externally directed and supported Communist conspiracy."[16] In an address in Omaha in 1966 Johnson made a similar point:

> South Vietnam is important to the security of the rest of all of Asia. A few years ago the nations of free Asia lay under the shadow of Communist China. They faced a common threat, but not in unity. They were still caught up in their old disputes and dangerous confrontations. They were ripe for aggression. Now that picture is changing. Shielded by the courage of the South Vietnamese, the peoples of free Asia today are driving toward economic and social development in a new spirit of regional cooperation. All you have to do is look at that map and you will see independence growing, thriving, blossoming, and blooming. They are convinced that the Vietnamese people and their allies are going to stand firm against the conqueror, or against aggression.
>
> Our fighting in Vietnam, therefore, is buying time not only for South Vietnam, but it is buying time for a new and a vital, growing Asia to emerge and develop additional strength. If South Vietnam were to collapse under Communist pressure from the North, the progress in the rest of Asia would be greatly endangered. And don't you forget that![17]

President Nixon likewise emphasized containment as a war aim guiding U.S. resolve in Vietnam, as the domino theory quote at the beginning of this chapter attests:

> if the United States leaves Vietnam … this will be immensely discouraging to the 300 million people from Japan clear around to Thailand in free Asia; and even more important it will be ominously encouraging to the leaders of Communist China and the Soviet Union … It will encourage them in their expansionist policies in other areas.[18]

In short, there is little doubt that containing communism, at the 38th parallel, the 17th parallel, the Berlin Wall, and elsewhere, was a major U.S. foreign policy objective and a shared Vietnam War aim for four U.S. presidents.

A second U.S. foreign policy principle that became a war aim in Vietnam was to spread, or hold, democracy in places where it existed. In the immediate aftermath of World War II the Western allies were frustrated by the many promises broken by Stalin, from lingering Soviet military detachments in Iran to the lack of free elections in Poland. Stalin similarly broke promises associated with the spheres of influence Churchill believed were agreed upon at the Fourth Moscow Conference in 1944.

At dinner that evening, without the American representative Averell Harriman present, Churchill jotted down percentages of shared influence in Greece, Romania, Yugoslavia, Bulgaria, and Hungary. For instance, in Greece the U.K. was to have 90 percent influence and the Soviet Union 10 percent influence, with the opposite holding true in Romania. Yugoslavia and Hungary were both supposed to be 50/50. Stalin ticked off the various elements on the napkin and then returned it to Churchill. Final details were haggled over the next day by Foreign Secretaries Eden and Molotov. Of course, little of this was allowed to proceed, as Soviet troops effectively held on to most of these countries. Just a few years later President Eisenhower observed that the

> truly virulent problems in international affairs spring from the persistent, continuing struggle between freedom and Communism ... this conflict reflects the truisms that freedom must be earned and defended each day ... External forces, thirsting for power, are always ready to destroy freedom. Witness the fate of Austria and Ethiopia before the opening of World War II and Hungary, Poland, North Vietnam, Czechoslovakia, Bulgaria, and others since its close.[19]

By 1947 the U.S. was so frustrated by Soviet expansionism that a set of institutions was set in place to prop up the global economy (e.g. the Bretton Woods system), rebuild Europe to be an effective buffer and counter radicalism (the Marshall Plan), establish collective security (NATO), and pledge support to democracies being destabilized by communist fifth columnists or external bullies (Truman Doctrine). The U.S. began to see such a formula as equally important in Asia, including support for democracy and development (modernization) activities, because these were seen as inextricably intertwined: unless a country's economy was modernizing and developing, that country would find it difficult to have successful institutions and consolidate democracy. Parallel to NATO, a collective security organization was also established for Southeast Asia (SEATO).

In the case of Vietnam, it was not U.S. policy to establish democracy in a place where it had not previously existed, nor was it U.S. policy to forcefully impose democracy across Indochina. The goal was to buttress the feeble but existing governing institutions that were being left behind as the French withdrew in the aftermath of Dien Bien Phu and the 1954 Geneva Conference, which brought together nearly a dozen countries with the goal of settling outstanding issues on the Korean peninsula and in Indochina.

Few people realize today that the original U.S. position, in support of South Vietnam (State of Vietnam), at the 1954 Geneva Conference, was for a unified Vietnam with perhaps some United Nations involvement and a guarantee of competitive elections. In contrast, it was the North Vietnamese (Democratic Republic of Vietnam) and their allies who made the original argument for partition. The position of the two sides is revealing. The U.S. seemed to have some faith in the democratic process and that if it could fully take root in a Vietnam not plagued by warring factions or communist fighting, the country might evolve into a democracy and be outside the direct influence of Moscow and Beijing. In contrast, the Chinese pushed the North Vietnamese hard toward a partition agreement because, despite the French loss at Dien Bien Phu, there remained over 400,000 French troops on the ground in Vietnam and the communists feared that the U.S. would intervene and shift the balance of power against the communists. Moreover, although the North Vietnamese tried to get their communist allies in Laos and Cambodia admitted to the conference and thus legitimized in newly organized governments there, this initiative failed. The reason that all of this gamesmanship is important is because it demonstrates that U.S. policy toward East Asia was concerned about both stability and democracy. South Vietnam did have some fledgling democratic institutions and the U.S. position was that a united Vietnam should chart its own course, in the future, through democratic mechanisms.

The U.S. was committed to not allowing democracies to fall if at all possible, but Washington was keenly aware of just how fragile new democracies, especially in poor countries, could be. CQ Press reports that it is "impossible to determine" the total cost of the Vietnam War, in part because U.S. military veterans are still being provided with healthcare services. But CQ Press records $138.9 billion spent on the military effort from 1965 to 1976.[20] When it comes to foreign assistance of other forms (e.g. development monies from USAID, democracy support through the State Department, etc.), billions were spent in Vietnam because the U.S. did believe in supporting Vietnamese democracy through development and the strengthening of government institutions. The U.S. Defense Department estimated that $28.5 billion was spent on democracy and development activities during the most active phase of U.S. involvement in Vietnam.[21]

Much more could be said about the Geneva Accords but it is clear to many observers that by the time elections were to happen in 1956, the trajectories of Saigon and Hanoi and their patrons were on a collision course. By the end of 1956 the governments of South Vietnam and the U.S. clearly had no immediate expectation of a democratic consensus taking hold over the entire region and thus anticipated a status quo of a divided Vietnam, like Korea with the South shielded by the U.S. and its allies, for years to come.

Investment in democracy and development were not secondary goals but primary objectives of U.S. policy in Vietnam. Kennedy's NSAM-52 pledged that "The U.S. will undertake economic programs in Viet-Nam with a view to both short term immediate impact and a contribution to the longer range economic viability of the country." Kennedy typically spoke in this language of security and economic development when speaking about Vietnam. In his budget message to Congress for fiscal year 1964, Kennedy wrote:

> We are steadfast in our determination to promote the security of the free world, not only through our commitment to join in the defense of freedom, but also through our pledge to contribute to the economic and social development of less privileged, independent peoples.[22]

President Johnson, whose focus on empowering the poor was both a domestic and an international policy goal, told an audience at Johns Hopkins University:

> The first step is for the countries of Southeast Asia to associate themselves in a greatly expanded cooperative effort for development … I would hope that the Secretary-General of the United Nations could use the prestige of his great office to initiate … a plan for cooperation in increased development. For our part I will ask the Congress to join in a billion dollar American investment in this effort as soon as it is underway … The task is nothing less than to enrich the hopes and existence of more than a hundred million people. And there is much to be done.[23]

Johnson famously compared the vast Mekong River Delta to the Tennessee Valley Authority (TVA), noting that the size and resources of the former could—if effectively managed in peace—provide electric power and other goods for millions of people, far beyond the TVA. Johnson, like his predecessor, firmly believed that only a modernizing Vietnam could develop rooted democratic institutions and meet the needs of its populace.

Finally, when it comes to President Nixon, there was little new in his annual budgets to Congress with regard to non-military funding. As Jeffrey Kimball writes, "Neither Johnson nor Nixon was willing to abandon the essential goal of U.S. policy—a viable, anticommunist government of an independent South Vietnam."[24] But in Nixon's case it is apparent that from the beginning he was committed to a policy of "Vietnamization": to develop, as quickly as possible, stable South Vietnamese government and military institutions while ruthlessly forcing the North Vietnamese to the negotiating table by powerful U.S. military intervention. This was an extrication strategy with conventional development and democratization elements rather than a moral commitment to some sort of democratic ideal.

A third U.S. war aim was to demonstrate U.S. resolve. At the end of World War II the United States was thrust onto the global stage as the mightiest country on the earth, and it was quickly locked into a long-term adversarial contest with the Soviet Union and its satellites. A basic principle of the doctrine of containment was vigilance to provide counter-force against the wily, aggressive tactics of the communists. It was a common communist maxim that Western governments were weak and effeminate, lacking the staying power to counter the scientific fact of communist progress. Eisenhower recognized the importance of resolve and credibility, arguing in his memoir that,

> over a period of eight years, with problems involving Iran, Trieste, Guatemala, Korea, Suez, Lebanon, the Formosa Strait, Vietnam, Laos, Austria, Cuba, and other areas … [we] tried always to create mutual confidence and trust, well knowing that without these ingredients alliances would be of little enduring value.[25]

Consequently, the U.S. government had at least three audiences that it felt it had to convince of its resolve. The first of those audiences was the communists themselves. The U.S. felt that it had to prove to the communists the depth of its commitment not to abandon its allies.

A second audience that the U.S. had to demonstrate the credibility of its security guarantees to was its own allies. This view aligns with that of General Maxwell Taylor, quoted above. The U.S. was deeply concerned not to appear as if it was vacillating in Vietnam because that could signal to other countries, such as the Philippines or those in Latin America or in Europe, that the U.S. lacked the will to come to their aid if they were similarly challenged by communism.

A third audience was potential allies. By the mid-1950s the idea of "non-aligned" countries had developed, given impetus by the 1955 Bandung Conference (the formal Non-Aligned Movement conference did not occur until 1961). Both Moscow and Washington wanted to pull such countries into their respective orbits, including potential powerhouses such as India, Egypt, and Indonesia. If the West did not support South Vietnam, the thinking went, the lack of resolve would turn potential allies away.

Successive presidents talked at great length about the importance of demonstrating the credibility of deterrence, the toughness of America's national resolve, and an overarching sense of purpose; that the U.S., in the aftermath of World War II, had reluctantly but decisively accepted the mantle of global leadership and it would not back down. For instance, President Eisenhower reflected in his memoir,

> I pointed out that in Korea, Indochina, Formosa, Greece, and elsewhere, the Communists had been stopped in aggressive action only by the interposition of Western resolution and force ... there was no hope of inducing the West to go into unwise ventures which would be interpreted by the Soviets only as weakness and invitation to further aggression.[26]

President Kennedy trumpeted, "Let every nation know, whether it wishes us well or ill, that we shall pay any price, bear any burden, meet any hardship, support any friend, oppose any foe to assure the survival and the success of liberty." It is noteworthy what comes next in his 1961 inaugural address, because he specifically lays out these audiences:

> To those old allies whose cultural and spiritual origins we share, we pledge the loyalty of faithful friends ...
>
> To those new states whom we welcome to the ranks of the free, we pledge our word that one form of colonial control shall not have passed away merely to be replaced by a far more iron tyranny ...
>
> To those people in the huts and villages of half the globe struggling to break the bonds of mass misery, we pledge our best efforts to help them help themselves, for whatever period is required—not because the communists may be doing it, not because we seek their votes, but because it is right. If a

free society cannot help the many who are poor, it cannot save the few who are rich.

To our sister republics south of our border, we offer a special pledge—to convert our good words into good deeds—in a new alliance for progress—to assist free men and free governments in casting off the chains of poverty. But this peaceful revolution of hope cannot become the prey of hostile powers. Let all our neighbors know that we shall join with them to oppose aggression or subversion anywhere in the Americas. And let every other power know that this Hemisphere intends to remain the master of its own house ...

Finally, to those nations who would make themselves our adversary, we offer not a pledge but a request: that both sides begin anew the quest for peace, before the dark powers of destruction unleashed by science engulf all humanity in planned or accidental self-destruction ... We dare not tempt them with weakness. For only when our arms are sufficient beyond doubt can we be certain beyond doubt that they will never be employed.[27]

When Kennedy responded two months later to the Laos crisis, he told the world that "no one should doubt our resolution on this point."[28] Historian William J. Rust reports that "resolve" was important to Kennedy across the entire Southeast Asian theater and that the President felt that Vietnam had "relative advantages" (as compared with Laos) for U.S. air and naval power to "be more easily brought to bear" if necessary. Rust writes, "To demonstrate U.S. resolve, Kennedy sent Vice President Lyndon B. Johnson on a trip to Asia to meet with pro-Western leaders."[29]

President Johnson similarly emphasized the importance of demonstrating U.S. resolve and how that resolution buttressed world order. In a 1965 speech in which he rhetoricized, "Why are we in South Vietnam?" he responded,

We are also there to strengthen world order. Around the globe, from Berlin to Thailand, are people whose well-being rests, in part, on the belief that they can count on us if they are attacked. To leave Vietnam to its fate would shake the confidence of all these people in the value of American commitment, the value of America's word. The result would be increased unrest and instability, and even wider war.

President Nixon told the American people in 1973,

For the future of peace, precipitate withdrawal would thus be a disaster of immense magnitude ... Our defeat and humiliation in South Vietnam without question would promote recklessness in the councils of those great powers who have not yet abandoned their goals of world conquest ... This would spark violence wherever our commitments help maintain the peace— in the Middle East, in Berlin, eventually even in the Western Hemisphere. Ultimately, this would cost more lives. It would not bring peace; it would bring more war.[30]

At this point, one might ask: but what about the Pentagon Papers? Didn't they prove that this was all meaningless rhetoric and that senior leaders were just pulling the wool over everyone's eyes? That the presidents knew we could not win in Vietnam? These questions are *a propos*, particularly since the year of the publication of this book coincides with a major Hollywood film on the Pentagon Papers, raising their profile and muddying the waters of fact about their relevance to this discussion. The Pentagon Papers were a classified study, conducted under the authority of Democratic Secretary of Defense Robert McNamara, studying U.S. involvement in Indochina from 1945 to 1967 and illegally released to *The New York Times* in 1971. This is important because the Pentagon Papers did not cover any of the presidency of Richard Nixon, although the Nixon administration tried vigorously to prohibit their release on national security grounds.[31]

The Pentagon Papers simply do not prove that senior U.S. officials knew that Vietnam could not be won. That is because most U.S. leaders, such as members of Congress, did not even have the appropriate security clearance to see classified materials in the first decade of U.S. support to Saigon. The diversity of documents from numerous agencies were not compiled in one place until this study was conducted; hence, most people only had a partial picture of the war effort—even at the White House and the Pentagon. Unfortunately, the Pentagon Papers have taken on a mythical significance of "proving" that U.S. presidents knew all along that Vietnam was unwinnable, and thus a waste of U.S. time and resources. This is just wrong.

But what the Pentagon Papers did reveal to the U.S. public was a much earlier, deeper level of involvement by the U.S. government in Southeast Asia. This is the true revelation of the Pentagon Papers, and there were elements of the record that either contradicted public statements by various administrations or surprised the public. The biggest examples of this include information that the U.S. had provided assistance to the French military as far back as the Truman administration; Kennedy's complicity with—or, better, turning a blind eye to—the assassination of South Vietnamese President Diem in 1963; the fact that President Johnson quietly ordered escalation in 1964 (which was apparently the continuation of a Kennedy policy) while telling campaign crowds that he would not significantly increase U.S. involvement; and analyses that early strategic bombing campaigns did not appear to dampen the ardor of the Viet Cong.

Do the Pentagon Papers somehow change the analysis of this chapter on stated presidential war aims? Not in the least. In fact, the Pentagon Papers seem to prove the point: U.S. presidents felt it a matter of vital national import to contain communism, support the weak government institutions in Saigon, and demonstrate U.S. resolve to the world, even if they had to take steps clandestinely to do so.

A fourth war aim, one that developed as the war was being fought, was the sanctity of national honor. Although Clausewitz was partly correct that "war is politics by other means," he missed the spiritual dynamic of war, because the moment that blood is spilt, war takes on a sacred character. Thus, a war aim that develops over time, and is a justification for continuing the war as blood and treasure are invested, is the vindication of national honor.

The word "honor" can mean to accord privilege and respect but it can also mean the fulfillment of an obligation. Both definitions are salient when speaking in the context of lost comrades in arms. The questions, when leaders spoke about Vietnam, were: whose honor? What is the nature of the obligation? And, how are we to think about the polar opposite of honor, shame, in political life? These questions are often overlooked in the just war literature.[32] The answer, at least to some of the questions, can be ascertained by looking at the rhetoric of political leaders during the Vietnam War, including statements by Richard Nixon over the course of an entire decade. In 1965 Richard Nixon made this claim in a *Reader's Digest* essay: "our nation and our honor have been committed, and our men are falling and dying every day." In the same article he said that a weak "negotiated settlement" would mean that "hundreds of Americans and thousands of Vietnamese who have given their lives in the fight against Communist aggression would have done so in vain."[33] As a candidate running for President, Nixon promised, "I pledge to you that we shall have an honorable end to the war in Vietnam."[34] And on January 23, 1973, in a televised address to the American people reporting on the successful outcome of the Paris Peace Conference, President Nixon used the word "honor" seven times,

> I have asked for this radio and television time tonight for the purpose of announcing that we today have concluded an agreement to end the war and bring peace with honor in Vietnam and in Southeast Asia ...
>
> Throughout the years of negotiations, we have insisted on peace with honor. In my addresses to the Nation from this room of January 25 and May 8 [1972], I set forth the goals that we considered essential for peace with honor ...
>
> And finally, to all of you who are listening, the American people: Your steadfastness in supporting our insistence on peace with honor has made peace with honor possible. I know that you would not have wanted that peace jeopardized ...
>
> The important thing was not to talk about peace, but to get peace—and to get the right kind of peace. This we have done.
>
> Now that we have achieved an honorable agreement, let us be proud that America did not settle for a peace that would have betrayed our allies, that would have abandoned our prisoners of war, or that would have ended the war for us but would have continued the war for the 50 million people of Indochina. Let us be proud of the 2 ½ million young Americans who served in Vietnam, who served with honor and distinction in one of the most selfless enterprises in the history of nations. And let us be proud of those who sacrificed, who gave their lives so that the people of South Vietnam might live in freedom and so that the world might live in peace.[35]

The idea of honor in the context of war is that political leaders have a responsibility to vindicate the sacrifices of those who have paid the ultimate price in battle. Their deaths should mean something. The fallen should not have died in vain. This concept of honor also extends to the fallen of one's allies, including thousands of French and South Koreans, hundreds of Australians, and well over a million South Vietnamese soldiers and civilians.[36] All of these resisted the depredations of the North Vietnamese and Viet Cong, from the mass graves found at Hue, to torture, assassination, and terrorism. Didn't the living owe something to the dead? And, by honoring their sacrifice, Nixon argued, we send a message to our friends and our adversaries about our character, our values, and our steadfastness.

The notion of honor also includes, whether stated or unstated, the idea of return on investment. The U.S. had invested heavily in Vietnam for a decade, and invested across Southeast Asia since the late 1940s. It is very difficult for leaders—especially can-do, pioneering, overcome-every-obstacle American leaders—to admit that there is an unmovable obstacle or unachievable goal. Americans put a man on the moon the year that Nixon took office! Certainly America could achieve an honorable peace in the rice paddies of Asia! Americans want to win: it is, or was, in the very DNA of the national culture. Moreover, it is very difficult to abandon sunk costs and all the sacrifice they represent.

At times, U.S. leaders used negative terms to describe the opposite of honor: humiliation, shame, and degradation. These concepts intersect with the war aim about credibility in the eyes of allies. Because the U.S. had not committed large numbers of troops to Vietnam during his presidency, President Eisenhower did not speak in terms of U.S. national honor, but he did speak of the sanctity of French lives lost. In a letter to the French President in 1954, Eisenhower memorialized:

> My dear President Coty:
> The entire free world has been inspired by the heroism and stamina displayed by the gallant garrison at Dien Bien Phu. Their devotion and the quality of their resistance have been so great that that battle will forever stand as a symbol of the free world's determination to resist dictatorial aggression and to sustain its right of self-determination and its dedication to the dignity of the human being. France has in the past suffered temporary defeats, but always she has triumphed in the end to continue as one of the world's leaders in all things that tend to bring greater richness to the lives of men. Those who fought and died and suffered at Dien Bien Phu should know that no sacrifice of theirs has been in vain; that the free world will remain faithful to the causes for which they have so nobly fought.
> With expressions of my personal regard,
> DWIGHT D. EISENHOWER[37]

In a parallel letter to the South Vietnamese leader, Eisenhower spoke of heroism and sacrifice:

> Our admiration for the gallant men of the Vietnamese forces ... [who] so heroically defended Dien Bien Phu against insuperable odds. It is sad indeed

that the fortress and its brave defenders have fallen to the enemy, but we can be heartened in the knowledge that their sacrifice has not been in vain … their heroic resistance to the evil forces of Communist aggression has given inspiration to all who support the cause of human freedom. Those brave men made their sacrifice in order that individual freedom and national independence for the people of Viet-Nam should not be lost to Communist enslavement. We of the free world are determined to remain faithful to the causes for which they have so nobly fought.[38]

John F. Kennedy spoke in a very personal way about honoring the sacrifice of the fallen in response to a letter from Mrs. Bobbie Lou Pendergass (March 1963). She asked if the death of her brother had any meaning and the President assured her that "he had not died in vain," "earn[ing] the eternal devotion of this Nation and other free men around the world." President Johnson used such language in his 1965 Johns Hopkins speech:

> We are there because we have a promise to keep. Since 1954 every American President has offered support to the people of South Vietnam. We have helped to build, and we have helped to defend. Thus, over many years, we have made a national pledge to help South Vietnam defend its independence. And I intend to keep our promise.
>
> To dishonor that pledge, to abandon this small and brave nation to its enemy, and to the terror that must follow, would be an unforgivable wrong.[39]

Nixon likewise spoke of the dishonor of not keeping international commitments, such as in his famous 1973 speech revealing the resolution of the Paris Peace talks to the American people: "A nation cannot remain great if it betrays its allies and lets down its friends."

Nevertheless, there is something different, in the way that "honor" was used, especially by President Nixon, than the notion of shame in front of one's allies. The underlying idea is that there is a national soul that must be tended by righteous and even heroic action, regardless of the cost.

Honor is not necessarily victory, but an honorable peace is certainly not surrender. In the case of Vietnam, debates raged, and continue to this day, about what winning might have looked like. But, at the time of the conflict, a secondary logic took hold that was beyond the narrow logic of containment found in the domino theory, and that logic was the logic of an honorable end to war that accorded with national dignity and the loss of the fallen. Elements of that honorable peace may be myth, such as America telling itself that it could have won had it "taken off the gloves" or unleashed nuclear weapons. But also key to that notion of honor was getting the North Vietnamese to go through the rituals of international diplomacy, such as publicly signing an agreement, publicly committing to peaceful conflict resolution, promises (even if they were not believed) of ceasefire and the end of hostilities, assurances that ultimate reunification of Vietnam would occur through democratic means, and the like. "Honor" meant that the U.S. had defended its ally, forcing the North Vietnamese to live up to international standards, and that it could leave along the lines first outlined by President Kennedy a decade earlier:

> In the final analysis, it is their war. They are the ones who have to win it or lose it. We can help them, we can give them equipment, we can send our men out there as advisers, but they have to win it, the people of Vietnam, against the Communists.[40]

In conclusion, the notion of honor in its most profound sense is not usually a strategic objective during the wrangling among governments in the high politics of international life. The back and forth of diplomacy, threats, sanctions, espionage, blockades, and other political theater may be high drama, but this is not the time that a statesman articulates a concept of honor. Rather, when the "last full measure of devotion" occurs and the lives of one's countrymen in uniform are lost, a new logic enters the arena of "politics by other means." That is the sacred logic of honor. Honor is about the national soul and its virtue. In the case of Vietnam there was a strong sense among American presidents, at least among Johnson and Nixon and many of their advisors, that any sort of peace had to be an "honorable" peace, not surrender.

A fifth war aim was the personal reputation for toughness of the President. Julius Caesar opined, "I love the name of honor more than I fear death." George Washington not only had a personal rule book of behavior but his diaries investigated his own ideas, actions, reputation, and plans. Hannibal, Napoleon, Genghis Khan, Douglas MacArthur … the list is endless of political and military leaders who saw war not just as a contest between opposing sides but also as a test of character for themselves and for their followers. A distinct, unspoken aim that may develop during a war has to do with the soul and reputation of leaders. It is impossible to fully quantify this element, although statements, interviews, and private diaries may provide compelling insight into the personal mindset of military officers and political leaders.

The issue of personal reputation was at work during the hottest phase of the Cold War, as American presidents countered communist aggression in Korea, Vietnam, Laos, Cambodia, and elsewhere in Southeast Asia. None wanted to be on duty during another "loss," like that of China, to the Red Army. This was a test of their individual resolve and initiative, not just against the enemy but in mobilizing the latent powers of the West against the threat posed by communism. With this in mind, a number of scholars have made the persuasive claim that vindicating the personal credibility, toughness, and leadership of individual U.S. presidents was a driver for continuing the Vietnam War.

This is not to argue that Presidents Eisenhower through Nixon sought war to demonstrate their personal determination. But, as Frederik Logevall has written in *Choosing War*, it is clear that U.S. presidents—as men and leaders—did not want to back down to Stalin, Khrushchev, Mao, and their ilk.[41] The Democratic

Party was stained with the loss of China to the Communists in 1949 and later Democratic presidents, Kennedy and Johnson, did not want to be seen as soft. They felt that their credibility as tough leaders and negotiators was crucial for the global balance of power, from East Berlin to Saigon. President Eisenhower was probably less concerned with this due to his outstanding war record as Supreme Allied Commander in Europe. Nixon, on the other hand, wanted to maintain a reputation for toughness (extending back to his days as an anti-communist on Capitol Hill and as Vice President) and believed that reputation to be crucial for getting an honorable deal on Vietnam.

In short, the social and political psychology literature is suggestive that a war aim that develops as a war goes on is the interplay between the character and reputation of the individual leader and the war effort's perceived success or failure. Because just war thinking begins with the idea of *legitimate political authority* and that authority is invested in flesh-and-blood humans, this dimension, which is typically overlooked in the just war literature, must be taken into account as a war aim, especially in the context of the Vietnam War. This is also important because the just war tradition, as distinct from the legal paradigm of the formal law of armed conflict, also emphasizes *right intention*. It is one thing to fight a war because there is a strategic concept of security and because one must honor promises to one's allies. It is an entirely different thing for a leader to be worried about the appearance of his personal toughness and for this to drive the push toward war (or peace).

President John F. Kennedy brought energy and confidence to the White House and was surrounded by a group of "can-do" "whiz kids." Insiders and observers reflect that there was a tone of pride, or conceit, in that group from the very beginning. David Halberstam writes, "A remarkable hubris permeated the entire time."[42] Kennedy advisor, and later historian, Arthur M. Schlesinger, Jr., noted, "Euphoria reigned; we thought for a moment that the world was plastic and the future unlimited."[43] Some see Kennedy's ego and need for conquest as rooted in a more complex and wider set of relationships, needs, fears, and desires. For instance, presidential historian Robert Dallek characterizes Kennedy as a "compulsive womanizer … whose insatiable urge for sexual conquests was fueled by a complex array of personal traumas."[44]

Whether for personal satisfaction or a cool calculation of international perception, one thing that drove Kennedy's Cold War policies was his perception of his relationship with Soviet Premier Nikita Khrushchev. From the beginning, and in the shadow of his predecessor, Kennedy felt that he had to portray toughness: "I have to show him that we can be just as tough as he is. I'll sit down with him, and let him see who he's dealing with."[45] During the Cuban Missile Crisis Kennedy told Walt Rostow, "That son of a bitch, Khrushchev … he won't stop until we take a step that will lead to nuclear war … there's no way you can talk to that fella into stopping until you have taken some really credible step."[46]

Kennedy's successor also thought a great deal about his reputation, in both his immediate context of Washington and the history books. Numerous Johnson observers have written about his machismo as well as his pride in his rags-to-riches

Texas story. Author Larry King, who worked on Johnson's campaigns, entertainingly writes:

> Where once he had argued the injustice of Vietnam being viewed as "his" war, Lyndon Johnson now brought to it a proprietary attitude ... no matter his periodic bombing halts or conciliatory statements inviting peace, because once he took a thing personally, his pride and vanity and ego knew no bounds. Always a man to put his brand on everything (he wore monogrammed shirts, boots, cuff links; flew his private L.B.J. flag when in residence at the L.B.J. ranch; saw to it that the names of Lynda Bird Johnson and Luci Baines Johnson and Lady Bird Johnson—not Claudia, as she had been named— had the magic initials L.B.J.), he now personalized and internalized the war. Troops became "my" boys, those were "my" helicopters, it was "my" pilots he prayed might return from their bombing missions as he paid nocturnal calls to the White House situation room to learn the latest from the battlefields ... His machismo was mixed up in it now, his manhood. After a cabinet meeting in 1967 several staff aides and at least one cabinet member—Stewart Udall, Secretary of the Interior—remained behind for informal discussions; soon L.B.J. was waving his arms and fulminating about his war. Who the hell was Ho Chi Minh, anyway, that he thought he could push America around? Then the President did an astonishing thing: he unzipped his trousers, dangled a given appendage, and asked his shocked associates: "Has Ho Chi Minh got anything like that?"[47]

Johnson's favorite biographer, and former staffer, Doris Kearns Goodwin writes:

> I knew from the start, Johnson told me in 1970, describing the early weeks of 1965, that I was bound to be crucified either way I moved. If I left the woman I really loved—the Great Society—in order to get involved in that bitch of a war ... I would lose everything. All my programs. All my hopes to feed the hungry and shelter the homeless ... if I left the war and let the Communists take over South Vietnam, then I would be seen as a coward and my nation would be seen as an appeaser ...
>
> ... everything I knew about history told me that if I got out of Vietnam and let Ho Chi Minh run through the streets of Saigon, then I'd be doing exactly what Chamberlain did in World War II. I'd be giving a big fat reward to aggression ... [it] would shatter my presidency, kill my administration, and damage our democracy ...
>
> ... there would be Robert Kennedy out in front leading the fight against me, telling everyone that I had betrayed John Kennedy's commitment to South Vietnam. That I had let a democracy fall into the hands of the Communists. That I was a coward. An unmanly man. A man without a spine ... every night when I fell asleep I would see myself tied to the ground ... I could hear the voices of thousands of people ... shouting ... Coward! Traitor! Weakling![48]

When it comes to analyzing personal reputation and ego in the case of Richard M. Nixon, there are multiple elements at play that are beyond the scope of this chapter, including his many years of public service in a changing political landscape, his long-term grievances with his portrayal in the media,[49] his symbiotic relationship with that tower of self-assurance Henry Kissinger, Nixon's psychology and personal ego, and his calculated strategy to appear a loose cannon in order to force Hanoi and its patrons in Moscow and Beijing to negotiate. What can be said is that Nixon was extremely image-conscious, understanding the powerful role that journalists and electronic media had in defining a candidate. One historian writes, "Few presidents have been so concerned with image, and even fewer have devoted so many hours to working on the public relations aspects of the presidency."[50] Nixon concurred in his memoirs: "In the modern presidency, concern for image must rank with concern for substance."[51]

Additionally, Nixon had great self-confidence as a leader and political guru. He dismissed Lyndon Johnson while asserting his toughness: "I'm not going to end up like LBJ, holed up in the White House afraid to show my face on the street. I'm going to stop that war. Fast."[52] One scholar commented, in ways similar to analyses of the early Kennedy White House: "[in 1969] Nixon and Kissinger set out to end the war with that sublime self-confidence common among men new to power."[53] In fact, that aggressive ego was on display when Nixon's alter ego, Kissinger, confidently told Quaker anti-war activists, "Give us six months, and if we haven't ended the war by then, you can come back and tear down the White House fence."[54]

Of course, one can point to the many times Nixon said that this was, at least in part, a strategic act. To his aide H.R. Haldeman he said:

> I call it the Madman Theory, Bob. I want the North Vietnamese to believe I've reached the point where I might do anything to stop the war. We'll just slip the word to them that, for God's sake, you know Nixon is obsessed about Communism. We can't restrain him when he's angry—and he has had his hand on the nuclear button—and Ho Chi Minh himself will be in Paris in two days begging for peace.[55]

Again, during the Christmas bombing in December 1972, Nixon told the Chairman of the Joint Chiefs of Staff, "The Russians and the Chinese might think they were dealing with a madman and so had better force North Vietnam into a settlement before the world was consumed by a larger war."[56]

Conclusions: Grand strategy, national honor, and ego

America's involvement in the Vietnam War has been examined using the lens of just war by serious thinkers, such as Paul Ramsey and Michael Walzer, as well as by countless less-thoughtful critics who reflexively echo that the war was "unjust." Those critics nearly always mean one of two things. The first charge is that the war was fought in an unethical manner, such as the use of chemical defoliants, individual acts that contravened the war convention (e.g. My Lai), and bombing across international boundaries in Cambodia and Laos. The second criticism is fuzzy but nonetheless has a moral dimension: the social, economic, and political costs of prolonging the war (e.g. the divisive anti-war protests, the financial costs to taxpayers, the lives of both troops and combatants, etc.) were so great that at some point it became immoral and unjust. Both of these critiques, regardless of their merits, are about how (*jus in bello*), rather than why (*jus ad bellum*), the war was fought. In contrast, the purpose of this chapter is to focus on the *jus ad bellum* elements of the ethical content and context that inspired a succession of U.S. presidents of both political parties to fight the war in Indochina.

Did the war aims of Presidents Eisenhower, Kennedy, Johnson, and Nixon meet the primary *jus ad bellum* criteria? Each of these men represented the legitimate political authority of the U.S. in its vital role as a global leader and each attempted to work with the South Vietnamese leadership toward a common purpose. Moreover, despite the weakness of Saigon's government, these presidents invested not only in armaments and military training but also in government institutions, education, political training, and wider economic development in order to buttress representative, legitimate political authority in South Vietnam. Each President truly believed that he was acting with appropriate just cause by supporting the self-defense posture of South Vietnam as well as the neutrality of Cambodia and Laos. This took place in a regional and global context of superpower rivalry and communist insurgency that was informed by the heuristic of the domino theory.

When it comes to the secondary, prudential *jus ad bellum* criteria, it is difficult to know in any specific case when have the protagonists arrived at last resort, what is the precise likelihood of success, and how one should definitively gauge the proportionality of ends and means. But clearly, at the time, these national leaders, informed by World War II and their knowledge of communism, and influenced by the domino theory, felt that these criteria were met.

U.S. presidents typically do not go about adumbrating specific just war principles, but these presidents did elaborate a number of specific war aims through speeches, policy documents, and private communications. This chapter identified the following five war aims:

1. Contain communism.
2. Spread democracy, or at least hold it in places where it already existed.
3. Demonstrate resolve to various foreign audiences.
4. Vindicate national honor.
5. Protect the personal reputation and credibility of the President.

Do these war aims meet the just war criteria?

The first three war aims are all limited yet robust national security objectives and accord with just war thinking. The containment doctrine was a vigilant, restrained framework for U.S. policy, and in the case of Indochina this appeared to be morally congruent with the local and regional context. The U.S. position, explicated at

Geneva in 1954 in the context of the recently ended Korean War, was to support international guarantees for the neutrality of Laos and Cambodia and the status quo of a divided Vietnam until free elections could be held. The U.S. did not try to conquer or absorb any of the countries in Southeast Asia, nor did it attempt to roll back communism in North Vietnam.

The second war aim, to support the economic development and democratic institutions of a fragile, developing Vietnamese democracy, also comports with just war thinking, both in terms of securing political authority and as a focus beyond military power to other elements of political stability (last resort). Vietnam was never going to be a U.S. colony—Eisenhower was the greatest anti-colonialist of the era, to the chagrin of London and Paris. Eisenhower saw the importance of containing communism and nurturing democracy wherever practicable. The U.S. invested massive amounts of money in the attempt to bring Vietnam's governance, education, and social structures—as well as security institutions—up to modern standards. An indicator of both U.S. commitment to, and frustration with, effective government in South Vietnam was when the Kennedy administration turned a blind eye to (or privately supported) a military coup that toppled the erratic, authoritarian President Diem.

U.S. investment in Vietnamese economic progress, government institutions, and security was seen as being of benefit to the local populace but also as having a global impact in terms of U.S. credibility. This idea of strategic resolve in high politics is something that is rarely addressed in the just war literature. In the 1960s Paul Ramsey thoughtfully discussed the morality of deterrence, but he was doing so primarily with nuclear weapons in mind. In contrast, a presupposition of the domino theory for those presidents was the example of Munich: the West had appeased Hitler, allowing him to knock down the dominos of Austria, Czechoslovakia, and the Rhineland without a fight. Stalin and Mao could not be allowed to do the same.

Although some have argued that the Munich analogy may have been overplayed in Vietnam, nevertheless it was real to the men in Washington at the time, and the idea of keeping promises and signaling credibility remains alive and well today. It is this basic idea of moral credibility that compelled President Bill Clinton to apologize for not intervening in Rwanda in 1994 and later compelled him to intervene in Kosovo in 1999. In both cases there was a sense of historical promise to not allow genocide to return to international life. The credibility of Barack Obama's foreign policy suffered significantly when he established a "red line" on Syrian chemical weapons but later refused to act when Damascus employed weapons of mass destruction (WMDs) on its own citizens.

In the Vietnam case, the fear was—as General Maxwell Taylor and Ralph White explained—that U.S. allies and potential allies would be disheartened and the communists empowered if the U.S. did not maintain its security guarantees. Also, thanks to the Geneva Accords (which the U.S. observed but did not sign) and the SEATO Treaty, the U.S. had made commitments in Asia that had global ramifications. Keeping these commitments was morally praiseworthy and strategically sound, although they were not a carte blanche for unrestrained war.

What about the war aim of national honor? In this instance we are not focused on fulfilling treaty commitments but instead on the idea of keeping faith with the sacrifice made by those who lost their lives on the battlefield and their families. Do not leaders owe victory, or at least "peace with honor," to the families, comrades, and memories of those who have lost their lives in the fight?

I am personally very sympathetic to this position. I have spent over twenty years as a military reservist and I have worked on post-conflict issues at the U.S. Department of State in Africa and Asia. Like many others, my visits to Gettysburg, Normandy, Baghdad, Kandahar, and elsewhere have had an otherworldly, spiritual dimension. No one wants to think that our sons, husbands, brothers, and fathers died in vain at Hue, Khe San, and Hamburger Hill. Many of us instinctively feel that every name carved into the black granite of the Vietnam Memorial was not a victim but rather a hero whose purpose we—the survivors—must somehow vindicate. President Johnson believed this: he had nightmares of being labeled as a "traitor" if he lost in Vietnam. Nixon believed this, and his belief was supported by a silent majority who gave him two major election victories in 1968 and 1972, despite the growing unpopularity of the war.

To be clear, the U.S. did not go to war to vindicate its national honor; honor becomes a war aim that prolongs a war after it has already started. By itself, regardless of its emotional and psychological power, the concept of national honor does not necessarily accord with just war thinking. Trying to uphold the sanctity of ephemeral national honor is morally perilous because it suggests additional cost and additional sacrifice, not in pursuit of victory, but to simply continue the fight. Those additional costs can become unrestrained: "no cost too great." National honor, by itself, is not a rationale for victory, nor is it synonymous with morality. Rather, national honor can become a rationale for prolonging the destructiveness of war. In its most perverse form, the honor justification begins to make the war itself the highest good and to make any and all sacrifice not only legitimate, but venerable. The perverted, extreme view of national honor does not accord with the individualistic, democratic sentiments of the U.S. because it can become the voice of Hitler and the kamikazes.

Nonetheless, there is something moral about invoking the sanctity of national honor, in at least two ways. The first way is that we do want national leaders to prioritize honoring the sacrifice of citizens and taxpayers, and so a focus on honor can actually become a limiting factor restraining other presidential war aims. We want presidents and generals to say: we will fight hard to win. We'll give your sons and daughters in uniform every tool to be successful. We'll care for them while in uniform and after they come home. And, we promise you, that if the calculus for fighting this war changes in some way, we will honor their service and your sacrifice by changing course. We won't dishonor the dead by needlessly adding more to their numbers. That is a formula for peace with honor.

The second way that national honor is moral and appropriate is in the aftermath of war. Leaders must honor the meaning and sacrifice of the survivors as well as that of the lost. "Peace with honor" should include establishing war memorials, rehabilitating veterans, ensuring the well-being of families of the fallen, not to mention reviewing the "lessons learned" and teaching these to military officers to prevent the re-outbreak of past wars. President Nixon was on to something morally complex but precious in speaking about honor when one thinks about the needs of veterans, especially those scarred by their service. This is an issue of national honor, not just for the government but for society at large in how it treats the veterans of its wars. A scandal in U.S. history is the way that so many Americans in the anti-war campaign spat upon those who wore the uniform.

Finally, the fifth war aim identified is that of personal reputation and toughness. Does preserving or advancing the personal reputation of a leader meet the just war standard? Of course not. None of these presidents started the Vietnam War to prove their mettle to themselves, their opponents, or history. Yet, some of them made decisions about grand strategy and Vietnam policy that were informed by considerations of image and reputation. Kennedy wanted to appear tough to Khrushchev and the cockiness of Kennedy and his wonder-boys is well documented. Kennedy did not want to be a "loser" like Truman in 1949, on whose watch the Soviets got the bomb and China fell to the Red Army. Johnson was a macho, aggressive male in the domestic political arena. He wanted to project that strength in the international arena but was bedeviled by insecurity about reputation, toughness, and his legacy in the conflicted politics of that time. Nixon was truly an impressive geopolitical strategist and after being exiled from public life he worked very hard to restore his image as a statesman through books, op-eds, public speeches, and the private Nixon Presidential Library in California. Not surprisingly, the transcripts of Nixon's recordings and the testimony of his closest associates demonstrate the role that ego played in some of his decisions about Vietnam, such as dismissing the expertise of senior leaders in government due to personal dislike and careful attention to his image.

Ambition, personal reputation, the psychology of leaders—all of this is extremely difficult to pinpoint and it has been neglected by military ethics and just war thinking. There exists an important social psychology literature, referenced above, that deals with Vietnam, and its focus is almost entirely on the role of Munich on the shared psychological schema of American policymakers at the time. Nevertheless, just war thinking can contribute due to its keen focus on "right intention" and its connection to "just cause." Augustine famously wrote that wars fought for greed, envy, hatred, vengeance, and the like were not just. If these presidents prolonged the war because of personal hatred, greed, or a desire for revenge, or to meet the needs of their own ego in some way, then that does not accord with just war reasoning. Of course, a leader's concern for immediate and historical glory does not mean that other war aims are necessarily tainted, but personal ego can have many distortive effects for the makers of sound policy, from damaging personal relationships among senior leaders (e.g. elected officials not trusting military leaders), to limiting the possibilities for diplomacy across borders, to distorting the mental reality and therefore the policy possibilities for peace and security. All of these are hazards and do not comport with just war thinking.

In sum, the Vietnam era of U.S. history was lengthy and costly. Tens of millions of Americans were directly involved, whether serving in government or in uniform or through being connected to those who did serve. The conditions that President Truman faced in Southeast Asia in the early 1950s evolved dynamically to the moments when President Ford watched the abandonment of the U.S. Embassy in Saigon on his television set in 1975. The decisions made across presidencies to fight and prolong the war had some sound strategic and ethical foundations, and yet there are morally troubling aspects to the war aims as well. Today, a half-century after the escalation of U.S. fighting in Vietnam, these controversial issues continue to be debated by policymakers and military officials in ways similar to how the lessons of Munich were considered by an earlier generation of Western leaders.

Notes

1 Dwight D. Eisenhower, "The President's News Conference" (April 7, 1954), Gerhard Peters and John T. Woolley, The American Presidency Project, available at: www.presidency.ucsb.edu/ws/?pid=10202. Throughout this chapter I have utilized the vast resources of the University of California at Santa Barbara's American Presidency Project, which provides presidential speeches and other materials for the entirety of U.S. history. I am grateful to John Woolley and Gerhard Peters for this spectacular, freely available resource available at my graduate alma mater: www.presidency.ucsb.edu.
2 Joint Resolution of August 10, 1964, Public Law 88–408, 78 STAT 384, to Promote the Maintenance of International Peace and Security in Southeast Asia. U.S. National Archives, available at: https://catalog.archives.gov/id/12009390.
3 John F. Kennedy, "The President's News Conference" (April 24, 1963), Gerhard Peters and John T. Woolley, The American Presidency Project, available at: www.presidency.ucsb.edu/ws/?pid=9165.
4 See Doris Kearns Goodwin's chapter on Vietnam in her *Lyndon Johnson and the American Dream* (New York: Harper-Collins, 1976), p. 258.
5 For those interested in the seeds of U.S. involvement under President Harry S. Truman, see Robert J. McMahon, "Harry S. Truman and the Roots of U.S. Involvement in Indochina, 1945–1953," in *Shadow on the White House: Presidents and the Vietnam War (1945–1975)*, ed. David L. Anderson (Lawrence: University of Kansas Press, 1993).
6 Quoted in Gary R. Hess, "Kennedy's Vietnam Options and Decisions," in Anderson, p. 69.
7 Quoted in Ralph K. White, "Misperception and the Vietnam War," *Journal of Social Issues*, vol. 22, no. 3 (1966), p. 66.
8 Ibid., p. 70.
9 For more on this debate, see "Kennan and Containment, 1947," Office of the Historian, U.S. Department of State, available at: https://history.state.gov/milestones/1945–1952/kennan (accessed January 1, 2017).
10 George Kennan, "The Sources of Soviet Conduct," *Foreign Affairs* (July 1947).
11 "A Report to the National Security Council by the Executive Secretary (Lay)" (April 14, 1950), Ofiice of the Historian, Department of State, available at: https://history.state.gov/historicaldocuments/frus1950v01/d85.
12 Dwight D. Eisenhower, *Waging Peace: 1956–1961* (New York: Doubleday and Company, Inc., 1965), p. 294.

13 Anderson, p. 43.

14 According to William J. Rust, "On March 23, 1961, Kennedy held a televised press conference in the State Department auditorium to dramatically portray the recent military gains of the Pathet Lao, the local Communist Forces. Using three large maps, he charged that in violation of Laotian neutrality, 'large-scale' Soviet airlifts and North Vietnamese 'combat specialists' had been providing ever-increasing support to the Pathet Lao: 'It is this new dimension of externally supported warfare that creates the present grave problem.' Kennedy explicitly warned that the U.S. was prepared to go to war: 'If these attacks do not stop, those who support a truly neutral Laos will have to consider their response … No one should doubt our resolution on this point.'" William J. Rust, *Kennedy in Vietnam* (New York: Charles Scribner's Sons, 1987), p. 28.

15 Herbert Y. Schandler, *Lyndon Johnson and Vietnam: The Unmaking of a President* (Princeton, NJ: Princeton University Press, 1977), p. 4.

16 Document available at the Federation of Atomic Scientists depository, https://fas.org/irp/offdocs/nsam-lbj/nsam-273.htm (accessed January 1, 2017).

17 "Address by President Johnson at Omaha Municipal Dock on June 30, 1966, 'Two Threats to Peace: Hunger and Aggression,'" *Department of State Bulletin* (July 25, 1966), p. 115. Available in *The Pentagon Papers*, vol. 4 (Boston: Beacon Press, 1971), pp. 655–656.

18 National Archives, available at: https://catalog.archives.gov/id/12009390 (accessed January 1, 2017).

19 Eisenhower, *Waging Peace*, pp. 624–625.

20 Vietnam Statistics at CQ Press, available at: https://library.cqpress.com/cqalmanac/document.php?id=cqal75-1213988 (accessed January 1, 2017).

21 USAID published a forty-page bibliography of its economic reports on its projects, from dam dredging to agricultural assistance, from this time period. It is available at: http://pdf.usaid.gov/pdf_docs/Pnaax020.pdf (accessed January 1, 2017). For the $28.5 billion figure, see: http://thevietnamwar.info/how-much-vietnam-war-cost/ (accessed January 1, 2017).

22 Annual Budget Message to the Congress, Fiscal Year 1964, Gerhard Peters and John T. Woolley, *The American Presidency Project*, available at: www.presidency.ucsb.edu/ws/?pid=12846.

23 *Department of State Bulletin*, LII (April 26, 1965), available at: www.vietnamwar.net/LBJ-2.htm (accessed January 1, 2017).

24 Jeffrey P. Kimball, "Peace with Honor: Richard Nixon and the Diplomacy of Threat and Symbolism" in Anderson, p. 157.

25 Eisenhower, *Waging Peace*, p. 624.

26 Ibid., p. 113.

27 Available at: www.jfklibrary.org/Research/Research-Aids/Ready-Reference/JFK-Quotations/Inaugural-Address.aspx.

28 Rust, p. 28.

29 Rust writes, "During the Laotian crisis, Attorney General Robert Kennedy had asked, 'Where would be the best place to stand and fight in Southeast Asia?' The answer was Vietnam. '[President] Kennedy had decided, out of these first four months of experience, that if he had to engage American forces in Southeast Asia, he would do so in Vietnam rather than Laos,' said [Walt] Rostow. 'Vietnam appeared to have relative advantages, which Kennedy once tersely ticked off to me in these terms: Relatively speaking, it was a more unified nation; its armed forces were larger and better trained; it had direct access to the sea; its geography permitted American air and naval power to be more easily brought to bear; there was the cushion of North Vietnam between South Vietnam and the Chinese border.'" Rust, p. 34.

30 Speech delivered on November 3, 1969.
31 For free access to the Pentagon Papers, go to the U.S. National Archive at: www.archives. gov/research/pentagon-papers. For background on these issues, two critical classics are H.R. McMaster, *Dereliction of Duty: Johnson, McNamara, the Joint Chiefs of Staff, and the Lies That Led to Vietnam* (New York: Harper Perennial, 1998), and David Halberstam, *The Best and the Brightest* (New York: Random House, 2002).
32 There was a time when the notion of honor was intrinsic to how many thought about just war. As James Turner Johnson recorded, the chivalric code of the Middle Ages included conceptions of honor. See his *Just War Tradition and the Restraint of War* (Princeton, NJ: Princeton University Press, 1981).
33 Richard M. Nixon, "Why Not Negotiate in Vietnam?," *The Reader's Digest*, vol. 12 (1965).
34 Richard Nixon, "Address to the Nation on the War in Vietnam" (November 3, 1969), Gerhard Peters and John T. Woolley, The American Presidency Project, available at: www. presidency.ucsb.edu/ws/?pid=2303.
35 Richard Nixon, "Address to the Nation Announcing Conclusion of an Agreement on Ending the War and Restoring Peace in Vietnam" (January 23, 1973), Gerhard Peters and John T. Woolley, The American Presidency Project, available at: www.presidency.ucsb. edu/ws/?pid=3808.
36 "UCDP/Prio Armed Conflict Database," Uppsala University, www.pcr.uu.se/research/ ucdp/datasets/ucdp_prio_armed_conflict_dataset/ (accessed January 1, 2017).
37 Dwight D. Eisenhower, "Exchange of Messages Between the President and the President of France on the Fall of Dien Bien Phu" (May 7, 1954), Gerhard Peters and John T. Woolley, The American Presidency Project, available at: www.presidency.ucsb.edu/ ws/?pid=9879.
38 Ibid.
39 *Department of State Bulletin*, LII.
40 Full quote: in September of 1963, President Kennedy declared in an interview, "In the final analysis, it is their war. They are the ones who have to win it or lose it. We can help them, we can give them equipment, we can send our men out there as advisers, but they have to win it, the people of Vietnam, against the Communists ... But I don't agree with those who say we should withdraw. That would be a great mistake ... [The United States] made this effort to defend Europe. Now Europe is quite secure. We also have to participate—we may not like it—in the defense of Asia." Available at: www.jfklibrary. org/JFK/JFK-in-History/Vietnam.aspx.
41 Frederik Logevall, *Choosing War: The Lost Chance for Peace and the Escalation of War in Vietnam* (Berkeley and Los Angeles: University of California Press, 2001).
42 David Halberstam, quoted in Hess, p. 69.
43 Ibid.
44 Quoted in Robert Dallek, *JFK: An Unfinished Life* (New York: Little and Brown, 2003), p. 201.
45 Quoted in Tanya Savory, *John F. Kennedy* (West Berlin, NJ: Townsend Press, 2010), p. 15.
46 Quoted in Dallek, p. 303.
47 Larry L. King, "Machismo in the White House: LBJ and Vietnam," *American Heritage Magazine*, vol. 27, no. 5 (August 1976), available at: www.americanheritage.com/content/ machismo-white-house (accessed January 1, 2017).
48 Kearns Goodwin, pp. 251–253.
49 In Nixon's case, reputation and image were tied to his combative relationship with the media, which he felt had treated him unfairly, from his 1952 Checkers speech to his 1960

failed presidential bid against Kennedy. He famously told the press that they would not have him to "kick around" any more when he left public life.

50 Melvin Small, "Containing Domestic Enemies: Richard M. Nixon and the War at Home," in Anderson, p. 133.

51 Richard M. Nixon, *RN: The Memoirs of Richard Nixon* (New York: Warner Books, 1978), p. 354. But the concern with not only results but credit for the results, and for an image of toughness were not only to force compromises from his communist enemies but also to beat the critics whom he loathed at home.

52 Kimball, p. 158.

53 George C. Herring, *Vietnam: America's Longest War*, fourth ed. (New York: McGraw-Hill, 2001), p. 354.

54 Marvin Kalb and Bernard Kalb, *Kissinger* (New York: Little & Brown, 1974), p. 120.

55 Kimball, p. 155.

56 Ibid., p. 173.

PART II

The ethics of how war is fought

The first section of this book looked at the just war criteria for going to war. From a political-military perspective, that is the realm of diplomats, elected officials, and military officers at the highest levels. These are the individuals who make the decisions about how and when to employ force at the strategic and grand strategic levels. The next section of this book focuses on the moral issues of how war is fought at the operational and tactical levels. These are the decisions made in campaigns and on discrete battlefields, usually by lower-level military officers.

Unfortunately, there is too much pop punditry on these issues. That is because a good deal of blogosphere and op-ed just war theorizing, especially of the quasi-pacifistic kind, focuses on criticizing the behavior of the troops: it is juvenilely easy to nitpick the actions of soldiers and police officers, when they are responding to danger and duress, from the comfort of a pundit's easy chair. It is far harder to carefully analyze the layers of dynamic, reflexive action that lead to specific decisions in unique contexts.

The *jus in bello* issues of proportionality and discrimination have been thoughtfully handled by scholars such as Michael Walzer, Paul Ramsey, and James Turner Johnson, and I have discussed them at length in a previous book entitled, *Just War Thinking.*[1] So, only two chapters of this book are focused on the intersection of political responsibility with the *jus in bello* criteria of *proportionality* and *discrimination*. Proportionality asks, "Are the battlefield tools and tactics employed proportionate to battlefield objectives?" Discrimination, often labeled "distinction" or, more narrowly, "non-combatant immunity," queries, "Has care been taken to reasonably protect the lives and property of legitimate non-combatants?" This section also raises a third criteria that is not a just war principle, but is a part of how national militaries and even the International Committee of the Red Cross teach these *jus in bello* concepts. That is the idea of *military necessity*.

Chapter 5 looks at three specific controversies in how the U.S. military fought the war in Mexico, the first of which has to do with the difference in behavior between volunteers (e.g. militia, Texas Rangers) and regular troops. A second issue is evaluating the methods by which military leaders in the field communicate moral objectives and restraint, such as through public letters, proclamations, and explicit statements of commander's intent. Of course, military leaders must not only adumbrate standards—they must also enforce discipline and punishment, as General Winfield Scott and his contemporaries did. Third, every battlefield has its trade-offs and the U.S. forces besieging Veracruz had decisions to make in order to balance the welfare of troops, achieving the mission, and forcing the enemy to surrender in a timely fashion. This is where military necessity meets proportionality and discrimination, and it is up to commanders on the ground to make these critical choices. The specific decision to be made by General Scott was whether or not to bombard a civilian population center that would not surrender in order to avoid being bogged down in an environment notorious for malaria, yellow fever, and other tropical diseases.

Chapter 6 looks at the nexus of presidential decision-making, *jus in bello* principles, and weapons of mass destruction during the height of the Cold War. Much of the literature criticizing nuclear weapons as immoral focuses on *proportionality* and *discrimination*: what action by our enemies could nuclear weapons possibly be a proportionate response to? Furthermore, aren't the real targets of nuclear weapons civilian population centers, making such weapons indiscriminate and thus immoral? This chapter focuses carefully on two separate issues. First, it considers President Truman's responsibility to the American people and the world at large to bring World War II to a speedy end. This is where the principles of legitimate authority, just cause, and right intention inform battlefield decisions. The latter part of the chapter then moves to a more nuanced conversation about different strategies of nuclear deterrence rooted in distinctions made by ethicist Paul Ramsey, concluding that it is entirely possible, however ironic, for a strategy of nuclear deterrence to be justified and just in *jus in bello* terms.

Note

1 James Turner Johnson, *The Just War Tradition and the Restraint of War* (Princeton, NJ: Princeton University Press, 1981); Michael Walzer, *Just and Unjust Wars: A Moral Argument with Historical Illustrations*, third ed. (New York: Basic Books, 2000); Paul Ramsey, *The Just War: Force and Political Responsibility* (New York: Charles Scribner's Sons, 1968); Eric Patterson, *Just War Thinking: Morality and Pragmatism in the Struggle against Contemporary Threats* (Lanham, MD: Lexington Books, 2007).

5

THE TEXAS RANGERS, YELLOW JACK, AND VERACRUZ

Proportionality and discrimination in the Mexican–American War

"From the halls of Montezuma, to the shores of Tripoli ...": the United States Marine Corps hymn begins with this phrase, words memorializing the role of U.S. Marines in the Mexican–American War, from America's first major amphibious landing at Veracruz through the later conclusive Battle of Chapultepec.[1] After Mexican forces attacked across the U.S. border in 1846, what appeared to be an inevitable clash between Mexico and the U.S. lasted for two years, with battles ranging from the Gulf of Mexico to the Pacific Ocean.[2] Although many of the underlying political issues of the time seem remote, such as Mexico's constantly failing democracy and the perennial question of whether U.S. slavery would advance west, nonetheless the war was of tremendous importance to the future of both countries. From the U.S. perspective, it was the training ground for the leaders of the future U.S. Civil War, including Robert E. Lee, Ulysses S. Grant, and George McClellan.

Although there was at the time, and remains today, debate about whether or not it was just for the U.S. to go to war[3] (*jus ad bellum*), the focus of this chapter[4] is on how the U.S. military fought the war (*jus in bello*): using means and tactics proportionate (*proportionality*) to battlefield objectives and which limit harm to civilians, other non-combatants, and property (*discrimination*). Robert E. Lee remembered that the troops "fought well and fought fairly ... in a manner no man might be ashamed of."[5] Ulysses S. Grant is well-known for having labeled the U.S. decision to go to war as "wicked"; however, his comments on the conduct of U.S. troops are proud: "The troops behaved well in Mexico, and the government acted handsomely about the peace ... Once in Mexico ... the people, those who had property, were our friends."[6]

Lee and Grant argued that the U.S. fought the war in a moral manner. This chapter evaluates their claims, asking: did the U.S. military fight this war justly? Did the leadership emphasize *proportionality* and *discrimination* to the rank and file? Were civilians and their property respected? Was customary international law complied with? Was the use of force proportionate at the battlefield level? When violations of the war convention occurred, how were they dealt with (e.g. swept under the carpet or court martial)?

On what basis are we to judge the efficacy of *jus in bello* criteria by U.S. troops during the Mexican–American war? In order for us to go back 170 years to analyze those military operations, we will look at three things, the first of which is what we today call "*commander's intent*." What do we know from the rules, proclamations, and conduct of senior U.S. military commanders, such as Generals Zachary Taylor and Winfield Scott? And were such rules and proclamations heeded by the troops and enforced by the chain of command? Such commander's intent will take two forms: first, any commands given about the active theater of battle, and second, directives about how occupying forces were to interact with non-combatants. One can imagine how different an appeal to "wipe out the barbarians" would be from a call to "best our noble adversary and protect his wives and children."

Second, and critically for the Mexican–American War, we will look at the issue of *who was doing the fighting*. The U.S. military force that was first attacked and then crossed the border into Mexico was made up of professional military personnel ("regulars") but was strengthened by "volunteers" such as Texas Rangers and state militia elements. This opens up a wider set of issues about the difference between professional, trained armed forces and the ethical training, and limitations imposed on, conscripts and/or militia personnel who may have had little to no training on the laws of armed conflict. The documentary record suggests that the volunteers were far more likely to violate the rules of armed conflict, but also that those rules were poorly defined at the time.

Third, *how was the war fought*? All in all, this was a conventional, set-piece war on land, although there were unconventional elements as well as siege warfare involved (not to mention the involvement of the U.S. Navy). It is beyond the scope of this chapter to look at every engagement, so we'll look at what many feel to be a uniquely controversial episode in the war: the bombardment of Veracruz, a major population center. Veracruz raises issues of proportionality and discrimination in unusual ways—in particular, how commanders balance the health and safety of their own troops with mission objectives and the presence of vulnerable non-combatants.

Mexico and the U.S. at war

On April 24, 1846, Mexican General Arista, acting on the express orders of Mexico City, sent 1,600 men to attack the U.S. Army under General Zachary Taylor on U.S. soil.[7] This attack, called the Thornton Affair or Rancho Carricitos, initiated the Mexican–American War.[8] Among the causes of the war were a sense of unfinished business since Texas had achieved its independence from Mexico a decade before, grievances on both sides regarding borders, bandits, Indians, the potential wealth of border territories, and the U.S. sense of manifest destiny that these thinly populated, almost ungoverned western spaces would fall into its orbit.[9]

Within a month of the Mexican attack at Ft. Texas, General Zachary Taylor had bested General Arista at Palo Alto, Resaca de la Palma, and Matamoros; in the meantime, President Polk had requested that Congress declare war, which it did on May 13, 1846 (Mexico had already declared war).[10] Following the take-over of Matamoros, General Taylor issued a proclamation outlining benevolent intentions to the Mexicans.[11] He specified that America had no quarrel with the Mexican people, but only with their tyrannical leaders.[12] Many could believe this, as Mexico had had constant turnover of governments for the previous twenty years. Taylor promised that churches would remain intact and untouched. He requested only food for the American army and promised monetary compensation. He also asserted his desire to disprove depictions of Americans as ruthless, asking for the chance for the Americans to prove themselves as civilized people.[13]

Overall U.S. strategy in the war was to quickly beat Mexico's armies in the field, on the assumption that the level of political instability and intrigue in Mexico City would result in a quick capitulation. This was originally to happen in two general theaters, one in the northeast along the Mexico–Texas border and eastern part of Mexico, with a second front in Alta California (today's U.S. state of California), to which small groups had marched overland (under John C. Fremont and Stephen Kearney) and at which a small naval force, under Commodore Stockton, had arrived by sea.

Mexico City, despite its vacillations and intrigue among various factions, did not quickly sue for peace. Consequently President Polk, who had secretly corresponded with Mexico's former dictator General Antonio López de Santa Anna, who was then in exile in Cuba, allowed Santa Anna to return to Mexico on the promise that Santa Anna would quickly end hostilities. In classic Santa Anna fashion he reneged on that promise to Polk and took the field, suffering major losses at the Battle of Buena Vista and elsewhere. By the autumn of 1846 it was clear to U.S. leaders that a speedy, conclusive blow was not to occur as defeated Mexican armies drew further and further back into the interior, and that a long, overland march across Mexico's deserts and mountains could decimate U.S. forces in numerous ways, not only at the hands of Indian attacks and the elements, but as three-month enlistments expired and as some Northern public opinion became more strident in its opposition to the war.[14] Consequently, as some armies trekked southward and westward, over 1,000 miles deeper and deeper into Mexico, a new force, under General Winfield Scott, made an amphibious landing at Veracruz, bombarded the city into submission, and then marched the short 250 miles toward Mexico City.

Battles raged on for the next eighteen months, including Monterey, Yerba Buena, Camargo, Tamaulipas, Tabasco, Buena Vista, and many others, in places as widely dispersed as the Gulf Coast, Santa Fe (New Mexico), Sacramento, and Mexico City. This culminated, on February 2, 1848, in the signing of the Treaty of Guadalupe Hidalgo, ending the war. The treaty established the Rio Grande as the Texas boundary and negotiated a new border for New Mexico and California from El Paso to the Pacific at the 32nd parallel for the price of $15 million.[15] Of the 104,556 regulars and volunteers who served in the U.S. Army, 1,551 (1.5 percent) were lost to combat and 12,229 (11 percent) were lost to disease, a death toll of 13,780. Mexican records are less precise: total military personnel, including soldiers and guerilla forces, was about 82,000. Approximately 14,700 Mexican soldiers and 2,100 guerillas fell in battle. At least 1,000 civilians died in combat and an untold number died due to disease or at the hands of U.S. and Mexican military personnel, Mexican guerrillas, and Indians.[16]

Who did the fighting? Regulars versus volunteers

The U.S. military that deployed to protect Texas and ultimately defeated Mexico was far different from the U.S. military of today. True, there was a cadre of trained officers from West Point, including individuals such as Robert E. Lee and Ulysses S. Grant, but almost none had experience in conventional warfare, as the War of 1812 had ended when Lee was eight years old; Grant was born in 1822. Some of the officers had experience fighting American Indians but much more of their work and training had been as engineers. Nonetheless, by all accounts, the majority of American professional "regulars" fought well and behaved appropriately.

Yet, the U.S. regulars were accompanied by a variety of other types of fighters, from scouts (e.g. Indian scouts, Texas Rangers) to militia with a variety of different levels of experience and expertise. This trend was a part of the American ethos of maintaining a small, established military and calling upon citizen-soldiers or "volunteers"—almost all of whom had some firearms proficiency—to rapidly augment the regular military. The terminology is confusing because today when we talk about "volunteers" we mean the professional, full-time members of the U.S. armed services.

In the 1840s the "volunteers" were usually members of state militias who may have had little or no formal training, may never have been mobilized, and may never have been deployed. Indeed, for many of the militia members in 1846–1848, their short enlistments (2–6 months) and modest expertise would have been familiar to George Washington, who wrote to Congress in 1776, "To place any dependence upon militia, is, assuredly, resting upon a broken staff." Official records place the number of regular army personnel at 31,024[17] and claim that the volunteers numbered 73,260, most of whom served near home.[18] Volunteers not only made up the ranks, but occupied many senior positions: President Polk appointed (and Congress subsequently confirmed) thirteen Democrats as volunteer generals. According to historian Richard Bruce Winders, Polk did this both for political reasons and because of his Jacksonian conviction that average Americans were "the best troops in the world, and would gain victories over superior forces of the enemy, [even] if there were not an officer among them."[19] These volunteers could be extremely helpful and it is likely that most followed the rules. But it is also apparent that militia members sometimes acted unlawfully and may have not feared repercussions because their immediate chain of command was less formal.

These distinctions are important because they reveal something about training and point to many contemporary issues, including the role of conscripts in modern warfare. It is unlikely that the militia forces heading to Mexico had much training, and the training of the time was often on formation procedures and marching technique as opposed to operations and the law of armed conflict. Furthermore, those who were engaged as foraging parties and scouts existed in the battlefield's twilight—constantly in danger themselves and at the same time able to operate with a large degree of impunity beyond the eyes of their superiors.

Many of the names we associate with the American Civil War were young officers in Mexico, and they typically had dismissive opinions of the volunteers. Lieutenant George Meade opined, "They cannot take care of themselves, the hospitals are crowded with them, [and] they die like sheep ... [they] require twice as much provisions as regulars do." Lieutenant George B. McClellan noted that the volunteers were incapable of caring for themselves and "died like dogs;" he also called them "Mohawks" and "Mustangs." Captain Phillip Barbour also called them "Mohawks," meaning that they behaved like savages. Lieutenant A.P. Hill, upon seeing a village attacked by volunteers, reflected, "'Twas then I saw and felt how perfectly unmanageable were volunteers and how much damage they did."[20]

Some of this criticism may have been the chauvinism of the regulars. So, in point of fact, how did the militia behave? General Zachary Taylor did not find it easy to impose order in the first months of the war.[21] A commander of 2,500 regulars augmented by "volunteers," he ascertained that maintaining order among his men was difficult and at times in the early months of the war looked the other way. Because Taylor had almost no regular cavalry or scouts, he relied heavily on Texas Rangers on short enlistments to serve as scouts, auxiliaries, and light cavalry, which they did very effectively. As we will see later, under the existing Articles of War and the vagaries of the volunteer system, he had little authority to prosecute a variety of types of crime and limited authority to try the volunteers under his command. In fact, Taylor attempted to give local Mexican judges jurisdiction in some of the cases, but the local judges were fearful of such a prospect.[22] It should be noted, however, that the failure to maintain order was not a result of pure cynicism or laziness on the part of General Taylor. Few U.S. military leaders had significant experience in traditional interstate war, the Lieber Code was two decades in the future, and Taylor lacked formal procedures to punish murder, assault, rape, or theft. In fact, American criminal courts that could punish such actions, under U.S. law, had no authority outside American soil.[23] To be fair, the U.S. was little different from other national militaries in this respect at the time.

What were the problems Taylor faced in those early months with his light cavalry and scouts drawn from Texas?[24] Some Texans wanted retribution for the blood spilled in the Texas revolution a decade earlier: recall that it was a total slaughter at the Alamo and there were other atrocities committed by the Mexicans as well.[25] Texans remembered that Santa Anna—after surrendering at San Jacinto—reneged on the terms of surrender to fight another day. They also remembered the infamous "black bean" incident when every tenth Texan prisoner was murdered by their captors.[26] On Palm Sunday, 1836, the Mexican Army—on Santa Anna's orders—executed 342 Texan soldiers who had surrendered at Goliad, and then burned the bodies.[27] In addition to a sense of vengeance for the past, the Texans believed that the Mexican army could not be trusted to comport themselves in accordance with the laws of armed conflict, and this was born out later at Buena Vista when the Mexican army wrongfully used a flag of truce to its advantage.[28]

One recent study of the Texas Rangers' involvement in the first months of the Mexican War reports that they initially enlisted as three-month volunteers, and re-enlisted as the first enlistment was coming due in order to fight at Monterey. According to the author, U.S. Army Captain Ian Lyles, the Rangers served as "mounted cavalry, scouts, counter-guerrilla elements, and mounted escorts to Taylor's infantry and artillery, making several important contributions" during the early phase of the war, "with few charges of ill-discipline … Those forces undoubtedly rendered significant operational and tactical contributions during this phase" because Taylor had almost no "regular" cavalry or dragoons.[29]

> The Rangers were a "mixed blessing" for Taylor because they were unpredictable and could lash out at the locals. For example, a Texas Ranger killed a Mexican soldier days after the battle had ended. The Rangers' leader, Colonel Hays, did arrest the individual and turned him over to the regular military authorities. But, herein lay one of the enduring problems of the Mexican War, no formal authority existed with which the army could punish troops for violation that would have fallen under the jurisdiction of civilian courts in the United States. Taylor lacked formal authority and he was unwilling to assume the informal authority necessary to deal with gross violations of the law [such] as murder, rape, and serious theft. Instead, Taylor wrote to the Secretary of War for guidance; what he received was the recommendation that the man be sent from the army since the crime was not specifically listed in the Articles of War. So, rather than deal effectively with the problem Taylor merely wished it away by granting the Texas Rangers their discharges on 30 September, disbanding the two regiments.[30]

Lyles concludes, "On 6 October, just twelve days after the end of the battle [for Monterey], Taylor wrote of the Rangers, '… with their departure we may look for a restoration of quiet and good order in Monterey, for I regret to report that some shameful atrocities have been perpetrated by them since the capitulation of the town.'"[31]

As the war went on, there did continue to be some violations against civilians' lives and property. Beyond the vengeance motive of Texans, other inducements for unlawful behavior included lawlessness by criminal elements within state militias, as well as a sort of "anything goes" attitude among some men craving adventure and serving far from the judgmental eyes of wives and neighbors. Luther Giddings of Ohio cataloged an instance when Gray's Texas Cavalry massacred twenty-four Mexican men in "reprisal" for some past grievance.[32] Giddings also reported that among Gray's Texans, one soldier accused the volunteers of disgracing the nation with their conduct when one of his comrades opened fire on a woman to test his rifle and another tore the earrings out of a Mexican woman's ears. According to Giddings, such actions went unpunished.[33]

Following the Battle of Monterrey in 1846, the Texas Rangers, under the command of Colonel Hays, went on a rampage that culminated in the murder of one hundred civilians, and the torching of peasants' huts.[34] In retaliation for an ambush on a U.S. wagon train near Cerralvo, which left forty Americans dead and one hundred and twenty wagons destroyed, "Mustang" Gray attacked the first Mexicans in sight. Eventually it was reported that two dozen Mexican men were murdered near an American camp.[35] Samuel Chamberlain claimed that this was part of a plan by General Taylor to unofficially "unleash" these waves of terror upon the people of Nuevo Leon and Tamaulipas in retaliation for the loss of the wagon train. Taylor claimed that his investigation into atrocities involving plunder, murder, and rape came up short. Chamberlain claims that those who witnessed the brutality failed to speak up for fear of facing the wrath of the perpetrators.[36]

General William Worth was made Military Governor of Monterey in September 1846, and was diligent in standardizing and enforcing discipline.[37] When it came to dealing with the locals, General Worth's administration would not convict Mexicans without legal proof and due process. This stopped individuals from taking advantage of Mexican businessmen or fathers who were trying to protect their daughters. Worth often employed draconian methods of punishment such as iron ball-and-chain and forced labor. Indeed, the pendulum had swung from permissive to harsh: senior U.S. military leaders rarely cracked down on U.S. officers who injured miscreant soldiers through tough punishments.[38] Desertion was punishable by hanging, but more often deserters were disciplined with imprisonment, branding, and hard labor.

One American almost died trying to stop volunteers from Louisville from committing "outrages upon the citizens."[39] The *Louisville Journal* of June 29, 1847, reported that the volunteers beat one Mr. Davis to death, although the instigating volunteer was later incarcerated for the crime.[40] An eyewitness observed that Company D, 1st Pennsylvania Infantry, was made up of a collection of troublemakers who called themselves "the Killers" and performed one disgraceful act after another.[41] They disrupted a theater performance, attacked and nearly killed a Spanish store owner, and robbed a Frenchman of his poultry and his pet deer and cooked them both. Before the Frenchman produced a warrant for the arrest of "the Killers," the quartermaster promised just compensation.[42] Ruben Davis lamented that upon swearing the soldier's oath, men lost all moral restraint except that which was connected to personal valor and their loyalty to the nation.[43] General Taylor echoed this sentiment in June 1847, noting that when it came to the volunteers, "There is scarcely a form of crime that has not been reported to me as committed by them."[44]

The U.S. military leadership did attempt to rein in volunteer brutality.[45] Early in the war volunteers were forbidden to occupy towns, and garrisons were quickly replaced by regular soldiers. At Veracruz the volunteers marched on the city as a second wave, sandwiched by regular troops before and behind. In fact, the difference between the regulars and the volunteers was apparently so obvious that the Mexicans were able to tell them apart from a distance.[46] While the official policies were favorable to the Mexican people, the decentralized disciplinary structure within the U.S. Army, particularly in the first several months of the war, obstructed the ability to crack down on individuals, especially those of volunteer units, who violated codes of conduct.

To this point I have attempted to demonstrate the types of violations of the ethics of how war is fought, which observers at the time and today's historians largely blame on volunteer forces during the first six months of the war. With these examples of violations of the principle of discrimination in mind, just how widespread were outrages by the volunteers? It is difficult to say with any precision, but the numbers and disposition of those volunteers suggests that actually they were limited. The volunteers constituted the *least* amount of the soldiers in the war when based on time in service and where they served.[47] There were 73,260 volunteer enlistments; 2 percent served for three months, 15 percent served for six months, 24 percent served for one year, and 46 percent served for the whole war. Many provided backfill to existing Army missions so that the regulars could deploy to Mexico. For instance, the Texas volunteers mostly did border patrol and Indian fighting, Floridian volunteers took over the posts that the regulars sent to Mexico had vacated, the Missouri militia maintained order on the Oregon Trail and in the Colorado and Kansas areas, the Camp Washington militia was never utilized (despite the fact that they surpassed their quota), and Iowa volunteers stuck to escorting Indians to new reservations and manning their own forts on the frontier. The majority of volunteers never actually made it to the Mexican battlefields; of those who did, many did not serve directly under the commands of Generals Scott and Taylor.[48] This is to say not that there was not "hell-raising" by many of the volunteers, but that much of it did not occur in Mexico. It is also not to say that there were no violations of the principle of discrimination: it has been clearly reported here that there were. Nonetheless, based on current scholarship, since the volunteers were responsible for the bulk of the outrages, and few of them were sent to Mexico, outrages against the Mexican populace were the exception rather than the norm and the regular U.S. Army—as noted by Lee and Grant—behaved well, particularly after the first several months of the war as volunteers either went home or were gradually assimilated into army life.

What are we to learn from all of this? At the most basic level, we can recognize that the U.S. military—as well as those of its neighbors and competitors in the 1840s—was far different than today's militaries. There was no Lieber code,[49] the provisions that were to emanate from the International Red Cross and later Hague Conventions were decades in the future, and the war convention was far less robust than today. Moreover, like any army consisting of poorly trained citizens, there was wide room for both error and violations. The challenge faced in Mexico by U.S. military leaders was not dissimilar to some challenges faced by some those superintending "volunteers," and especially conscripts, in wars around the world, including later U.S. wars in Europe, the Pacific, Korea, and Vietnam.

So, one lesson, and moral challenge, for national governments is how best to prepare their militia and non-traditional recruitment base (e.g. conscripts) to adhere to the protocols of military discipline and law of armed conflict. There are answers to this question—answers that have largely developed in the past half-century. One is for countries to have a mandatory service obligation, as Israel and Switzerland have and Sweden recently reinstituted, that provides a common level of training in the profession of arms across a wide swathe of the citizenry.[50] This also provides for a common set of ethical expectations for when the uniform is worn. A second model, more germane to recent U.S. experience, is to ensure that militia forces (e.g. state national guards and the federal reserve forces) have high levels of professional training. This is clearly the case in the U.S. today, where the reserve forces receive essentially the same training as the active-duty military and are expected to adhere to the same standards—a far cry from the experience of Harry Truman and other militia members who marched around with broomsticks and played poker on drill weekends before World War I.[51]

A third model, one that has its weaknesses, is to rapidly mobilize a conscripted force from the general citizenry, with hasty, standardized training, as the U.S. did at the outset of World Wars I and II and for the hottest phases of Vietnam. In 1942 there were tremendous incentives for average Joes to become GI Joes, and although the training was very rapid, there were elements both at boot camp and then in the theater designed to emphasize appropriate behavior by the troops. One of the famous examples of this was the small booklets developed for U.S. forces in North Africa that provided a few words in Arabic and prohibited soldiers from molesting the local Arab population.[52] In contrast, as the Vietnam War dragged on, the conscript force fighting in the jungles was far more diverse in its views on the war and what appropriate behavior should be—particularly as the enemy often fought in dastardly, unconventional ways. But perhaps what differentiates the situation of the U.S. military in 1846 and again in 1860 is the lack of federal oversight and standardization of these forces. Militias often elected their own leaders at the local level and there was often no standardized military training or expectations. This proved problematic for Union units in the early part of the U.S. Civil War due to the ineptitude of the "political generals." At least by the twentieth century, state militias, volunteers, and conscripts were folded into the regular army in most cases before being deployed abroad.

In any event, the Mexican–American War, with these subsequent examples in mind, forces us to reflect on the responsibility of sending officials—sovereign political authorities—in preparing the troops for battle in line with the *jus in bello* principles that are enshrined in a country's legal codes and the war convention, as well as the responsibility of the troops to act in accordance with common humanity, proportionality, and discrimination. The U.S. Army had to learn in motion while in Mexico and it took creative, decisive leadership—such as General Scott's martial law (see below)—to move beyond the ad hoc to a formal set of rules and procedures governing behavior.

Commander's intentions, proportionality, and discrimination

Military commanders and political leaders have long given speeches or general orders at the outset of a battle. These statements may have a variety of purposes, from inspiring the martial spirit to emphasizing the mission and restraint. The most famous of such general orders in U.S. history is that given by General George Washington on March 1, 1778, at one of the lowest moments of the American War for Independence, following the long, bleak garrison at Valley Forge.

> The Commander in Chief again takes occasion to return his warmest thanks to the virtuous officers and soldiery of this Army for that persevering fidelity and Zeal which they have uniformly manifested in all their conduct. Their fortitude not only under the common hardships incident to a military life but also under the additional sufferings to which the peculiar situation of these States have exposed them, clearly proves them worthy of the enviable privilege of contending for the rights of human nature, the Freedom and Independence of their Country …
>
> Surely we who are free Citizens in arms engaged in a struggle for every-thing valuable in society and partaking in the glorious task of laying the foundation of an Empire, should scorn effeminately to shrink under those accidents and rigours of War which mercenary hirelings fighting in the cause of lawless ambition, rapine and devastation, encounter with cheerfulness and alacrity, we should not be merely equal, we should be superior to them … American soldiers … will despise the meanness of repining at such trif-ling strokes of Adversity, trifling indeed when compared to the transcendent Prize which will undoubtedly crown their Patience and Perseverance, Glory and Freedom, Peace and Plenty to themselves and the Community; The Admiration of the World, the Love of their Country and the Gratitude of Posterity![53]

Today, such statements of the "commander's intent" are distributed by email, posted on the walls of military installations, and distributed through a variety of media, with a variety of purposes, from inspiring the troops to providing specific battle-field guidelines to propaganda designed to influence one's enemy (as well as critics at home).

We will focus on the key military statements made by U.S. generals in Mexico that demonstrate their intentions regarding the conduct of their troops as well as appropriate behavior toward enemy combatants, civilians, and private property. The evidence suggests that U.S. military leaders, for moral and pragmatic reasons, truly wanted their troops to obey customary law and act with restraint toward the lives, livelihoods, and way of life of Mexican civilians. These proclamations were important messages designed for multiple audiences in a dynamic environment and clearly indicate that from the very outset of the conflict, U.S. commanders called for discrimination and proportionality. For instance, after Mexican forces crossed

---

BOX 5.1 HEADQUARTERS, ARMY OF OCCUPATION, CORPUS CHRISTI, TEXAS, MARCH 8, 1846, ORDER NO. 30

The Army of Occupation being about to take position on the left bank of the Rio Grande, under the orders of the Executive of the United States, the General Commanding deems it proper to express his hope that the movement will prove beneficial to all concerned, and that nothing may be wanting on his part to ensure so desirable a result, he strictly enjoins on his command the most scrupulous regard for the rights of all persons who may be found in the peaceable pursuit of their respective avocations, residing on both banks of the Rio Grande; no person under any pretense whatever will interfere in any manner with the civil rights or religious privileges of the people, but will pay the utmost respect to both. Whatever may be required for the use of the army will be purchased by the proper Departments at the highest market price. The General Commanding is happy to say that he has entire confidence in the patriotism and discipline of the army under his command, and feels assured that his orders, as above expressed, will be strictly observed.

Source: "Gen. Zachary Taylor's General Order on Respecting the Rights of Mexicans," The Mexican War and the Media Project at Virginia Tech, available at: www.history.vt.edu/MxAmWar/Newspapers/Niles/Nilesa18441846.htm# NR70.11218Apr1846ArmyofOccupation (accessed May 22, 2017).

---

the Rio Grande and attacked U.S. troops, initiating the war, General Zachary Taylor led the U.S. Army into Mexico. At the time he issued the terse General Order No. 30 (March 8, 1846).

Within just two months, Taylor's army had beaten the Mexican army at Palo Alto and Resaca de la Palma. Mexican forces quietly withdrew from the advancing American army, allowing Taylor to peacefully take the major city of Matamoros (May 18, 1846) without bloodshed. Taylor then issued a lengthy proclamation to the general Mexican public, laying out the reasons for the war and U.S. objectives. He gave specific pledges regarding appropriate treatment of the civilian population, writing:

> It is our wish to see you liberated from despots, to drive back the savage Comanches, to prevent the renewal of their assaults, and to compel them to restore to you from captivity your long lost wives and children. Your religion, your altars, your churches, the property of your churches and citizens, the emblems of your faith and its ministers, shall be protected, and remain inviolable—hundreds of our army, and hundreds of thousands of our citizens are members of the Catholic Church. In every state, and in nearly every city and village of our Union, Catholic churches exist, and the priests perform

their holy functions in peace and security under the sacred guarantee of our constitution. We come among the people of Mexico as friends and republican brethren, and all who receive us as such, shall be protected, whilst all who are seduced into the army of your dictator shall be treated as enemies. We shall want from you nothing but food for our army, and for this you shall always be paid in cash the full value.[54]

Earlier in this chapter we saw how General Taylor, in 1846, lacked specific guidance from the War Department on how to handle a number of crimes. With the problems of the volunteers in mind, in February 1847 General Winfield Scott issued very specific instructions (General Order No. 20) that he defined as "martial law" designed to flesh out what we would today call the rules of engagement.

BOX 5.2 GENERAL ORDER NO. 20

1st It can be feared that many and grave crimes not foreseen in the act of Congress *establishing the rules and articles for the Government of the United States Army*, approved on April 10, 1806, can be committed by individuals of those armies or against them in Mexico during the war between the two republics. Those atrocious crimes that, if committed in the United States or in its organized territories, would be precisely judged and severely punished by the Nation's ordinary or civil courts, are mentioned here.

2nd Murder, premeditated murder, injuries or mutilation, rape, assaults and malicious beatings; robbery, larceny, desecration of Churches, cemeteries or houses, and religious buildings; and the destruction of public or private property that was not ordered by a superior officer, are crimes of this nature.

3rd Good service, the honor of the United States, and the interests of humanity imperatively demand that all the above-mentioned crimes be punished severely.

4th Yet, the written code, commonly called the rules and articles of war, as mentioned earlier, does not prescribe the punishment for any of these crimes ...

5th It is evident that article 99, independent of all reference to the restriction in article 87, is null in respect to any of those grave crimes.

6th Consequently, all the offenses enumerated above in the 2nd paragraph, which can be committed in another country, in the army, or by the army or against the army, absolutely need a supplemental code.

7th This unwritten code is *Martial* Law, an addition to the written military code, which Congress ordered to be observed in the *rules and articles of war;* it is an unwritten code that all armies are obligated to follow in enemy countries, not only for their own safety, but also to protect the inoffensive inhabitants and their properties within the theater of military operations, from offenses committed against the laws of war.

8th Martial law has been declared because of this supreme necessity; it is a supplemental code for all camps, military points, and hospitals that are occupied by whatever part of the United States forces in Mexico and by all the columns, escorts, convoys, guards, and detachments of the expressed forces, while they are engaged in continuing the present war in and against the aforesaid Republic.

9th Consequently, any crime enumerated in paragraph No. 2 that is committed: first, by any Mexican inhabitant, denizen, or traveler against the person or property of any individual adherent to or dependent on the United States forces; 2nd By any individual adherent to or dependent on said forces against the person or property of any Mexican inhabitant, denizen, or traveler; 3rd By any individual adherent to or dependent on said forces against the person or property of any other individual adherent to or dependent on said forces, will be punctually judged and punished according to the expressed supplemental code.

10th With this objective, all the delinquents in the above-mentioned cases are ordered to be promptly apprehended, imprisoned, and denounced in order to be judged by a *military commission* that will be named to this effect.

Source: "General Headquarters of the Army, General Order #20," Rice University (last modified June 7, 2010), available at: https://scholarship.rice.edu/jsp/xml/1911/27562/3/aa00208tr.tei.html.

General Scott's General Order No. 20 was circulated across the country and was a critical tool for commanders for the rest of the war. Two months later, after American forces had taken the strategically vital port of Veracruz, General Scott wrote an open letter, publicized widely, "To the good people of Mexico … I think myself called upon to address you":

Mexicans—Americans are not your enemies, but the enemies, for a time, of those men who, a year ago, misgoverned you, and brought about this unnatural war between two great republics. We are the friends of the peaceful inhabitants of the country we occupy, and the friends of your holy religion, its hierarchy and its priesthood. The same church is found in all parts of our own country, crowded with devout Catholics, and respected by our government, laws and people.

For the church of Mexico, the unoffending inhabitants of the country, and their property, I have from the first done everything in my power to place them under the safeguard of martial law against the few bad men in this army.

My orders, to that effect, known to all, are precise and rigorous. Under them, several Americans have already been punished, by fine, for the benefit of Mexicans, besides imprisonment, and one, for a rape has been hung by the neck.

Is this not a proof of good faith and energetic discipline? Other proofs shall be given as often as injuries to Mexicans may be detected.

On the other hand, injuries committed by individuals, or parties of Mexico, not belonging to the public forces, upon individuals, small parties, trains of wagons and teams, or of pack mules; or any other person or property belonging to this army, contrary to the laws of war—shall be punished with rigor; or if the particular offenders be not delivered up by Mexican authorities, the punishment shall fall upon entire cities, towns or neighborhoods.

Let, then, all good Mexicans remain at home, or at their peaceful occupation, but they are invited to bring in, for sale, horses, mules, beef, cattle, corn, barley, wheat, flour for bread, and vegetables. Cash will be paid for every thing this army may take and purchase, and protection will be given to all sellers. The Americans are strong enough to offer these insurances—which, should Mexicans wisely accept this war may soon be happily ended, to the honor and advantage of both belligerents. Then the Americans, having converted enemies into friends, will be happy to take leave of Mexico and return to their own country.[55]

There are plenty of other documents to look at, but these are representative and they demonstrate that the U.S. military leadership was attempting to specify restraint in terms that we recognize as proportionality and discrimination (i.e. noncombatant immunity). General Zachary Taylor began his first general order calling for the protection of non-combatants: "he strictly enjoins on his command the most scrupulous regard for the rights of all persons who may be found in the peaceable pursuit of their respective avocations." This theme was picked up by all of the subsequent orders and proclamations: seeking to protect private citizens, private property, and religious institutions as much as possible. This was no mere window-dressing: a wider look at how the battles were fought—largely as conventional battles between opposing armies on the battlefield—demonstrates that there was a high level of both proportionality and discrimination practiced on the battlefield as well. Battlefield tactics focused on winning local and theater-specific goals with explicit limits on destruction, such as keeping transportation routes open and protecting civilian government buildings.

Finally, these proclamations make it clear that there are direct links between these *jus in bello* criteria and the *jus post bellum* ideas of stable, secure post-conflict environment. All of the commanders recognized that even during occupation, there would be a symbiotic relationship between the occupied (e.g. selling foodstuffs to the troops) and occupiers (as protectors of law and order). In the longer term, General Scott talked of "converting enemies into friends" and all accepted that, whatever the war's outcome, the U.S. and Mexico would continue to be neighbors in perpetuity. A smart, restrained war and limited peace settlement—which included how the Mexican people were treated during the war—was critical to ending the war decisively and well.

Jus in bello and the bombardment of Veracruz

Democrat President James K. Polk and his senior military advisor, General Winfield Scott (a Whig), wanted a rapid victory. As this did not happen in the first six months of the war, the decision was made to plan an assault on the Mexican capital. But U.S. armies already on the ground in the north would have to transverse vast deserts to get there, so Scott advocated for America's first major amphibious landing at the strategic port of Veracruz on the Gulf of Mexico. This would allow U.S. troops to cut inland across the Sierra Madre plateau and march on Mexico City itself, assuming they could get past the citadel of Veracruz, the harsh environment, and any Mexican armies in the way.

Although historians say that Polk—a shrewd politician and former Speaker of the U.S. House of Representatives—did not want to provide a platform for a victorious Whig General to challenge him for the presidency a few years later, nonetheless Scott's exquisite planning of the operation from Washington, DC, made him the obvious choice to direct the invasion. Scott's plan called for U.S. troops to be at Veracruz in January 1847 in order to not be defeated by his greatest foe: yellow fever.

Scott knew that the tropical climate of Veracruz was extremely dangerous for his troops and that the American forces needed to be in the Sierra Madre region by about April 15 in order to not have the dreaded "yellow jack" decimate the army.[56] However, to Scott and his fellow commanders' dismay, the U.S. War Department bungled the dispatches, manpower, and supplies for the operation, making it impossible to arrive at Veracruz until the first week of March 1847, two full months after the original rendezvous date.[57] This meant that Scott had to land his troops, engage and defeat the Mexican forces, and then force the march inland to get out of the tropical zone with its mosquitos and various diseases. Scott had to have in mind the ill-fated French expedition to Haiti forty years earlier, in which an army of 25,000 was decimated by disease. Only 3,000 French made it home alive.[58]

This was not expected to be an easy task. Veracruz (Vera Cruz—the True Cross) was considered the most heavily fortified city in the entire Western hemisphere, able to withstand major pirate assaults. Scott would have about 10,000 troops at his command; the Mexican army had nearly 4,000 in the city. Moreover, Scott knew that in a short time the enlistment of many of his volunteers would expire and they would return home. Upon arrival, Scott learned that another Mexican army, perhaps under General Santa Anna himself, was on the march toward his position. It took Scott several days to land his troops (on March 9), invest positions around the city, coordinate artillery with the naval elements, and prepare for the next phase.

What were Scott's choices? He had three. He could lay siege to the city and attempt to wait it out, causing starvation and disease to erode the city's morale and defenses. He could attack it straight on, throwing his armies at its gates and walls, and hope that somehow his army could break through. Or, he could shell it with artillery, blasting it into submission.

Scott demanded immediate surrender of Veracruz, but Mexican Brigadier General Juan Morales refused to comply.[59] As late as March 22, Scott urged surrender, but General Morales said no and the cosmopolitan city, which included various foreign consuls, businesspeople, and members of the Mexican elite, expected a protracted siege. Although the details of various skirmishes, the role of a Mexican artillery battery on a nearby island, raiding sorties issuing out of Veracruz, and the engineering efforts of Captain Robert E. Lee and his subordinates (including Lieutenants Joe Johnston and George McClellan) are all of interest, those complexities are beyond the scope of this chapter.[60] Scott made the decision to bombard the city, despite its large civilian population, from that point on because the Mexican authorities would not surrender. Two days later, the foreign leaders in the city sent a request to Scott to allow the women and children to leave, but he refused, citing previous opportunities that would have saved civilian lives.[61] This may have been a delaying tactic to allow Mexican reinforcements to arrive, and Scott, with his eye on the calendar, was interested in surrender not delay. Now the blood was on the hands of the Mexican military.

History tells us that within a short time Mexican General Morales resigned, citing health problems, and his second-in-command quickly surrendered to the American army. Reports indicate that Mexico lost 1,100 people, including civilians, while Scott's army of 10,000 suffered only 68 dead and wounded.[62] Scott rapidly put in place General Order 20, quoted in this chapter, and established order in the city, going as far as to attend mass in order to demonstrate his goodwill to the Catholic population.[63] In fact, Scott's benevolence became so renowned that it led some Mexicans to beg for him to become their new ruler.[64] A few weeks later, when Scott's army arrived at Puebla, they were welcomed "almost cordially, 'more like travelers than enemies,' in the words of the Spanish minister."[65] Because elements of his army had marched ahead and beaten a 2,000-member Mexican force that had come to cut them off, General Scott was free to move the bulk of his army toward the healthy foothills of the Sierra Madre, leaving the dreaded coast with its tropical diseases behind him.

Veracruz and proportionality

Proportionality is about stewardship, restraint, and limiting destruction. It is also about thoughtfully attempting to link battlefield options and actions with battlefield objectives. But, what is often missed in thin discussions of military ethics, at least by armchair philosophers, is how a specific battle is interwoven with a larger set of trends and campaigns. In other words, there is a mid-range of "proportionality" that is bigger than tactical battlefield engagements in a specific time and place, that connects what happens in that engagement with campaign and theater objectives. In other contexts, great battles like Antietam and D-Day mattered, but not just as discrete battles: they also were connected to larger campaign and war aims. Thus, when it comes to the overall strategic objective— taking Mexico City and bringing a more rapid ending to the war—the attack on Veracruz was a proportionate activity. This is an important point when thinking about more recent wars. Perhaps one of the reasons that some battles in Iraq and Afghanistan had to be refought and won was that senior leadership at the highest level was unwilling to authorize decisive battlefield actions (i.e. due to very limited rules of engagement) that would have linked enduring victory in one location with wider, longer-term victories that could be held and built upon elsewhere. This is likewise a criticism of some of the campaigns of the Vietnam War: it seemed that the issue of proportionality could be so limited, particularly under President Johnson, in terms of how many bombs in what place at what time on what target, that the entire strategic notion of proportionality in a the-ater or strategic sense was entirely missing.

At Veracruz, Winfield Scott understood this. He knew that decisive victory at Veracruz was more than just tactical operations against the city. It had to do with creating a sea-based line of communication (for the short term), creating a path to Mexico City, opening a third major front in the war, and saving the lives of his own troops. This is strategic proportionality. Scott did not seek a scorched-earth cam-paign but he did seek rapid, decisive victory using all of the tools at his disposal. Thoughtful proportionality means recognizing that whatever men and materiel that he lost in the short term at Veracruz would not be resupplied for some time, so the resources that he wisely conserved in the short bombardment were going to be available to fight another day. This, of course, was the problem the Confederacy ultimately faced in the U.S. Civil War: pyrrhic victories with no reserve resources to fall back on, in contrast to what appeared to be a never-ending supply of men and armaments from the Union.

Finally, a more conventional view of proportionality, one that simply focuses on the relationship of battlefield tactics in achieving battlefield objectives, also suggests that the course of action chosen by Scott was proportionate. His army did not just overcome a major military obstacle ("military necessity") but did so in a way that appropriately employed the resources at his disposal in order to secure this critical objective, with an eye on time, manpower, and materiel. It is noteworthy that this *sui generis* action by General Scott demonstrated his resolve to the Mexican military and political class and thereby ultimately saved lives: there were no similar urban bombardments by the U.S. Army throughout the remainder of the war.

Veracruz and discrimination

When it comes to the issue of discrimination, there are a number of issues worth considering. First, was a rapid, hammer blow to Veracruz likely to result in more or less destruction than a long-running traditional siege? Second, does the principle of discrimination mean that Scott's only humanitarian objective was to protect civilian life and property in the city, or did he have some responsibility to his own troops (many of whom were volunteers), particularly in the face of yellow fever and other disease? Third, if an opponent's military is using human shields—and one could argue that Veracruz is such an instance—who is actually responsible for the deaths of those civilians?

We do not fully know what Scott was thinking at the time, although his memoirs (written years later) indicate that he believed that a short, dramatic bombardment would force the capitulation of Veracruz and actually limit human suffering. The weapons of the time, from army and navy artillery to Congreve rockets, were a far cry from the discriminating smart missiles of today. However, the English Consul both condemned Scott's action as barbaric and simultaneously conceded that the bombardment probably resulted in fewer casualties in the city than a traditional siege would have.[66] Part of the reason for the Consul's complaint was that civilians and foreigners were not allowed to leave the city at some point after the bombardment began: the historical record is blurry about at what point Scott said that civilians were no longer going to be allowed to leave the city: Scott demanded surrender, not truce, from the outset of the bombardment.

Interestingly, in the last twenty years a scholarly literature has developed looking at a parallel set of questions regarding armed humanitarian intervention. The reason this is *a propos* is this: is it more discriminating to attack with resolve and massive force, or is it more discriminating to besiege a military-civilian center and slowly denude it of not only the lives of its inhabitants but also its institutions and infrastructure? For instance, Mathew Krain, with the Balkans wars of the 1990s in mind, concludes that in some instances, slow escalation results in more civilian deaths and greater destruction of institutions and infrastructure due to the measured but relentless downward spiral of devastation, and it may even escalate it by signaling apathy or consent.[67] This battlefield logic seems to hold true in an instance such as the Veracruz operations: both sides probably had lives saved due to the city rapidly falling to bombardment rather than enduring a long-term siege dragging out through the months when starvation and "el Vomito," yellow fever, would attack indiscriminately. This was the reluctant view of the British Consul, who denigrated the bombardment of Veracruz but conceded that in the long run it saved lives.[68]

Much of the discussion about loss of life centers on how indiscriminate artillery, aimed at a city, will kill both combatants and non-combatants. A second question, posed too infrequently by academic observers, is: what was the moral responsibility Scott had to provide safety and security to his own troops? One of his options at Veracruz was to attack the Western hemisphere's most impregnable city head on, with waves of soldiers marching on the city to be picked off by Mexican soldiers inside. This hardly made sense either in terms of military necessity or in terms of military ethics. The other option was a protracted siege, but with the specter of disease ravaging his troops. This is an important point because the majority of men who died in the Mexican–American War died from disease. According to official records, 1,192 were killed in action, with an additional 529 dying later of wounds received in battle. But 11,155 died of disease (e.g. yellow fever, smallpox, malaria, etc.).[69] Scott was wise to protect his own troops, as much as possible, from disease, not just as human "tools" of war, but also keeping in mind that many U.S. troops were citizen-soldiers on short enlistments who would be eligible to return to their homes, farms, and businesses in just a few short months. Unfortunately, some of the recent literature on military ethics seems to suggest that soldiers' lives are worth far less than those of citizens, but this is a problematic line of reasoning that needs more attention, particularly when citizen-soldiers have responded, voluntarily, in self-defense to an attack on their country.[70] As will be discussed in the next chapter, consider U.S. service personnel serving in the Pacific theater in 1942–1945. Most of them were average citizens going to work or school the first week of December 1941; they little expected to have to fight a war against the Axis powers following Pearl Harbor. Their lives matter—just because they put on a uniform does not make them cannon fodder and the enemy's civilians somehow far more valuable morally. This is an area where greater attention is needed in just war thinking when it comes to conscription, reserve forces, and "volunteers."

Finally, although Mexican authorities may have not been thinking in terms of what we today call "human shields," nonetheless Veracruz is an excellent example of a problem faced by moral military commanders. What is a commander to do when one's enemy deliberately uses the principles of humanity and discrimination callously, by employing child soldiers, hiding bombs in the folds of a woman's garments, using a house of worship or hospital as a military emplacement, or daring an attack that would result in the deaths of women and children? Veracruz seems to have been a case where locals had confidence that the presence of the city's many European inhabitants and a sense of American *noblesse oblige*— rather than the skill of the Mexican military—would protect the city. Western militaries have been facing these problems for the past half-century, from Vietnam to Serbia to Iraq. In Scott's case, the Mexican General may have tried to outlast Scott by expecting Scott's honor to make it impossible for the Americans to bombard the city.

Such battles are cases of the opponent attempting to manipulate the ethics of the situation by putting moral blame on the adversary. But who is really morally obligated in such a situation? Just as a bank robber who holds civilians hostage has primary moral responsibility for their safety—not the police officers who have responded to the alarms—so too the Mexican leadership had the primary responsibility to protect civilian lives and property. We do not know all of the early communication that occurred between Scott and General Morales, nor do we fully know the thinking behind the walls of Veracruz when they saw U.S. ships on the horizon in early March, but certainly the Mexican leadership should have taken actions to protect civilians. In this case, what is particularly craven—at least when one allows one's mind to explore the possibilities—is that the Mexican leadership did not try to come to an arrangement early on to protect civilians, but only did so after refusing substantive parley at the beginning of the siege and bombardment.

It was only later that the Mexican leadership attempted to use civilians as a trump card against Scott's forces.

The human shield motif is complex and no two situations are alike, but it has been the declared policy of individuals like Saddam Hussein and Slobodan Milosevic to assume that Western forces would be shackled by their military and political ethics (and CNN) and thus not respond with robust force against them. This is not new: U.S. GIs encountered it in the Pacific during World War II, in Korea, and in Vietnam. In such instances, Western leaders must take human life and property into account, on both sides of the conflict, but not necessarily be stymied by such nefarious, inhumane actions. The primary moral responsibility lies on those leaders for putting their citizens into such situations.

In conclusion, General Scott's Veracruz Proclamation of April 11, 1847, promised to protect the Catholic Church of Mexico, and offered monetary compensation for all things purchased or taken, as well as protection to all merchants. In this same proclamation Scott acknowledged that there were miscreants in the American army and punished them. One was fined and imprisoned for his offense, while another was hanged for rape. Scott called these public punishments "proof of good faith and energetic discipline" and promised further examples should American troops wrong the Mexican people. The Veracruz Proclamation also decreed that Mexican towns would collectively suffer if they did not surrender private civilians who injured the American army by violating the laws of war. Finally, Scott used the Veracruz Proclamation to communicate his hope that America would convert her Mexican enemy into a friend at the closing of the war.[71] Scott and his successor, General Worth, distributed rations and eliminated extortion through the employment of fair scales for food. Stores reopened and commerce flourished. Within ten days the physical effects of the bombardment were all but eliminated.[72] It appears that General Scott found a balance between military necessity, proportionality, and discrimination.

Conclusion: Assessing the record, lessons for today

Sadly, every war has its violations of the war convention, so what are we to conclude about the ethics of how the U.S. military fought the Mexican–American War? One way to get at the general tenor of the war's ethical climate is to consider the view of first-hand observers and critics. The evidence they present is that the U.S. military did a good job in terms of restraint. For instance, Theodore Parker, a vocal American critic of the war, conceded that it was "conducted with as much gentleness as a war of invasion can be."[73] Robert E. Lee, a veteran of the war, remembered that the Americans "fought well and fought fairly … in a manner no man might be ashamed of."[74] As noted above, Ulysses S. Grant remarked, "The troops behaved well in Mexico, and the government acted handsomely about the peace."[75] Despite his misgivings about going to war, Grant suggested that it would have been best for everyone involved if the United States absorbed Mexico entirely, a view shared by some Mexican political liberals and many of the business class. Grant reflected,

We could have held Mexico, and made it a permanent section of the Union with the consent of all classes whose consent was worth having ... The Mexicans are a good people. They live on little and work hard ... The country is rich, and if the people could be assured a good government, they would prosper. See what we have made of Texas and California—empires. There are the same materials for new empires in Mexico. I have always had a deep interest in Mexico and her people, and have always wished them well ... When I was in London, talking with Lord Beaconsfield, he ... said he wished to heaven we had taken the country, that England would not like anything better than to see the United States annex it ... Now that slavery is out of the way there could be no better future for Mexico than absorption in the United States.[76]

Foreign opinion weighed in heavily on the matter as well. Francis Giffard, the British Consul, lamented that despite Taylor's grand pronouncements, his poor enforcement of order early in the war provided "perfect impunity" for the worst of human behavior for a time.[77] Giffard also considered Scott's bombardment of Veracruz to be an example of unnecessary brutality, but conceded that his shelling tactic succeeded in forcing the surrender.[78] Lerdo de Tejada, a renowned Mexican historian, conceded that Veracruz endured little more than foreign occupation, an occupation that allowed the city to gain "several profits."[79] Gutierrez de Estrada, a highly regarded Mexican diplomat, observed that the Americans provided Mexicans with greater security of life and possession than their native government, which had been in never-ending intrigue and tumult since independence from Spain a quarter-century earlier.[80] Percy William Doyle, British *chargé d'affaires*, surveying the populace from Veracruz to Mexico City noted that, "From the account of the Mexicans themselves [the American Army] seemed to have behaved very well."[81] Finally, the Mexican historian Roa Barcena opined, "The elevated and kindly character of Taylor and Scott lessened as far as was possible the evils of war."[82] In short, although this was an imperfect war—as all are—the evidence is clear that the U.S. military generally acted with restraint toward non-combatants, narrowed its military objectives to critical targets, and imposed on its own troops some discipline for poor behavior. The restraint appears to have been particularly true of trained soldiers, as distinct from volunteer (militia) forces. This is not a surprising finding, and it accords with what one sees in poorly trained, conscript militaries around the globe and those that operate beyond the strict reins of authority.

The Mexican–American War thus provides an opportunity for deeper analysis and learning on the intersection of ethics training, professionalism, leadership, and battlefield restraint in times of war and uncertainty. How can commanders and political leaders best demonstrate their resolve to fight decisively yet with an expectation that those under their command behave within the laws of armed conflict? Certainly there are elements of training, public statements of policy, and respect for the rule of law that must be considered. More examination needs to be given to how poorly trained military forces are integrated, as well as irregular troops, to ensure that atrocities do not occur, such as the crime of UN peacekeepers in Congo raping the very people they were supposed to protect, or vigilante violence by armed Shia militias (allied with Baghdad) in Iraq. This is particularly important when one looks at the list of top UN peacekeeper contributors, many of which are poor countries: Bangladesh, India, Pakistan, Ethiopia, and Rwanda were at the top of the list in 2018.[83] The Mexican–American War reminds us that there are numerous models for national militaries, from Israel's national service require- ment to Switzerland's highly trained, self-defense posture, to militaries made up of conscripts, criminals, or those so poor that the military is an avenue to basic food and clothing. But how should a government train, integrate, and restrain its non- regular force or allies? This is a contemporary issue, from the *contras* and *mujaheddin* in the 1980s to today's Kurdish *peshmerga* and Arab paramilitaries fighting Islamic State. Western militaries, and the UN Security Council, need to more explicitly consider these ethical factors and the challenge of limits when working with such armed groups. In the U.S., there has been a quiet revolution in the military over the past two decades, as its reserve and National Guard forces have trained to the point of no longer being a traditional reserve but often being just an additional option for activation and deployment.

Finally, in the heat of battle, these issues of commander's intent, restraint, and forecasting (or gambling on) how different battlefield tactics will protect one's soldiers and the enemy's civilian population—whether at Veracruz or Baghdad or Sarajevo—will continue to be worked out by leaders on a case-by-case basis. Leaders have to keep in mind not only the immediate, local issues of proportion- ality and discrimination, but how discrete battlefields are connected to the wider campaigns and theater of war. These issues are particularly salient today in an era when targeted air strikes are the first choice of civilian leaders: how does this action connect to future outcomes? What is the basis for evaluating the discrimination and proportionality of such activities, or are they really just "blowing off steam" in order to be seen as "doing something?" In some ways, the Mexican–American War is a faded portrait of an almost forgotten past; in other ways it remains a trove of poten- tial lessons for war-making, and peace-making, today.

Notes

1 Some argue that the first major amphibious operation was at "the shores of Tripoli"; however, this phrase refers to a force of eight Marines allied with mercenary forces that marched overland from Alexandria, Egypt, to Derna in the Tripolitan State in 1805. Much of the U.S. struggle with the Barbary pirates took place at sea and in harbors. See Joseph Wheelan, *Jefferson's War: America's First War on Terror 1801–1805* (New York: Public Affairs, 2004).

2 The legal and moral status of the territory's future was quite different from today. As Timothy Henderson notes, international law was far less robust then about poorly governed territory and there were almost seven times as many Anglo "squatters" in what had been the Texas territory as there were Hispanic Mexicans at the time of Texas' war for independence. He writes that the entire region from Guatemala to Oregon

only had 7 million inhabitants and thus "Mexicans were keenly aware of how vulnerable those territories were." See Timothy J. Henderson, *A Glorious Defeat: Mexico and Its War with the United States* (New York: Hill & Wang, 2007), pp. 35, 65.

3 One thing that is poorly defined in the literature on whether or not there was a just *casus belli* for the U.S. or for Mexico (or both) has to do with the politico-security arrangement of the area. Scholars should reconsider whether or not the area of Texas was, for all intents and purposes, an anarchic frontier or a "stateless space" that needed political organization and functioning security arrangements. Such stateless spaces, including the high seas, the deserts of Yemen, some jungles of East Asia and the Pacific, the tribal areas of Pakistan, and parts of the Great Lakes regions of Africa, are clearly outside state control and have been the subject of ethics-of-war debate for the past decade, when they have provided the staging ground for terrorism like that of Abu Sayyaf, Joseph Kony's Lord's Resistance Army, and al Qaeda. Certainly the anemic Mexican state was not providing much security prior to Texan independence; a study that begins with the security parameters of people living in Texas at the time might make for an interesting new approach to considering the ethics of going to war in the first place, at least on the part of Washington, DC. One author who points to the insecurity of the region is Brian DeLay, in *War of a Thousand Deserts: Indian Raids and the U.S.–Mexican War* (New Haven, CT: Yale University Press, 2008), p. xv.

4 I would like to thank my research assistant, Bryan Ballas, for important work on the background of the Mexican–American War, particularly his careful reading of diaries and histories from the decades after the conflict and bringing to my attention the profound differences between "regulars" and "volunteers." I also appreciate the editorial assistance of Peter Purcell.

5 Fitzhugh Lee, *General Lee* (New York: D. Appleton and Co., 1894), p. 43.

6 John Russell Young, *Around the World with General Grant: A Narrative of the Visit of General U. S. Grant, Ex-President of the United States, to Various Countries in Europe, Asia, and Africa in 1877, 1878, 1879; To Which Are Added Certain Conversations with General Grant on Questions Connected with American Politics and History*, vol. 2 (New York: The American News Co., 1800), pp. 447–448.

7 The treaty ending the war ensuring Texas' independence had stated that the Rio Grande was Texas' southern boundary; Timothy Henderson notes that this was the treaty's provision and "an audacious land grab by the Texans" because previously the Nueces River had been the provincial boundary. Subsequently, this became an issue between the warring parties. Henderson, p. 98.

8 Ibid., pp. 154–155.

9 Harvard University scholar Brian DeLay reports that northern Mexico was almost ungovernable, "a land of a thousand deserts": "In the early 1830s ... the Comanches, Kiowas, Apaches, Navajos, and others abandoned imperfect but workable peace agreements [with Mexico] ... killing and capturing people they found and stealing or destroying the Mexican's animals and property ... Mexicans responded by doing the same ... through the 1830s and 1840s until much of the northern third of Mexico had been transformed into a vast theatre of hatred, terror, and staggering loss for independent Indians and Mexicans alike. By the eve of the U.S. invasion these varied conflicts spanned all or parts of ten states." See DeLay, p. xv.

10 Ibid.

11 John Frost, *Life of Major General Zachary Taylor; With Notices of the War in New Mexico, California and in Southern Mexico* (New York: D. Appleton & Co., 1847), pp. 104–106.

12 Ibid.

13 Ibid.

14 The primary voices of opposition usually argued that this was a war of conquest, led by Southerners, with the express intent of expanding slavery.

15 Ibid.

16 Mark Crawford, David Stephen Heidler, and Jeanne T. Heidler, *Encyclopedia of the Mexican–American War* (Santa Barbara, CA: ABC-CLIO, 1999), p. 68.

17 U.S. Congress, House, Military Forces in the Mexican War: Letter from the Secretary of War, 31st Cong., 1st sess., 1850, Exec. Doc. no. 24, 3.

18 Richard B. Winders, *Mr. Polk's Army: The American Military Experience in the Mexican War* (College Station: Texas A&M University Press, 1997), p. 72.

19 Ibid., p. 36.

20 Ibid., pp. 196–197.

21 Justin H. Smith, *The War With Mexico*, vol. 2 (New York: MacMillan, 1919), p. 211.

22 Ibid., pp. 211–212.

23 Erika Myers, "Conquering Peace: Military Commissions as a Lawfare Strategy in the Mexican War," *American Journal of Criminal Law*, vol. 35, no. 2 (2008), pp. 210.

24 Smith, p. 211.

25 Amy S. Greenberg, *A Wicked War: Polk, Clay, Lincoln, and the 1846 U.S. Invasion of Mexico*, (New York: Alfred A. Knopf, 2012), p. 9.

26 Thomas J. Green, *Journal of the Texian Expedition Against Mier* (New York: Harper, 1845; reprint, Austin: Steck, 1935); Sam W. Haynes, *Soldiers of Misfortune: The Somervell and Mier Expeditions* (Austin: University of Texas Press, 1990).

27 Henderson, p. 97.

28 Ian B. Lyles, *Mixed Blessing: The Role of the Texas Rangers in The Mexican War, 1846–1848* (Ft. Leavenworth, KS: U.S. Army Command and General Staff College, 2003), Kindle ed., location 508.

29 Ibid., location 703.

30 Ibid, location 705.

31 Ibid.

32 Paul Foos, *A Short, Offhand, Killing Affair: Soldiers and Social Conflict During the Mexican American War* (Chapel Hill: The University of North Carolina Press, 2002), p. 114.

33 Ibid., p. 116.

34 Ibid., p. 121.

35 Ibid.

36 Ibid., p. 123.

37 Ibid., p. 213.

38 Ibid.

39 "Mexican–American War and the Media," Virginia Tech Department of History, available at: www.history.vt.edu/MxAmWar/Newspapers/Niles/Nilesb1846MayJuly.htm#NR70.325-326July251846wantof (accessed January 1, 2016).

40 Ibid.

41 John Jacob Oswandell, Nathaniel Cheairs Hughes, and Timothy D. Johnson, *Notes of the Mexican War: 1846–1848* (Knoxville: University of Tennessee Press, 2010), pp. 9–10, 18, 20.

42 Ibid, p. 21.

43 Reuben Davis, *Recollections of Mississippi and Mississippians* (Boston: Houghton, Mifflin and Co, 1890), p. 237.

44 Smith, p. 212.

45 Foos, pp. 120–121.

46 Ibid.

47 Ibid., p. 72.

48 Ibid.

49 "The Lieber Code: Limiting the Devastation of War," American Red Cross, available at: www.redcross.org/images/MEDIA_CustomProductCatalog/m16240360_Lieber_Code_lesson.pdf (accessed May 23, 2017).

50 "Sweden Brings Back Military Conscription amid Baltic Tension," BBC online (March 2, 2017), available at: www.bbc.com/news/world-europe-39140100 (accessed May 1, 2017).

51 David McCullough, *Truman* (New York: Simon and Schuster, 1993), p. 72.

52 Rick Atkinson, *An Army at Dawn* (New York: Henry Holt and Co., 2002), p. 117.

53 "Washington Speech to Rally the Troops," UShistory.org, available at: www.ushistory.org/valleyforge/youasked/017.htm (accessed May 23, 2017).

54 "Forgotten Woes," Center for Latin American Studies at The University of California-Berkley (last modified August 13, 2015), available at: http://clas.berkeley.edu/research/us-mexican-war-forgotten-foes.

55 "Edgefield Advertiser, May 5th, 1847," United States Library of Congress, available at: http://chroniclingamerica.loc.gov/lccn/sn84026897/1847-05-05/ed-1/seq-1/ (accessed May 22, 2017).

56 "Yellow Fever and the Strategy of the Mexican–American War," Montana State University, available at: www.montana.edu/historybug/mexwar.html (accessed May 24, 2017).

57 John S.D. Eisenhower, *So Far From God* (New York: Anchor Books, 1990), p. 371.

58 "Yellow Fever and the Strategy of the Mexican-American War."

59 Oswandel et al., p. 44.

60 K.J. Bauer, *The Mexican War, 1846–1848* (New York: MacMillan, 1974).

61 Crawford et al., p. 252.

62 Ibid., p. 286.

63 Smith, p. 221.

64 Crawford et al., p. 253.

65 Henderson, p. 168.

66 Smith, pp. 211–212.

67 Matthew Krain, "International Intervention and the Severity of Genocides and Politicides" *International Studies Quarterly* (September 2005). Also see Philip Gourevitch, *We Wish to Inform You That Tomorrow We Will Be Killed with Our Families: Stories from Rwanda*, first ed. (New York: Farrar, Straus, and Giroux, 1998); Alison Des Forges, "Confronting Evil: Genocide in Rwanda," *Leave None to Tell the Story: Genocide in Rwanda*, March 1, 1999, Human Rights Watch, available at: www.hrw.org/report/1999/03/01/leave-none-tell-story/genocide-rwanda (accessed July 5, 2018); Samantha Power, *A Problem from Hell: America and the Age of Genocide* (New York: Perennial, 2002), p. 353; Gerald Caplan, *Rwanda: The Preventable Genocide*, The Report of the International Panel of Eminent Personalities to Investigate the 1994 Genocide in Rwanda and the Surrounding Events (n.p.: Organization of African Unity, 1998); Barbara Walter, "The Critical Barrier to Civil War Settlement," *International Organization* , vol. 51, no. 3 (1997); Eric Patterson, "Rewinding Rwanda: What If? (A Counterfactual Approach)," *Journal of Political Science*, vol. 33 (2005).

68 Smith, pp. 211–212.

69 According to "Yellow Fever and the Strategy of the Mexican–American War," another 362 died of accidental death.

70 This is my critique of the work of David Rodin and Henry Shue. See David Rodin, "Moral Inequality of Soldiers," in *Just and Unjust Warriors*, ed. David Rodin and Henry Shue (Oxford: Oxford University Press, 2008).

71 Winfield Scott, *Head Quarters of the Army, Veracruz, April 11, 1847. Major General Scott, General-in-Chief of the Armies of the United States of America: To the Good People of Mexico—Proclamation*. 1847, available at: http://dspace.uta.edu/handle/10106/9188.
72 Smith, pp. 221–222.
73 Ibid., p. 324.
74 Lee, p. 43.
75 Young, pp. 447–448.
76 Ibid.
77 Smith, pp. 211–212.
78 Ibid, pp. 33–34.
79 Ibid., p. 221.
80 Ibid., p. 232.
81 Ibid., pp. 231–232.
82 Ibid., p. 324.
83 See the UN Peacekeeping monthly accounting, available at: https://peacekeeping.un.org/sites/default/files/1_summary_of_contributions.pdf (accessed March 1, 2018).

6

TRUMAN, HIROSHIMA, AND CONTEMPORARY NUCLEAR ISSUES

The intersection of *jus ad bellum* and *jus in bello*

It has been seventy years since the United States finally forced Japan to capitulate subsequent to the use of atomic weapons against the Japanese homeland. President Harry S. Truman famously stated that he never lost a night's sleep over dropping the bomb because American military strategists had estimated at least 1 million U.S. casualties, not to mention millions of Japanese deaths, if and when the United States invaded the Japanese homeland.[1]

The advent of the atomic age resulted in a quarter-century flurry of moral and political debate on the morality of using nuclear weapons, some of it rather silly but much of it quite sophisticated. For the general public and many of the commentators debating the issues surrounding atomic and nuclear weapons, the focus was primarily on *jus in bello* criteria of proportionality (could nuclear weapons really be proportionate to some sort of battlefield scenario?) and, especially, discrimination (aren't nuclear weapons targeted at civilians and their cities in the first place?). There exists a voluminous literature on these issues.

Why, then, this chapter? The purpose of this chapter is to consider an element of the morality of nuclear weapons that is largely left out of today's debates, although it was keenly recognized by just war theorist Paul Ramsey in the 1950s and 1960s as the fundamental issue that Western leaders, especially Roosevelt and Truman, faced at the very advent of the atomic age. That issue is also the foremost challenge that those concerned with the contemporary use of nuclear weapons face. Perhaps "issue" is the wrong word, because the thing that I have in mind is so foundational, so essential, that it is taken for granted and overlooked in most discussions of using nuclear weapons in any form. It is a principle that harks back to the beginning of the just war tradition and it is the bedrock principle of the international system, at least since 1648. That concept is legitimate political authority. Early thinkers on nuclear weapons assumed that national leaders had to act to protect their populaces, and to them the issues of just cause and right intention did matter.

More specifically, this chapter does two things. First, it will explicate the basic contours of the early Cold War debates about the ethics of governments choosing to utilize nuclear weapons by focusing on some of the just war arguments that ethicist Paul Ramsey was making at the time.[2] Ramsey provides an introduction to a massive, but often polemical, literature still relevant today. We will focus on the development of doctrines of "mutually assured destruction" (MAD) and flexible response in the period before Vietnam, when it was entirely conceivable to anyone who had lived through World War II that atomic weapons might be used again; this seems possible again today due to North Korean bullying and the tense standoff between India and Pakistan. Much of our focus in this chapter will be about how governments can best defend their citizens, and thus the principles of *just cause* (i.e. self-defense) and *right intention* (is it moral to deceive the enemy?) come into play. This chapter also briefly introduces more nuanced perspectives on *proportionality* and *discrimination*, again as adumbrated by Paul Ramsey, demonstrating how these are not such simple ideas when it comes to nuclear ethics.

The debates over just cause and right intention as well as proportionality and discrimination bring us to the second contribution of this chapter: the issue of legitimate political authority, often lost (or assumed) in the early Cold War debates and its intersection with contemporary nuclear security debates. This section starts with a look at the Truman dilemma: what was he to do as President of the United States to advance international security, save American and Allied lives, and stop Imperial Japan? The issue here, often lost in debates about just cause and right intention, has to do with an ethic of political responsibility—the classical notion of political authority providing order and justice.

The most potent WMD threats Western societies face today are not from opposing blocs of state powers threatening, and fearing, a global thermonuclear holocaust. Instead the most likely threats faced by an American President or European Prime Minister today come from rogues brandishing a nuclear device, whether it be a religious (Iran, Pakistan) or totalitarian (North Korea) outlaw state acting alone, or a nuclear device being activated by a non-state actor, whether to destroy an enemy or usher in the apocalypse. The chapter proceeds thus: rather than replay all the nuanced exchanges of the golden era of strategic nuclear thinking (roughly 1945 to 1970), we will use the basic just war framework to highlight the key debates surrounding the use of nuclear weapons and interstate conflict.

Just nuclear war thinking: MAD and flexible response (1945–1970)

Jus ad bellum: Just cause and right intent

How does all of this apply to controversies over nuclear weapons? It is important to start at the beginning and recall the context of the classical nuclear deterrence debates. At the end of World War II the world was almost immediately thrust into the Cold War due to the belligerence of Soviet Russia, which dropped an "iron curtain" on Eastern Europe; supported communist parties and movements in Central and Western Europe; garrisoned troops in breach of treaty obligations (e.g. in Iran and northern Japan); and supported insurgents and clients in Turkey, Greece, and the Far East (e.g. North Korea, China). Although the United States had a monopoly on atomic weapons for a short time, it did not attempt a first strike by either conventional or nuclear means to crush the growing Soviet threat. A counterfactual is in order here: one wonders if Moscow would have practiced such restraint had the roles been reversed.

The next two decades witnessed a nuclear arms race that was largely defined, at least until the 1960s, in terms of mutually assured destruction. The essence of MAD was the widely shared conviction that any conventional war between the Soviet-led Warsaw Pact and the West would rapidly and inexorably escalate to a full thermonuclear exchange targeting opponents' cities. The thinking underlying MAD developed in tandem with rapid developments in nuclear weapons. The first atomic devices in the 1940s were as powerful as 20,000 tons of TNT, but the first thermonuclear weapon ("hydrogen bomb") tested by the U.S. in the early 1950s was 500 times more powerful. Consequently, the destructive power of the world's arsenals could be thought of no longer in terms of an individual city (Hiroshima or Nagasaki) but rather in terms of the extinction of entire national groups.

The Kennedy administration called for a new framework called "flexible response" with the corollary of "graduated deterrence." Flexible response was an attempt to disrupt the assumptions leading to rapidly escalating MAD: the U.S. would not rely on a cookie-cutter, one-size-fits-all protocol to respond to every provocation by the Soviet Union. Instead, it would reserve the right to be flexible in its policy response. Such an approach was apparent in the Kennedy administration's handling of the Cuban Missile Crisis in 1963. The nuclear corollary to flexible response was "gradual" or "graduated" deterrence. The idea here was that the response to most forms of Soviet aggrandizement would be the slow, deliberate ratcheting up of pressure, including tactical use of nuclear weapons. Graduated deterrence was based on analysis of the nature of specific provocations and was intended to focus first on military targets and thus stop the pell-mell race to MAD.

It is worth noting that Western publics, including many religious leaders, bear some of the blame if there is to be any for MAD becoming the default doctrine of Western powers. In the late 1940s and 1950s Western citizens were tired of war and wanted a peace dividend. To achieve this there was wide consensus to drastically cut military spending and demobilize the massive militaries fielded through 1945.[3] In contrast to Western demobilization, the Soviet Union continued increasing its military strength at an alarming rate, stationing forty-five army divisions along the Western front ready to invade Central Europe.[4] Consequently, the looming Soviet threat combined with the reluctance of Western countries to invest in the sort of conventional weapons necessary to counterbalance Soviet power (as well as millions of Chinese Communists in the Far East) made the West fall back on nuclear weapons as the only economical answer to its security dilemma.

Classical just war thinking begins with *jus ad bellum*: the ethics of the decision to go to war. During this period of writing on nuclear ethics (1945–1970) there was considerable ink spilled on how global government might solve the world's security dilemma, but this utopia was unrealistic. When it came down to it, little debate occurred on the principle that *legitimate political authorities* are responsible for the security of their own people. This is a point that will be returned to later in the chapter because its nuances were largely overlooked at the time, particularly when one considers the decision that confronted President Truman.[5]

The principle of just cause was given renewed urgency by the advent of atomic weapons. This seemingly rhetorical question, asked sometimes sincerely and at other times with self-satisfied moral force, was potent in the 1950s: if we know that war is going to rapidly escalate to counter-city nuclear war, then can there ever be a just cause? Paul Ramsey took critics to task on this point because it seemed they were conflating two different Augustinian points about just cause. Augustine sagely illuminated just causes as being protection (self-defense), righting a past wrong (justice), or preventing wrong. Ramsey's antagonists were arguing that it could not be rational to try to right a wrong in a world where one's opponent held the nuclear trump card. In other words, it could not be moral or rational for the U.S. to go to war against a nuclear-armed Russia. Ramsey argued that even if this was the case for *justice* as a just cause (and he did not agree with them on this point), this did not take away *self-defense* as a just cause. In other words, even in the nuclear era there is still at least one just cause to go to war; nuclear weapons do not abolish the right, and political responsibility, of self-defense. U.S. presidents had a responsibility to take a self-defensive nuclear posture against the Soviets.

The second debate of that era concerned *right intent* and here it is tied to the *jus in bello* principle of discrimination or non-combatant immunity. MAD seemed to assume that conventional warfare would quickly and inevitably escalate into nuclear counter-city warfare, and since the West preferred not to keep pace with the Eastern Bloc's arms build-up, proponents of MAD argued that the threat of counter-city nuclear attack seemed like the only possible way to deter the Soviet army from blitzkrieging through Central and Western Europe. The moral dilemma here is whether the West's intention was immoral from the outset: did MAD mean that the West intended, from the outset, to obliterate Russian cities?

Paul Ramsey dealt with this dilemma in at least two ways. First, the linked doctrines of flexible response, counter-force targeting, and graduated deterrence meant that by the 1960s, policymakers had many more options at their disposal than simply annihilating all major communist cities. For instance, conventional warfare and even small tactical nuclear weapons could be employed on the battlefield to destroy advancing Soviet forces as well as military bases in the Soviet rear. Major Russian cities need not be the primary targets. Second, Ramsey consistently argued that the West's intention should never be counter-*city* warfare ("it is always immoral") but rather counter-*force* warfare: using nuclear weapons—even strategic ones if appropriate—against military units and installations. He advocated Washington publicly taking a stand against counter-city warfare, but he also argued there was such ambiguity about how the U.S. would respond to provocation that it would heighten the potency of deterrence. In other words, the Soviets would never be able to predict with certainty just how the U.S. would react to a communist first strike.

For Ramsey, the U.S. was obligated to assume a strong nuclear posture and develop strategies for fighting all levels of warfare, but should openly say that its intention was not to harm civilians if at all possible. This is an important point for Ramsey: the notion that nuclear deterrence has a certain inherent ambiguity. Does this mean our intentions or our policies are a lie to deceive the enemy? How much should be publicly stated about our national security intentions? Ramsey distinguished between outright falsehood (telling something that is untrue, a lie) and withholding information. These are two different ways of defining the word "deception": to lie versus to withhold information. Ramsey argued that a policy of nuclear deterrence, like all the elements of national strategy, should include enough elements of ambiguity to keep the enemy guessing, and yet can remain ethical in its *right intent* to never directly target civilians (*discrimination*). In sum, Ramsey provided an important and sophisticated account for how Western democracies, threatened by the ideology and actions of global communism, could ethically live up to their responsibilities as sovereign political entities, with just cause and right intention, in the nuclear era.

Jus in bello: Proportionality and discrimination

Strangely, the prudential *jus ad bellum* criteria of *likelihood of success*, *proportionality*, and *last resort* are often muddled when it comes to the debates on MAD. This has to do with the difference between MAD as a strategic deterrence doctrine and MAD as an operational concept. Is MAD, as a wartime strategy, proportionate to the end of peace? To the goal of survival? The purpose of nuclear deterrence, including MAD, is to prevent war from actually breaking out at the interstate level in the first place. Moreover, what is MAD's likelihood of success? MAD is successful as a deterrence threat, but it is clearly a failure if it has to be employed. Is this consistent with the just war principle of last resort? By definition, MAD has to be considered a first resort: our enemies have to be, at the outset, concerned that we are resolved to go all the way to doomsday in order for MAD to work. In short, MAD works well strategically; MAD is a disaster if triggered operationally.

However, the type of flexible response and graduated deterrence noted earlier are far more consistent with *jus ad bellum* principles, which makes the histrionics of many mainline ethicists in the 1960s seem ridiculous. Graduated deterrence can be intended as a counter-force strategy: only using nuclear weapons against an adversary's military targets. Thus, ownership of, and even tactical use of, nuclear weapons can contribute to a successful outcome that is *proportionate* to the end of a secure peace and can be part of a political strategy that sees war as a *last resort*.

All of this brings up the debates over *jus in bello* issues of proportionality and discrimination. On the issue of *proportionality*, two of the most significant debates at the time regarding MAD had to do with strategic first strikes and tactical nuclear weapons. The first is an assumption that the introduction of nuclear weapons by the U.S. would be proportionate to the enemy's action because both sides, under the logic of MAD, would quickly escalate to some form of nuclear blackmail ("surrender or we nuke London and New York") or actual nuclear strikes. Moralists and theorists long debated the ethics and efficacy of first-strike strategies, typically deciding that strategic first strikes were never moral but the massive second-strike capabilities (e.g. submarine-launched ballistic missiles) could add a strong level of deterrent insurance. The second proportionality issue had to do with the battlefield itself: was the introduction of tactical nuclear weapons justified in the case of Soviet invasion of Western Europe? To be even more theoretically clinical, there were discussions at the time about using small tactical nuclear weapons against ships at sea where there would be no collateral damage: would such be ethical?

These debates about *proportionality* typically ended up conflating proportionality with the real *jus in bello* principle under consideration, *discrimination*. We should spend less time asking the question of "proportionate to what?" and instead focus on questions of distinction. Can nuclear weapons ever be seen as discriminating? Can we ever imagine the targeted and limited use of some form of nuclear weapons away from civilian population hubs? Certainly this was inconceivable under MAD, although many Americans thought the answer was "yes" under flexible response. The Europeans typically did not agree, worrying that a Soviet invasion across the Fulda Gap would result in millions of civilian casualties in Germany and its neighborhood due to tactical nuclear weapons. In other words, Moscow and Washington (and Beijing and London) would remain safe while Central Europe became a radioactive wasteland. This was not very comforting or very discriminating.

This takes us back to the presuppositions people had at the time when discussing discrimination. The majority of the ethical discussions at the time about nuclear weapons were centered solely on non-combatant immunity, because almost everyone believed that nuclear weapons were purposefully designed to target civilians. It is worth noting that in the context of the time, all those writing had good reasons to expect World War III to be unrestrainedly destructive. This was not simply due to the grotesque nature of the communism that massacred and enslaved people in Russia, China, and Eastern Europe but was also informed by the experience of World War II, including the Japanese "rape of Nanking" and brutality in the Pacific theater, the Nazi-led Holocaust, and the fact that from the very beginning of the war the Germans targeted cities such as London and Warsaw. Hence, for a variety of reasons, the Allies responded in kind to the Germans and Japanese at Dresden and Kyoto, and thus the advent of nuclear weapons suggested that civilians and their property could never be safe.

It is worth taking a step back to the very foundations of just was thinking at this point when considering the context of 1950s MAD doctrine. Classical just war thinking, such as that of Cicero and Augustine, begins with the notions of political order and justice. Political authorities are compelled out of responsibility or neighbor love to defend their citizens and, when possible, prevent wrong and correct some past wrongs. MAD is a conundrum: it promises to violate the long-standing injunction against harming civilians and, in doing so, to actually save civilian lives. As noted earlier, for Paul Ramsey neither our intent nor our actions in warfare need deliberately target the civilian population centers of our adversaries; nuclear weapons were plenty destructive against strategic military targets, and the inherent ambiguity of the weapons combined with the potential irrationality of leaders made deterrence robust.

In conclusion, the advent of the atomic age introduced incredibly potent weapons, but their use seemed to follow the total war model of World War II. The 1950s assumed mutually assured destruction, and there were vigorous debates about the morality of nuclear deterrence through the 1960s. Apart from the hordes of wishful thinkers who somehow thought unilateral disarmament would win the Cold War, just war thinkers like Paul Ramsey were able to thoughtfully address the issues of just cause, right intent, and discrimination. What they often left out of their deliberations, which is important for contemporary discussions of nuclear ethics, is the principle of legitimate authority. I believe this is because they simply took "authority" for granted: nuclear weapons were so large and so expensive that no one imagined a non-state actor such as Che Guevara or the Mau Mau or the Palestinian Liberation Organization getting their hands on an atomic device. The second generation of anti-nuclear activism associated with some religious and aca-demic thinkers, the nuclear freeze movement of the 1980s, was based on similar presuppositions about counter-civilian warfare and MAD. Indeed, as James Turner Johnson has recently reported, the 1980s pacifist movement associated with Pax Christi grew over the years to shun the Roman Catholic Church's historical just war teaching.[6]

In any event, whether in the 1950s or 1980s, the debates were largely about Washington facing another state actor with modern nuclear weapons. We live in a different world today. The breakdown of effective and authentic political authority is a contemporary crisis and it has significant ramifications for all forms of weapons of mass destruction in the twenty-first century.

Contemporary issues

Today's fundamental moral issues involving nuclear weapons revolve around the responsibilities and legitimacy of political authority, the first just war principle. More specifically, when it comes to national security in its most general sense, American presidents are faced with the Truman dilemma: what, if anything, does a U.S. president "owe" foreign enemies when he is trying to care for his own citi-zenry? The second authority issue in contemporary life is the non-legitimacy of those political actors most likely to utilize a nuclear device and the risks this poses to international security.

Just war thinking is rooted in the classical and Christian ideas of political order, political responsibility, and justice. The fundamental responsibility of political authorities—the key to their legitimacy—is providing order and security for their populace. Their second important task is to promote justice. In a republic, leaders are selected by the populace within a framework of law to protect and promote the lives, livelihoods, and way of life of the citizenry. Call it a social contract, political compact, or whatever one likes, this is the arrangement upon which Western polities, particularly the U.S., are built.

This brings us back to Harry S. Truman. President Truman was the first U.S. president to have fought under the conditions of modern warfare as an Army National Guard artillery officer in World War I. He knew that war could be hell, and he rightfully felt a tremendous responsibility to the U.S. service personnel who were fighting in World War II. Moreover, as President he was briefed daily on the ongoing Pacific war, most notably the way that the Japanese military fought to the last man island by island, at great cost to U.S. and Allied invasion forces. Intelligence had surfaced in 1945 that the Japanese would likely annihilate all prisoners of war under their control in the final days of the war, including thousands of Americans, British, Australians, and other allies. Intelligence estimates suggested that there would be as many as a million U.S. casualties if the Japanese homeland was invaded. Furthermore, the number of dead Japanese in such an eventuality is difficult to imagine.[7]

As President, what was Truman's responsibility? It was first of all the protection of American lives. This included not only American civilians on the home front, but also the thousands rotting away in Japanese concentration camps. It also included U.S. troops. This is an important point. Sometimes the literature on the ethics of war suggests that military personnel are second-class citizens. I disagree with this characterization, but its roots are important to understand. The just war "contract" is that individuals, who are under the authority of the state and clearly demarcated by uniforms, control structures, and the like, have license to kill under wartime conditions. They can also be killed. This separates them from civilians who are not supposed to kill (that would make them criminals) and who have non-combatant immunity from the battlefield.

Much of the philosophical literature of the past thirty years has put soldiers into such a box as to make them almost morally inconsequential: their job is to protect civilians and they seem to have no rights. Soldiers must go to extraordinary lengths to protect civilians, even if it puts them at serious risk.[8] Again, I disagree. Particularly in a democracy, soldiers have moral value as citizens. World War II is an important case in point. Nearly all of those soldiers, airmen, Marines, and sailors fighting Japan had been civilians on December 7, 1941. They entered the military out of self-defense. They were citizens first, not second- or third-class persons. For President Truman, their lives should and did matter. Indeed, his first responsibility was to American lives, in and out of uniform, not to Japanese civilians. The care of Japanese civilians was the first duty of the leadership in Tokyo, not of that in Washington, DC. It was the actions of those in the Japanese leadership in Tokyo that put their civilians at risk, not those of President Truman.

With this in mind, it is apparent that there was moral urgency for President Truman to act decisively to bring World War II to a close and stop the killing of

American and Allied personnel. The U.S. alone had lost approximately 400,000 troops by this time, and this does not account for Allied forces from the U.K., Australia, China, and elsewhere or the many civilian deaths at the hands of the Japanese, especially in China. Moreover, by this point the Japanese had lost close to 2 million military personnel. The bomb provided an opportunity to intervene dramatically and bring the war to a close. It worked. The dropping of bombs on Hiroshima and Nagasaki caused the Japanese empire to finally surrender. Indeed, we now know that even in the immediate aftermath of the second bomb, Japanese military leadership did not want an imperial surrender. The U.S. cause was just (self-defense following Pearl Harbor). The vast majority of U.S. fighting in the Pacific campaign followed just war principles. Dropping the bomb to hasten the war's end was just. Then, consonant with the principles of *jus post bellum* discussed elsewhere, the U.S. brought order, justice, and even conciliation to the people of Japan.[9]

Let's turn to today's security dilemmas. U.S. presidents continue to face the Truman challenge of how to protect and promote the security of U.S. citizens in an uncertain world. This is an issue of legitimate political authority. Today's threats posed by nuclear weapons typically derive from weak, failing, and/or illegitimate political authority.

Although Russia and China maintain adversarial relationships, to some degree, with the U.S. and although they both hold significant nuclear arsenals, few security experts suggest that the U.S. has much to fear today from a Russo- or Sino-MAD-style attack. Of course, the Far East is increasingly tense and dangerous, but employing nuclear weapons is bound to backfire locally due to the proximity of Beijing, Seoul, Tokyo, and other national capitals.

The only real state-to-state nuclear face-off today is between Pakistan and India, and this is a frightening prospect. The question is: why? Why do we worry about Islamabad vs. New Delhi instead of London vs. Paris? The reason has to do with weak structures of political authority and legitimacy, particularly on the Pakistani side. The fear on the Indian subcontinent is rapid escalation to nuclear weapons led by illegitimate (or religio-inspired) elements in the Pakistani military. When one considers the lack of oversight, influence of violent Islamists, governments-within-governments, and atavistic pronouncements of some in Pakistan, the situation is frightening, particularly because there are some in India spoiling for a fight. This is a scenario that clearly violates the fundamental presuppositions of the legitimate authority principle: how can it be in the best security interests of one's people to nuke a nuclear-armed neighbor?

There are other rogue regimes with access to nuclear technology: North Korea and Iran. Again, by most measures of political legitimacy, these are illegitimate political systems that do not necessarily have the best interests of their citizenry at heart. This is unqualifiedly true for North Korea. Because these regimes routinely violate international norms and blackmail their neighbors, all three erode international security. A case in point is the distribution of Pakistani nuclear technology to Pyongyang. All three governments operate under a certain irrationality that places goals other than the security of their citizens at the forefront of their foreign policies. They lack some measure of legitimacy and they are irresponsible when it comes to the security of their people. This makes their ownership of nuclear weapons extremely problematic.

Finally, perhaps the greatest threat today involving a nuclear event comes from non-state actors. One can imagine a variety of "dirty bomb" scenarios, most of which involve Islamist extremists of the al Qaeda or ISIS variety, although there are other likely suspects, such as "lone wolf" types who want to usher in the apocalypse. These outlaws thrive in stateless and failing-state spaces, they oppose widely accepted structures of authority, and they are pledged to harm and destroy Western publics and their governments. All of this is chilling, particularly in the era of 9/11 and bombings in Madrid, London, Moscow, and elsewhere.

The point here is that the moral and legal framework for restraint—the just war principle of legitimate authority with its attendant political responsibilities for international and national security—is broken in these cases. This is where the nuclear dilemma is at its most pressing because neither MAD nor graduated deterrence are likely to deter a nuclear 9/11. Just war thinking tells us quite clearly what the fundamental problem is and reminds U.S. leaders what their responsibilities are. But, just war thinking does not prescribe short-term, operational solutions to these evolving insecurities—political leaders must use creativity to find solutions to the dilemmas of international security within the bounds of the just war framework.

Conclusion

This chapter has provided the basic contours for how classical just war thinking provides a coherent perspective on the use of nuclear weapons by state actors, particularly in the context of interstate war. For reasons of space and cogency, it has focused on the major ethico-strategic debates of the high point of the Cold War and not on later influences, such as U.S. Catholic bishops' *The Challenge of Peace* (1983) and the nuclear freeze movement, which largely regurgitated arguments against MAD but may deserve consideration elsewhere. The place to begin with considerations of morality and the use of nuclear weapons by governments in the context of interstate war is with the issues of authority, political order, self-defense, and justice. Clearly, it is conceivable that nuclear weapons could be used in ways that meet just war criteria, although one hopes it never happens again. Unfortunately, over the past three decades there has been a decided lack of clarity on what the substantive issues at hand are, as writers have been distracted by ephemera such as whether nuclear weapons were inherently evil in and of themselves (divorced from the human decision-making component), weak conflations of nuclear-powered civilian energy (as an evil) with the potential destructiveness of thermonuclear weapons, *ad hominem* attacks on U.S. presidents (i.e. Reagan) as warmongers, quasi-religious claims about the sanctity of Mother Earth (Gaia), and the like. In contrast, the key questions for just war thinking have to do with the categories of *jus ad bellum* and *jus in bello*: what are the moral considerations for going to war and how is war to be fought? These are the fundamentals, whether one is speaking of sword-play or mutually assured destruction. Indeed, the ancients knew about MAD—just ask the Carthaginians.

This chapter has argued that the Cold War presupposed that nuclear weapons would be in the hands of political authorities, even if they were tyrannical regimes like those in Moscow and Beijing. However, today's outlaw regimes and rogue non-state actors demonstrate that nuclear weapons may fall into the hands of those who do not respect the boundaries of the just war tradition and international law. What we need today is intelligent ethical thinking and clever policy approaches to dealing with these actors so that we never get to the point where the West is reacting to a nuclear weapons incident perpetrated by its enemies, and to have protocols in place for appropriate response should the worst happen.

Notes

1 From Curtis E. LeMay and Bill Yenne's book *Superfortress: The Story of the B-29 and American Air Power*, quoted in Gar Alperovitz and Sanho Tree, *The Decision to Use the Atomic Bomb* (New York: Vintage Books, 1995) p. 341.

2 Paul Ramsey, *The Limits of Nuclear War* (New York: Council on Religion and International Affairs, 1963) and *War and the Christian Conscience* (New York: Scribner's, 1961).

3 There is considerable literature on this; a quick visit of these details is available in Robert W. DeGrasse, Jr., *Military Expansion, Economic Decline. The Impact of Military Spending on U.S. Economic Performance* (New York: M.E. Sharpe, Inc., 1983).

4 See William Thomas Lee and Richard Felix Staar, *Soviet Military Policy since World War II* (Stanford: Hoover Press, 1986).

5 There was a political authority debate at the time that is important, but somewhat different and seemingly arcane today. Many scientific and other voices argued that atomic energy could provide splendid civilian energy resources to benefit humanity while at the same time registering deep concern over chauvinistic national governments holding on to atomic weapons and spiraling into out-of-control arms races. These ideas—of a neutral international atomic energy agency with goodwill for all and the abolition of nuclear weapons from the hands of individual governments—never fully matured. For more on these considerations, see Robert L. Brown, *Nuclear Authority: The IAEA and the Absolute Weapon* (Washington, DC: Georgetown University Press, 2015); Erwin Häckel and Gotthard Stein, eds., *Tightening the Reins: Towards a Strengthened International Nuclear Safeguards System* (New York: Springer, 2011); John Simpson, *The Independent Nuclear State: The United States, Britain, and the Military Atom* (London: Palgrave-Macmillan, 1983).

6 James Turner Johnson, "Force and Christian Responsibility," unpublished paper delivered at Catholic University conference, March 22–24, 2018, The Catholic University of America, Washington, DC.

7 LeMay and Yenne, quoted in Alperovitz and Tree, p. 341. Laura Hillenbrand's *Unbroken*, a recent national bestseller listed in the bibliography, provides lengthy documentation on these issues in narrative form.

8 For an example of these arguments, see David Rodin and Henry Shue, *Just and Unjust Warriors: The Moral and Legal Status of Soldiers* (Oxford: Oxford University Press, 2010).

9 See Eric Patterson, *Ending Wars Well: Order, Justice and Conciliation at Post-Conflict* (New Haven, CT: Yale University Press, 2012).

PART III
Bringing war to a morally and politically satisfying end

In 2004 I was a young Assistant Professor fresh out of graduate school. I asked a nationally known military ethicist, "We have *jus ad bellum* and *jus in bello*, but what about the end of war and its aftermath? What is that? Would it be called *jus post bellum*? How do I learn more about that?" He replied, "I have never really thought about it … it is not part of the classic just war tradition." On the one hand, this is accurate: the language of *jus post bellum* is something that I, philosopher Brian Orend, and a few others have pioneered in the wake of the wars of the 1990s and especially since 9/11. But on the other hand, elements of *jus post bellum* have always been a part of the just war tradition. As James Turner Johnson has reminded me on numerous occasions, the purpose of a just war, its objective or goal, is "the end of peace." In other words, *jus post bellum* may not even need to be explicated as a distinct category because it was there all the time.

Although I agree that *jus post bellum* is inherent, in some way, in classical just war thinking, it nonetheless was implicit rather than explicit. We need an explicit model for *jus post bellum*—the ethics of war's end—in order to provide morally and politically satisfying policy guidance to leaders. Peace settlements should deal with both the past and the future, and this is the goal of what Michael Walzer called "justice in endings." Furthermore, an explicit model for *jus post bellum* will be useful to diplomats, aid workers, and military officers as they work to bring specific conflicts to termination.

The model that I assert focuses on categories similar to Thomas Aquinas' order, justice, and peace. More specifically, there are three critical elements of *jus post bellum*:

- *Order.* Beginning with existential security, a sovereign government extends its roots through the maturation of government capacity in the military (traditional security), governance (domestic politics), and international security dimensions.

- *Justice*: Getting one's "just deserts," including consideration of individual punishment for those who have violated the law of armed conflict and restitution policies for victims when appropriate.
- *Conciliation*: Coming to terms with the past so that parties can imagine and move forward toward a shared future.

As I have written elsewhere, I am skeptical that most conflicts will get to justice, much less conciliation. Indeed, time is often a factor in coming to terms with the past and ushering in some form of conciliation, such as modest German–Polish rapprochement following Willy Brandt's decision to kneel at a war memorial in Poland during his Ostpolitik era, more than two decades after the end of World War II. At the same time, a lesson from Afghanistan, Iraq, and elsewhere is just how difficult to achieve, and precious, a modicum of enduring order is. Figure III.1 helps us to visualize that it is only in a fraction of cases that some sort of significant justice follows the establishment of order, and it is only in tiny fraction of cases that some form of conciliation occurs between former belligerents.

The following chapters focus on how wars end. Chapter 7 analyzes the work of Governor General William Howard Taft and his eponymous commission, which strove to bring not only peace but also long-term prosperity to the Philippines after the Spanish–American War. Taft famously called the Filipino people his "little brown brothers," and it was meant affectionately. Taft invested years in seeking the long-term welfare of Filipinos, Cubans, and others by attempting to move their political and economic systems toward democracy and market capitalism through education, training, and infrastructure initiatives. His efforts demonstrate that there are military (traditional security), governance (domestic politics), and international security conditions to a basic post-conflict order that must be met and extended if there is to be lasting peace. The case of the Philippines provides us with a unique case study; regrettably, it is a poorly understood part of U.S. history but a good lesson on nation-building and what today are labeled "reconstruction and stability operations."

Chapter 8 looks at three different models for how World War I should have ended. France wanted to bludgeon the German people for the horrors of the war;

FIGURE III.1 *Jus post bellum*: Order, justice, and conciliation

England wanted revenge but its leadership was savvy enough to seek a middle road that kept Germany out of the orbit of revolutionary Communism; and Woodrow Wilson took up a crusade to reimagine a post-colonial, self-determined, liberal world order. When one considers order, justice, and conciliation, how do the political goals of each of the Big Three rate? When one considers the provisions of the Versailles Treaty, was it a force for order, justice, and conciliation, or something else? What is the difference between vindication and vengeance? Justice and revenge? These questions will be considered by looking at both the policy stances and the political outcomes of 1919.

Finally, Chapters 9 and 10 take us to the frontiers of just war thinking. Chapter 9 considers whether or not it is moral to seek victory, as well as asking why it is that Western governments no longer seem to take public stands in favor of victory. That chapter elucidates three ways of thinking about victory: the Fabian strategy of not allowing one's opponent to win, beating one's opponent outright, and the vindication of one's values. Just war thinking typically assumes that there are appropriate types of victory, such as in cases of self-defense and armed humanitarian intervention. Related to this are the changing dynamics of contemporary warfare, including terrorism, cyber-security, and a host of technology-related vulnerabilities. Chapter 10 looks at the frontiers of just war thinking and suggests a research agenda for the next decade on these and similar critical issues.

7

THE TAFT COMMISSION IN MANILA

Political order, justice, and conciliation after the Spanish–American War

"The American flag has not been planted on foreign soil to acquire more territory, but for humanity's sake."[1] Thus read a campaign poster for the re-election of President McKinley in 1900. The McKinley-Theodore Roosevelt campaign was arguing that the Spanish–American War was humanitarian in focus, liberating Cubans from Spanish *reconcentrado* (concentration) camps, despite the fact that it resulted in the U.S. acquiring the territories of Cuba, Puerto Rico, Guam, and the Philippines. The campaign advertisement was buttressed by the well-known fact that President McKinley was skeptical about going to war until the destruction of the USS *Maine* in Havana Harbor, as well as the political fact of the 1898 Teller Amendment, in which Congress

> hereby disclaims any disposition of intention to exercise sovereignty, jurisdiction, or control over said island [Cuba] except for pacification thereof, and asserts its determination, when that is accomplished, to leave the government and control of the island to its people.[2]

Like many wars, however, the Spanish–American War had a number of unintended consequences, most notably U.S. trusteeship of the Philippines for much of the next half-century. The fundamental question that the Spanish–American War raises is how a victor is supposed to act at war's end. In other words, what post-conflict policies most comport with the just war tradition? This chapter will look at the motives of the U.S. and the actions that it took after defeating the Spanish, particularly with regard to the Philippines. The U.S. won the war to liberate Cuba, but unexpectedly became involved in putting down an insurgency, integrating rebels into government, and what today could arguably be called nation-building. Did the U.S. implement actions consistent with establishing *jus post bellum* principles of *order*, *justice*, and *conciliation*?

Just war thinking and *jus post bellum*

The purpose of this chapter is not to evaluate whether or not the *casus belli* of the Spanish–American War was just (*jus ad bellum*), although few would argue that liberating Cubans from concentration camps was not a moral imperative. Nor is the purpose of this chapter to evaluate the ethics of how the war was fought (*jus in bello*), though the war was clearly constrained within the laws of armed conflict. Rather, the purpose of the chapter is to consider the aftermath of the war and the policies involved in the post-conflict phase. Were the *jus post bellum* policies designed not only to promote U.S. interests but also in the best interests of those on the ground in these environments? This is an important point for two reasons. First, the U.S. post-war work, particularly in the Philippines, was clearly what today would be called "stability and reconstruction" operations; one could even call it "nation-building." Thus, there is salience in reporting on U.S. motives and actions at the time for comparison with contemporary work in places such as Afghanistan and Iraq. Second, the case allows us to consider an outline for three *jus post bellum* principles that try to actualize just war ethics in post-conflict environments: order, justice, and conciliation. The argument of this chapter is that the U.S. post-bellum policies can be understood as having a moral dimension—a sense of brotherly obligation (neighbor love) toward the Filipino people—and the specific policies, led by the Taft Commission, did establish a robust order, move beyond issues of immediate justice, and effect a conciliation locally and internationally.

The fundamental responsibility of political actors, in war or peace, is to work toward *order*. In post-conflict settings, order begins with stopping the killing and the exercise of sovereignty by a single point of authority. Order extends its roots through the maturation of government capacity and services. There are military (traditional security), governance (domestic politics), and international security conditions to a basic post-conflict order that must be met and extended if there is to be lasting peace.

The military dimension regards the definitive termination of "hot" conflict, with the tools of warfare resting solely in the hands of legitimate authorities. This means that all belligerents have agreed to the cessation of conflict; there are no organized, armed spoilers or insurgents lurking in the countryside to destabilize the peace deal. All parties must support the new security arrangement by no longer challenging it via military force. Military considerations of order also begin to take account of the appropriate structuring of military strength and forces to sustain a robust defense without undermining the security of formal rivals.

All of these efforts to confirm military aspects of post-conflict orders should work in tandem with domestic and international political objectives while being careful to buttress, rather than erode, the basic peace settlement. Hence, the governance dimension of order is the imposition and maintenance of the domestic rule of law. It implies a national political entity which exercises sovereignty over the legitimate use of force at home, as well as political sovereignty over its policies at home and in relations with its neighbors. However, in some cases the resumption of sovereignty follows a period of political rehabilitation, whether in the aftermath of military defeat (post-World War II Japan) or political tutelage and reconstruction (East Timor). In either case, order means focusing on the fundamental tasks of governance, including responsibility over the economic sector.

The third dimension of order is the international security dimension, which means that the state no longer faces an imminent threat from an internal or external foe, nor is the country a threat to the peace and security of its neighbors (e.g. through refugee flows). The international security dimension is intertwined with and reinforces both basic internal security and efforts at governance. In sum, the very first steps toward a longer-term, more robust domestic and national situation of security begins with the grueling task of implementing order in these three dimensions.

Just getting to order can be a herculean ordeal. Order is most likely to occur when one side convincingly defeats its adversary on the battlefield, as the Union battered the Confederacy; the Entente defeated the Triple Alliance in 1918; and the Allies crushed the Nazis and Imperial Japan in 1945. More recently, as discussed in Chapter 9, we have seen decisive victories by the Rwandan Patriotic Front in Rwanda (1994) and by the Sri Lankan government (2009). Decisive victory allows a window for uncontested elimination of threats to security and establishment of the basics of political order. History testifies to how costly and difficult such victories can be to win, as in each of these cases, but they do provide an opportunity to found a secure post-conflict order.

It is even more expensive to win outright victory and then fail to establish the peace. Victors have an obligation to practice restraint yet impose order—admittedly a difficult balance—as Rwanda experienced from 1994 to 1998. It is not difficult to squander the moment of victory and thus lose the peace, as occurred in Iraq in 2003. More recently, Sri Lanka's government won a 25-year-long civil war against the Tamil Tigers in 2009, but seems determined to throw away the momentum for lasting peace through factional infighting, poor post-conflict planning, disregard for the adversary's survivors, and an unwillingness to pursue justice or national reconciliation. In short, Sri Lanka seems determined to cripple the order it achieved after a quarter-century of bloodshed.

To end well, all wars must establish order—whether or not there is an avenue for *justice*. But in some cases, an approximation of justice is possible and appropriate. However obvious this sounds, the actual application of "just deserts" is extremely difficult in practice. The most promising venue for justice is at home—the prosecution of violations of the war convention by one's own soldiers. The U.S., for example, has punished its own in recent years, including prison terms, fines, dishonorable discharge, and hard labor for the guards at Abu Ghraib. Another form of justice is the punishment of those elites responsible for planning and implementing aggressive policies, such as Napoleon's exile to St. Helena or the execution of Saddam Hussein. Punishment restrains those actors from further aggression, punishes them for their misdeeds, and avenges the victims.

Punishment is justice focused on the crimes of aggressors, but there is another side to justice that focuses on victims: restitution. Restitution attempts to acknowledge that wrong was done and compensate victims for their losses. In practice, though, reparations tend to be paid as government-to-government indemnities rather than amends to individual citizens, and in many cases—such as in post-World War I Germany (see Chapter 8) or Iraq in the 1990s—draconian reparations have been used as a bludgeon to punish perpetrators in a way that is destabilizing. Hence, restitution in post-conflict, like punishment, is an applied principle of justice that must be considered carefully on a case-by-case basis.

The third element of the *jus post bellum* framework is *conciliation*. Admittedly, real efforts at national and international conciliation are rare. This is due, in part, to the misperception that the path to peace and security begins with justice and reconciliation. It does not. Order must precede conciliation, but—and this is a critical point—order and conciliation can be intertwined and reinforcing. In the few cases of international conciliation, acts of conciliation occurred well after the hot conflict and followed from changes in the strategic interests of former belligerents. The rapprochement of France and Germany, occasioned by Allied occupation and the Soviet threat, ultimately led over time to the conciliatory policies of German Chancellor Willy Brandt in 1970–1972.

In cases of civil war, a model of conciliation based on changing interests, an evolving security situation, and some sort of political "forgiveness" policy (e.g. amnesty) may reinforce order, ameliorate justice claims, and transcend the status quo security dilemma. This is the sort of peace that is desirable, but it is extremely rare. A study by Long and Brecke found less than a dozen real attempts at political forgiveness and national reconciliation in civil conflicts out of hundreds of possible cases since World War II. Of those, a third failed.[3]

The Spanish–American War: From Cuba to the Philippines

To most Americans, the Spanish–American War was about Cuba, although some savvy political leaders in Washington—most notably then-Assistant Secretary of the Navy Theodore Roosevelt—recognized a larger geopolitical context that included Hawaii and the Philippines. Cubans had been agitating for independence since at least 1868; Cuban experts consider the period 1868–1878 the "Ten Years War" for Cuban independence. This effort failed and many Cuban dissidents relocated to the United States. Despite the fact that abolitionists promoted U.S. intervention in Cuba to end slavery there throughout the 1870s (slavery was abolished in 1886), a war-weary American public was not supportive of a foreign war.

Cuba continued as the key remaining Spanish colony due to its sugar wealth, but had become increasingly ungovernable by the 1880s. Over the next decade, various efforts at independence took root, including the founding of the Cuban Revolutionary Party by José Martí in 1892 and a full-scale rebellion in 1895. U.S. policy under President Grover Cleveland was neutrality. This second Cuban war of independence, the *Grito de Baire*, was a period of some of the worst atrocities associated with Spanish rule, including infamous *campos de reconcentracion* under the notorious General Valeriano Weyler. The motto of the revolutionaries became, "Independence or Death!"

While all of this was occurring, the Philippines was undergoing its own struggle for independence. For instance, in 1872 three Filipino priests were condemned as subversives and executed by garrote. A decade later, José Rizal's *Touch Me Not* became a national epic, recording the struggles and aspirations of Filipinos.

In October 1897, Práxedes Mateo Sagasta took over as Spanish Prime Minister. Among his first acts were the recall of General Weyler from Cuba and the closing of concentration camps, but local agitation continued. In this period of uncertainty and violence, the U.S. ordered the battleship USS *Maine* to Havana to protect U.S. interests in Cuba (January 1898). Three weeks later (February 15) the *Maine* exploded in Havana Harbor, killing 266 individuals. To this day there remains conjecture about the actual cause of the explosion, but "Remember the Maine!" became the rallying cry for direct intervention in Cuba. On February 25, Assistant Secretary of the Navy Roosevelt ordered Commodore Dewey to move into position in order to be ready to go to battle with Spanish forces in the Philippines. A U.S. naval blockade of Cuba, initiated on April 21, and the subsequent Spanish declaration of war (April 23) initiated the war formally.

On April 19, Colorado Senator Henry M. Teller proposed an amendment that became known by his name, which articulated that the U.S. did not intend to annex Cuba. The Teller Amendment promised to grant Cuban independence; a subsequent piece of legislation (the Platt Amendment) actually did so just a few years later. Teller's legislation articulated:

> [The U.S.] hereby disclaims any disposition of intention to exercise sovereignty, jurisdiction, or control over said island except for pacification thereof, and asserts its determination, when that is accomplished, to leave the government and control of the island to its people.[4]

By August 13, the Spanish fleet in the Philippines had been destroyed and Manila had surrendered; Guam, Puerto Rico, and Cuba had surrendered and the U.S. Congress voted to annex Hawaii. Six weeks later, a peace conference was convened in Paris.

The Treaty of Paris was signed on December 10, 1898. It is a short document and it essentially did two things. The first was to acknowledge in law what was already a fact: the U.S. had beaten the Spanish military and had control of Cuba, the Philippines, and other territories such as Guam and Puerto Rico. These territories now belonged to the U.S., to include government properties (e.g. wharves, buildings), and the U.S. accepted responsibility for law and order.[5] The second theme in the document is the protection of individual and commercial rights, such as patent protection and religious freedom for citizens (including those of Spanish descent) now living under U.S. jurisdiction. The U.S. was to pay Spain $20 million dollars in compensation for Puerto Rico and its Pacific possessions within three months of a signed treaty.[6]

Concluding the war in Cuba

The focus of this chapter is long-term U.S. policy in the Philippines, from a bloody insurrection to institution-building under a trusteeship to eventual independence over the course of four decades. But the Spanish–American War began with Cuba, so what about the Cuban campaign? As promised under the Teller Amendment, U.S. troops departed Cuba in 1902 under the terms of a second proviso, the Platt Amendment.[7] This amendment to a military appropriations bill, sponsored by Senator Orville Platt of Connecticut, laid out the terms for U.S. withdrawal from Cuba. The U.S. commanding General in Cuba, Leonard Wood, liaised with the new Cuban legislature on the details, which became part of the Cuban constitution.

The Platt Amendment operated from the perspective that the U.S. had come to the aid of the Cuban people and liberated them from Spanish-colonial oppression. Nearly 3,000 U.S. troops had died (90 percent from disease, notably yellow fever).[8] The U.S. did not want to see Spain or any other European power entangled in Cuban affairs or Cuba to become a lawless place, threatening U.S. security and commercial interests. Thus, the Platt Amendment specified that U.S. troops would depart—consistent with the obligations under the Teller Amendment—but that Cuba would not allow foreign militaries to operate there and would provide or lease land for a coaling and naval station (ultimately the Guantanamo Bay facility), and that the Cuban government must improve sanitary conditions on the island (a project already begun by General Wood). The influence of the U.S. on the new Cuban Constitution also included an emphasis on government institutions, the rule of law, and enfranchising much of the population. From a strategic perspective, the U.S. guaranteed that it would protect Cuban independence and intervene should the country descend into lawlessness.

The U.S. did intervene again in Cuba in 1906, and for a short time William Howard Taft served as Governor General (following his work in the Philippines with the Taft Commission). However, for the most part Cuba was a weak, independent, poor developing country for the next several decades—a post-conflict story not unlike that of many countries around the world when there is inadequate support for a robust order after political independence is achieved. There is scholarly, and partisan, debate about the role of the treaty, American commercial interests in Cuba, and the like; but it is also true that the U.S. liberated Cuba and departed: it did not annex Cuba nor hold it in trusteeship for any length of time. In 1934, as part of the "Good Neighbor" policy, the Roosevelt administration abrogated the treaty in order to remove any suggestion of quasi-imperialism in Cuban–American relations.

The U.S. in the Philippines

By Christmas 1898 the U.S. had won the Spanish–American War and put Cuba on a path to independence. As in many wars, the initial *casus belli* was different from the war's evolving aims (e.g. expanding commercial and strategic interests in the Pacific) and ultimate conclusion. Few could have expected in February 1898 that within a year the U.S. would not only have fought and beaten the Spanish and liberated Cuba, but would also now control several other territories, to include the Philippines. Nor did most people anticipate that by February 1899 the U.S. would be trying to quell a guerrilla movement in the far-off Pacific.

The peace negotiations between Madrid and Washington were held in France, with no Cuban or Filipino representation, despite the fact that Admiral Dewey had brought Filipino revolutionary Emilio Aguinaldo to the Philippines from Hong Kong (where he was in exile) in May 1898. Indeed, at the time, Aguinaldo had unilaterally declared Filipino independence, and he went on to besiege Manila with local troops. But, by January 1899 it appeared to some Filipinos that they were simply exchanging one colonial master for another. A group of Filipinos convened in January 1899 and declared a Filipino Republic with Emilio Aguinaldo as President, but this was not recognized abroad. By February 1899 an insurgency blazed, with Aguinaldo as a key leader, and very quickly hundreds of U.S. troops had been killed or wounded. President McKinley sent a five-man commission to evaluate the situation, but it arrived after hostilities had commenced. After the first months of warfare, U.S. Army personnel were increasingly at a loss about how to respond to the unconventional tactics of Aguinaldo and his troops, who would slip out of the jungle in the darkness, attack quickly, and then vanish. The poorly armed guerrillas, often operating with ancient rifles and machetes, would often leave behind mangled corpses, inflaming American troops.

The war quickly became a tit-for-tat exercise as U.S. troops began to move forcefully against Filipinos in the interior. During 1899 the U.S. military slogged its way through difficult terrain to the interior of Luzon, but the rebels continued to move and withdraw into the jungle. The U.S. began to censor reporting of conditions in the Philippines because there was loud, though minority, sentiment against the war in many quarters. The Anti-Imperialist League purchased newspaper advertisements opposing the war and discouraged re-enlistment of military personnel. Although it is clear that a majority of U.S. citizens did not have a strong aversion to the war, an increasing number of people were uncertain if it was in the nation's interest. As Andrew Carnegie said, "The Philippines will be to the United States precisely what India is to England, a nation of incipient rebels."[9] He offered the Treasury $20 million to purchase the independence of the Philippines.

Nonetheless, in 1899–1900 most eyes were not on the Philippines. McKinley was a popular President, there were a host of other pressing issues, and most newspapers focused more on Cuba than the distant Philippines. Moreover, all eyes were on the coming election of 1900. Yet, the war continued well beyond the election and into 1901. In March of that year, U.S. soldiers captured rebel leader Emilio Aguinaldo. On April 19, 1901, Aguinaldo swore allegiance to the U.S., calling for an end to the rebellion and peace with the Americans.[10] He said, "I saw my own soldiers die without affecting future events," meaning that it was apparent to him that guerrilla

warfare was not going to beat the Americans and deliver an independent, pros-
perous Philippines.[11]

In September 1901 President McKinley was assassinated, changing the political dynamics of American foreign policy forever as Theodore Roosevelt assumed
the presidency. Less than two weeks later, Filipinos in Balangiga on the island of
Samar attacked a local garrison of U.S. soldiers, brutally killing most of them with
machetes. This led to one of the bloodiest campaigns in the war, with U.S. troops
taking revenge against insurgents and civilians across much of the island of Samar.
Similarly, in Batangas province, U.S. forces pushed much of the civilian population into concentrated zones; those outside these areas were considered rebels. To
Filipinos, and many Americans, this smacked of the Spanish concentration camps, and
ultimately it would result in the court martials of three American leaders involved.

It was not until April 1902 that the rebels finally surrendered to U.S. forces. Like
the end of the U.S. Civil War, there was no grand retribution against rebels; in most
cases people were told to go home. A general amnesty was issued in July 1902. The
Taft Commission, appointed in 1900 and led by federal judge William Howard Taft,
had arrived and had developed an ambitious program for moving the Philippines
beyond its pastoral and Spanish-colonial past to a twentieth-century future that
included medicine, sanitation, an enfranchised citizenry, and most importantly, lit-
eracy. Taft became the first Governor of the Philippines on July 4, 1901, and was
confirmed in that position a year later (July 1902) when the U.S. Congress passed
an organic act setting up the institutions of the government of the Philippines. It
is to the analysis, plans, and execution of the Taft Commission that we turn for an
analysis of *jus post bellum*.

The Taft Commission and *jus post bellum*

In 1901 William Howard Taft "assured President McKinley that 'our little brown
brothers' would need 'fifty or one hundred years' of close supervision 'to develop
anything resembling Anglo-Saxon political principles and skills.'"[12] Taft's statement
was not in the least racist, at least not by the standards of the day. He loved the
Filipino people and was genuinely loved by many of them. However, his affec-
tionate belief regarding his "little brown brothers" was that illiteracy, poverty, ignor-
ance, and five centuries of Roman Catholic domination had not at all prepared the
Filipino people to operate a modern democratic country in the global capitalist
world. In contrast to Taft's belief that the U.S. could help the Filipinos through fra-
ternal guidance, the U.S. military greeted Taft's assertion "that 'Filipinos are moved
by similar considerations to those which move other men' with utter scorn."[13]

Taft's vision became the basis for a massive program, one that today in places like
Afghanistan and Iraq would be called "post-conflict reconstruction" or "stability
and reconstruction operations." Six years later, on October 16, 1907, Taft returned
to the Philippines (having served in Cuba in the interim) to do a stock-taking
of the efforts of what came to be known as the Taft Commission. That day he
was addressing the inauguration of the Philippine National Assembly, a legislative

body elected by the citizenry, and he was proud to claim that U.S. tutelage and investment was a "great experiment" that had never been tried before in world history: the "improvement" of a people and society that would "logically end … U.S. sovereignty" (over the Philippines) and result in a stable, democratic Filipino country. Taft candidly said that he believed the full evolution would take "considerably longer than a generation," but that the first steps toward enduring political order and justice had been taken:

> The avowed policy of the National Administration under these two Presidents has been and is to govern the Islands, having regards to the interest and welfare of the Filipino people, and by the spread of general primary and industrial education and by the practice in partial political control to fit the people themselves to maintain a stable and well-ordered government affording equality of right and opportunity to all citizens. The policy looks to the improvement of the people both industrially and in self-governing capacity. As this policy of extending control continues, it must logically reduce and finally end the sovereignty of the United Sates in the Islands.[14]

Taft's speech then considered major challenges to U.S. policy over the previous six years, including how those challenges were overcome. Among those challenges were:

(a) an insurrection;
(b) the problems posed by the Roman Catholic Church (e.g. largest landowner with 60,000 tenants; controlled weak, parochial education; contemporary schism within the church; the way the Church operated outside civil law);
(c) related to political instability, an arcane set of laws and political structures dating back to the sixteenth century;
(d) unwillingness of foreign capital to invest due to instability;
(e) limited access of Filipino sugar to U.S. market;
(f) agricultural disaster, most notably rinderpest killing 75–80 percent of cattle.

These were the strategic challenges faced by the Taft Commission when it began to take up legislative powers on September 1, 1900, and took on increased executive powers over the subsequent year (Taft assumed the role of Civil Governor in July 1901). With this in mind, let's consider the model of order, justice, and conciliation presented earlier in this chapter and the activities taken toward long-term security and prosperity.

Establishing order

"Government is a practical, not a theoretical, problem," stated Taft in his Inaugural Address as Civil Governor in Manila on July 4, 1901. The date had been specifically chosen by the administration in order to make it perfectly clear to all just what U.S. intentions were: establish civil order and help the Filipino people transition into a modern, democratic society and friend of the United States. This was no small feat considering the human and topographical geography of the area: the Philippines is made up of over 7,000 islands and multiple ethnic groups, with at least eight major languages or dialects and no single ethnic group representing more than a third of the population.[15]

The first practical problem was the establishment of order. The U.S. essentially took over the Philippines at the beginning of 1899, but, as noted above, an insurgency immediately broke out. Over the subsequent year and a half the U.S. military was the principal political authority trying to quell the violence, defeat the rebels, and install public order. There was little international threat, although various Pacific actors did watch the Philippine drama with interest. But there were two challenges. The first was to stop the bullets—end the insurgency and provide basic domestic security. The second order challenge was to establish a functioning, modern political order within which domestic institutions, education, and the economy could flourish.

On the civil-political side, President McKinley established a five-man commission to first study the situation in the Philippines and make recommendations, and then take over as the legislative and executive body until indigenous institutions were fully functioning. The report of the United States Philippine Commission, usually known as the "Taft Commission," was published in early 1901. The Commission had arrived in the Philippines in June 1899 and taken on some legislative and minor executive functions as of September 1, 1900. In the interim it had prepared a massive report on its findings, with hundreds of recommendations therein (108 pages of text; over 200 pages of "exhibits" reporting on everything from agricultural and climatological reports, to a report on the condition of the national mint, to a "historical resume" of the administration of justice in the Philippines by the local supreme court chief justice, to abstracts of imports/exports in various ports).

The first problem encountered after traditional security needs were met was a socio-political order question: what to do with the Roman Catholic Church? The Commission reported, "the whole Government of Spain in the islands rested on the friars." Four large religious orders (Augustinians, Dominicans, Franciscans, Recoletos) were the principal landholders and controlled many aspects of civic life. According to an article in The Yale Review at the time, these religious orders had gained tremendous wealth through deathbed bequests.[16] Furthermore, their members might serve in one area for decades, whereas Spanish military personnel rotated every four years. The modest schooling available to most Filipinos outside of Manila was through a hodge-podge of Church schools. The Commission firmly believed that the religious orders were hated, although the Catholic faith beloved: Catholicism as religion but also as a socio-political structure was intertwined into every part of Filipino life.

The Commission did not want to get into a church–state controversy, but moved to redistribute land in order to make it available to the 60,000 tenants on Church land. Taft noted in his 1907 speech that in the U.S. there is a strict separation of issues of church and state and that the Commission was reluctant to get involved in matters of faith, but the real issues here were land ownership, redistribution, and access to public education. The Commission did work out a land redistribution scheme as well as a way for untitled tenants ("squatters") to finally gain title to the lands they had tenanted for the Church (he notes that during 1907, 4,000 homestead settlements were reached "under the law."). This is clearly both an issue of social and political order and one of justice.

At the same time, the military government—through General Order No. 40—and later the Commission tried to deal with the antiquated local governance structure. The Spanish had imposed a sixteenth-century colonial model on the Philippines, with archaic laws. Civil servants were poorly paid, making them susceptible to bribery or corruption (according to the Commission). Thus, the military government and then the Commission revised municipal laws on an American model in order to emphasize local accountability, promote anti-corruption measures, and transform society from a dependency model to one of responsive government.

The Commission noted in its report the mineral and other natural forms of wealth (e.g. forestry) inherent to the Philippines, but argued that the lack of laws made investors wary about getting involved. Part of the complication was the arcane nature of Spanish Crown concessions on land and mineral rights. The Commission argued for a "tribunal" to take up these issues and make recommendations on appropriate legal mechanisms.

The Commission considered the Philippines a potential market for American products. Although the Commission could imagine a robust trade situation developing, it indicated that there was little real market as yet for American products, despite the obvious need. The report even looked at where Filipinos got their sewing machines, paint, pianos, and other items (Germany), noting that restrictive tariff barriers on goods from the Philippines entering U.S. markets hurt trade, just as did the lack of infrastructure, uncertainty over crime and insurgency (until 1901 at the least), and other primitive features of the islands. However, the Commission imagined a time when highways and railways had been built alongside other infrastructure, which would allow the Philippines to take off.

The Commission looked at banks (there were three principal banks in Manila) and urged a rational scheme based on U.S. law for managing the banks. It looked at taxes, customs, duties, registration costs, and other fees, arguing for major revisions to the tax code that would make it more rational, provide monies at the municipal level, and encourage people to actually pay their taxes.

Finally, a major section was devoted to the issue of education. Although the Spanish were to have two teachers allotted for every 5,000 pupils, the actual statistic was about one teacher for every 4,200 students. Obviously, only a few children would have access to this instruction, most of which was provided by religious orders rather than communities or the central government. Taft noted with some satisfaction that 1,000 American teachers were to arrive at some point to teach

English and other subjects. The Commission's view on education demonstrates how keenly the Commission felt about education:

> Undoubtedly, a well-directed system of education will prove one of the most forceful agencies for elevating the Filipinos materially, socially, and morally and preparing them for a large participation in the affairs of government.[17]

In conclusion, in 1907 Taft reflected on that first phase of the work, the period we might call a late-conflict transition, as one seeking "peace and good order." He candidly noted in his 1907 speech that:

> there still remained present in the situation in 1901 the smoldering ashes of the issues which had led the people to rebel against the power of Spain—I mean the prospective continuance of the influence of the regular religious orders in the parochial administration of the Roman Catholic Church in the Islands and their ownership of most valuable and extensive agricultural lands in the most popular provinces ... [as well as] the religious and property controversies arising out of the Aglipayan schism[18] and the disturbances it caused, added much burden to the Government.[19]

In 1907 Taft proudly chronicled investment and efforts in the areas of education, including bringing hundreds of American teachers to the Philippines to teach English, public health (most notably sanitation and fighting disease), and the creation of a modern, independent law enforcement that included both American and Filipino members in the judiciary and an effective constabulary that was not corrupt. Taft listed numerous public improvements, such as work on Manila's harbor and to roads, telegraph, electricity, and the like. For instance, in 1902 there were only 120 miles of railroad; Taft forecasted there would be 1,000 miles of working railroad by 1912. Finally, he talked at length about the formal rule of law as well as how to encourage and promote human capital and investment, from protecting patents (10,600 applied for), to fairly awarding mineral rights, to reforming the tax and municipal codes.

And all of this occurred over the course of two different U.S. presidencies, two national elections, the assassination of President McKinley, and efforts by the American opposition to derail long-term U.S. involvement in the Philippines. Taft attacked the opposition: "this ... prolonged the war ... [so] that during the educational process there has been a continuing controversy as to the political capacity of the Filipino people." For the modern reader, this observation is reminiscent of similar controversies during the recent wars in Afghanistan and Iraq.

Instituting justice

When it came to issues of justice, the Commission spent little time worrying over post-conflict treatment of former insurgents or engaging with Filipino violations of the war convention. Part of this is the milieu of 1900, but part of it also is the working assumption that insurgent leaders would be defeated on the battlefield and that the foot soldiers would return home and accept an amnesty. By the autumn of 1901 much of the country had been "pacified" and the Commission was far more interested in considering the establishment of native troops and constables, as well as reform of the civil code and reorganization of courts. All of this was necessary due to the desultory, inefficient, corrupt organization of the previous regime, where government functionaries had to bleed their own constituents in order to make a living due to poor pay.

Another justice factor, closely related to public order, was the issue of land titles and registration as discussed above. This is more an issue of the building or rebuilding of law enforcement and juridical structures than one of punition and restitution based on what happened during the hot war, and thus has been discussed as part of the long-term efforts at building an enduring order.

A final note on justice is that American military personnel were held accountable on occasion for violations of the military code of ethics. For instance, three officers were court-martialed for the bloody, indiscriminate killing of civilians as a retaliatory measure against guerrillas.[20]

Working toward conciliation

With regard to conciliation, the American view was to quickly move beyond the past to a partnership designed to enhance the relationship in a mutually advantageous fashion. The face of the insurgency, Emilio Aguinaldo, had been captured, sworn allegiance to the U.S., and been granted amnesty in April 1901. Most insurgents simply went home. This just what the U.S. expected, and it may be based on experience: in both the U.S. Civil War and the recent experience in Cuba, a general amnesty allowed most people to simply go home without punishment. This is precisely what happened for the vast majority of Filipinos involved in the insurgency. Moreover, the U.S.' investment, as well as obvious efforts at partnership by individuals such as Taft, meant that there was a sense of partnership, despite the fact that a group of Filipino leaders wanted quick independence rather than a trusteeship.

Taft concluded his 1907 speech to the Philippine National Assembly with a solemn promise to the people of the Philippines, one which may surprise the modern reader but helps give a window onto the issues of the time:

> I refer to the statement that the American Government is about to sell the Islands to some Asiatic or European power. Those who credit such a report little understand the motives which actuated the American people in accepting the burden of this Government. The American people are still in favor of carrying out our Philippine policy as a great altruistic work. They have no selfish object to secure ... I do not hesitate to pronounce the report that the Government contemplates the transfer of these Islands to any foreign power as utterly without foundation.[21]

Taft consistently argued that at some point in the future the Philippines would be fully ready to be an independent sister republic. It is hard to imagine a better example of conciliation than such a partnership based on mutual respect. Moreover, in this speech he proudly took personal responsibility for the inauguration of the assembly:

> I can well remember when that section [of the Organic Law, pertaining to the legislature] was drafted in the private office of Mr. [Elihu] Root in his house in Washington. Only he and I were present. I urged the wisdom of the concession and he yielded to my arguments and the section as then drafted differed but little from the form it has today. When the law passed the U.S. House of Representatives but was stricken by the Senate, I … urged its adoption upon both committees, and, as the then Governor of the Islands, had to assume a responsibility as guarantor in respect to it which I have never sought to disavow … it is not too radical in the interest of the people of the Philippine Islands. Its effect is to give to a representative body of the Filipinos the ability to initiate legislation, to modify, amend, shape or defeat legislation proposed by the Commission.[22]

Taft was proud of these accomplishments, proud of the peaceful election of the National Assembly (which included a small majority of those favoring outright independence from the U.S.), and he wished them success while warning them about corruption:

> As you shall conduct your proceedings and shape your legislation on patriotic, intelligent, conservative and useful lines, you will show more emphatically than in any other way your right and capacity to take part in the government … Upon you falls this heavy responsibility. I am assured that you will meet it with earnestness, courage and credit.[23]

Conclusion

The Spanish–American War pulled a reluctant U.S. President and citizenry from the shadows of the U.S. Civil War and into the early twentieth century's global competition for influence and raw materials. This was the period of Europe's final scramble in Africa, the building of the Panama Canal, and the rise of new global competitors such as Imperial Japan and Teddy Roosevelt's United States. In this time of rapid social and technological change, an unexpected consequence of the liberation of Cuba was U.S. possession of the Philippines. What was to be done?

This chapter reports on post-conflict efforts of the United States in the Philippines, led at first by, and immeasurably influenced by, William Howard Taft. Taft applied similar principles in Cuba and elsewhere and was a literal and figurative giant in American politics and law during this era. When it comes to the Philippines, he was extraordinarily proud of U.S. efforts to push what he considered to be a backward, primitive society toward secure independence in the modern world. Taft used terms like *order* and *justice* in ways consonant with the *jus post bellum* model outlined in this chapter. Taft believed he was operating from principles of Christian civilization as well as prudence and there is little doubt as to the tremendous investment made by the U.S. in the Philippines at the time and in the years that followed.

In sum, the Philippines case demonstrates the utility of an approach to post-conflict, following in this case decisive victory, in which thoughtful efforts at building a secure and just environment can result in long-term local and international *conciliation*. Indeed, when one considers the relative health of the Washington–Manila relationship for the past century, it demonstrates a significant difference from the post-colonial relationships between European powers and many of their former dependencies. This is due to an emphasis on the principles of order, justice, and conciliation.

Notes

1 See "The Administration's Promises Have Been Kept," available at: http://en.wikipedia.org/wiki/File:The_Administration%27s_Promises_Have_Been_Kept.jpg.

2 Benjamin R. Beede, *The War of 1898, and U.S. Interventions, 1898–1934: An Encyclopedia (Military History of the United States)*, vol. 2 (New York: Taylor & Francis, 1994), pp. 119–121.

3 William J. Long and Peter Brecke, "War and Reconciliation," *International Interactions*, vol. 25, no. 2 (July 1999), pp. 95–117.

4 "Teller and Platt Amendments," Library of Congress, available at: www.loc.gov/rr/hispanic/1898/teller.html.

5 "Chronology for the Philippine Islands and Guam in the Spanish–American War," Library of Congress, available at: www.loc.gov/rr/hispanic/1898/chronphil.html.

6 The $20 million is stipulated in Article 3 of the treaty, which defines the Philippine landmass and concludes, "The United States will pay to Spain the sum of twenty million dollars ($20,000,000) within three months after the exchange of the ratifications of the present treaty."

7 See letter from the American Minister to the Secretary of State, March 18, 1913, available at: https://history.state.gov/historicaldocuments/frus1913/d295.

8 Patrick McSherry, "Casualties During the Spanish American War," The Spanish American War Centennial Website, available at: www.spanamwar.com/casualties.htm.

9 Edwin Palmer Hoyt, *America's Wars and Military Encounters: From Colonial Times to the Present* (New York: Da Capo Press, 1988), p. 229.

10 It is noteworthy that Aguinaldo had done the same things with the Spanish, taking exile in Hong Kong rather than execution. However, while there he mobilized weapons for the insurgents at home.

11 "Emilio Aguinaldo," Bibliography.com, available at: www.biography.com/people/emilio-aguinaldo-9177563?page=2.

12 Stuart Creighton Miller (1984). *Benevolent Assimilation: The American Conquest of the Philippines, 1899–1903* (New Haven, CT: Yale University Press, 1984), p. 134.

13 Ibid.

14 Taft's speech can be found among the annual reports of the Philippines Commission to the U.S. Government, including *Report of the United States Philippine Commission to the*

Secretary ..., part 1 (1908), which is available electronically as a Google book at: https://books.google.com/books?id=H3goAAAAYAAJ&dq.

15 For contemporary figures, see the CIA World Factbook, available at: www.cia.gov/library/publications/the-world-factbook/geos/rp.html (accessed June 4, 2016).

16 This issue was discussed at length in tenth edition of *The Yale Review*. See Nathaniel T. Bacon, "Some Insular Questions," *The Yale Review*, vol. 10 (May 1901–February 1902), pp. 159–178.

17 *Report of the United States Philippine Commission.*

18 This was a religious schism within local Catholicism.

19 *Report of the United States Philippine Commission*, p. 16.

20 See Louise Barnett's *Atrocity and Military Justice in Southeast Asia: Trial By Army* (New York and London: Routledge, 2010), chapters 1–2. The first two chapters of this book focus on the Philippines court martials in 1901–1902 whereas the rest of the book focuses on post-World War II issues such as Vietnam.

21 *Report of the United States Philippine Commission*, pp. 22–23.

22 Ibid.

23 Ibid., pp. 41–42.

8

VINDICATION OR VENGEANCE IN 1919?

The contrasting policies of Wilson, Clemenceau, and Lloyd George

During the Christmas season of 1918, the holiday spirit in Western capitals was bittersweet. After four and a half years of war and the deaths of an estimated 9 million combatants and as many as 7 million non-combatants, the Allied powers of the West had bludgeoned their way to victory over Germany and its allies. The losses were staggering: on average, 10,000 Americans died every month of U.S. involvement in the war; the British Empire and France lost over a million soldiers; Germany and Austria-Hungary had as many as 4 million warriors die. This does not count the civilians lost to bombing, rapine, disease, and starvation. Moreover, the nature of the warfare was so grotesque, from poison gas to trench warfare to ethnic cleansing in the Balkans and Ottoman regions, that historians talk of a golden era, the "beautiful time" (La Belle Époque) being shattered by 1914, and being replaced by the Lost Generation of the 1920s.[1]

What next in a world of titanic shifts? Already the Romanov empire had fallen to Lenin's communism, or better, was tearing itself apart in a civil war. Western publics demanded vengeance on the Hun. At this writing, during the centennial anniversary of World War I, we well remember the two sides of the debate: on one hand those who wanted punishment and revenge; on the other hand, the vision, or utopianism, of Woodrow Wilson's Fourteen Points which called for victory, moral vindication, rehabilitation, and transformation of the world order.[2]

This chapter looks at the political and moral context within which the peace treaties that ended World War I were written. In order to consider different approaches to post-war peace and security using the *jus post bellum* framework of *order*, *justice*, and *conciliation*, the chapter looks at the bargaining position and objectives of the Big Three: Clemenceau, Lloyd George, and Woodrow Wilson. With the war having been fought primarily on French soil, Clemenceau demanded vengeance: heavy reparations from the Central Powers and the neutering of the military power of Germany. Lloyd George, sensitive to public opinion at home but also with an eye on the strategic future of Europe, took very seriously his constituents' demands for vengeance while at the same time trying to initiate policies of order and targeted, limited justice. In contrast, Woodrow Wilson viewed 1918 as a moment to break the power politics of the past and transcend history, with novel efforts at conciliation through self-determination, restorative justice, and political revolution. What were the possibilities open to the victors at the time? Could they have chosen a path that would not have led to a second great war?

Jus post bellum and the Versailles treaties

Most people think that World War I ended with a single Treaty of Versailles, signed by all members of the Entente, imposing war guilt and reparations on Germany and resulting in Germany's economic implosion in the 1920s, to the satisfaction of all its enemies. This state of affairs, the tale continues, resulted in German resentment, the rise of Hitler and his Nazi Party, and ultimately a second world war, exacerbated in part by Western Europe's pusillanimity and American isolationism. Popular history suggests that had World War I ended with unconditional surrender (rather than armistice), a Marshall Plan (for economic restoration), and Nuremberg trials (targeted justice) rather than national "war guilt," perhaps World War II would have been averted altogether.

This tale is not exactly false, but it is simplistic to the point of being misleading. There was not a single treaty, but a set of individual peace treaties directed at each of the Central Powers (Germany, Austria, Hungary, Bulgaria, and the Ottoman Empire).[3] Each of these treaties included in its text the Charter of the League of Nations, so the U.S. government ultimately did not ratify any of them, instead declaring unilaterally an end to the war in the Knox–Porter Resolution (1921) and signing thin bilateral peace treaties with Germany, Austria, and Hungary in 1921. Moreover, although it is left out of most history books, there was an effort made to hold senior leaders, such as Kaiser Wilhelm II, accountable via war crimes tribunals (e.g. the Leipzig Trials) and the Dawes Plan brought U.S. financial assistance to Germany in the 1920s so that Berlin could pay war reparations to Britain and France.

The point is this: the end of World War I was an extremely complex, dynamic environment that shattered four European empires, rearranged the map of three continents, and awakened new nationalistic and ideological influences on a global scale. The motivations and policy approaches of victors and vanquished clashed. One way to consider the moral challenges of bringing the war to resolution is to consider the *jus post bellum* criteria of order, justice, and conciliation and see if the political objectives of leaders and the political outcomes (i.e. treaties and their aftermath) that resulted at war's end were intended to promote these principles. The previous chapter outlined how the *jus post bellum* criteria can be implemented in practice: establishing the *military*, *governance*, and *international security* dimensions of a basic post-conflict order, such as buttressing local law enforcement; investing in *governance* (domestic politics and institutions) and the rule of law; and ensuring a positive *international security* dimension, which means that the state no longer faces an imminent threat from an internal or external foe. In some cases it is possible to move beyond order to justice, with a focus on the responsibility of aggressors (*punishment*) as well as the needs of victims (*restitution*). In some cases it is possible to come to terms with what occurred in the past and imagine some form of conciliation with past adversaries.

A look at the bargaining positions of the Big Three suggests that Woodrow Wilson was zealous about transcending this conservative model. Wilson envisioned revolutionary change. He did not want to rehabilitate Germany—he wanted to transform the world and earnestly believed that he had a divine mission to do so.[4] David Lloyd George was in tune with the vengeance demanded by the British public, while secretly ordering his negotiating team to seek outcomes that would restore Germany to its place as a British trading partner and counterbalance to Soviet Russia. Meanwhile, Clemenceau represented French and Belgian opinion: grind the Germans in order to punish them and hold them down in perpetuity. In order to see how this all played out, we shall consider the text of the Treaty of Versailles and its counterparts.

The treaties

There was no single treaty that ended World War I, but because the most important treaty was signed by the Allied powers with Germany at Versailles, and because the text of each of the other treaties was for the most part identical, historians speak of "Versailles" to mean not only the German treaty but also those with the other Central Powers. This chapter will follow this custom for the sake of simplicity. Recall that World War I began with the Austro-Hungarian Empire going to war against Serbia, and Vienna's ally, Germany, joined the fray immediately and enthusiastically. Bulgaria and the Ottoman Empire later joined the Central Powers as well. At war's end, the Ottoman Empire lost significant territory in the Treaty of Sevres (1920),[5] Austria was split from Hungary to become a land-locked, minor country (Treaties of Saint-Geneve-en-Lope and Trianon), and Bulgaria had its own treaty (Neuilly-sur-Seine).[6] Millions of people found themselves living, happily or unhappily, in newly created countries such as Romania or under a new colonial overlord (e.g. the Middle Eastern "mandates" of Britain and France).

Each of these versions of the Versailles peace treaty followed a common model, running to hundreds of pages of text. The table of contents for each treaty looked essentially like this:

> Preamble
> Part I: The Covenant of the League of Nations
> Part II: Frontiers of Germany
> Part III Political clauses for Europe
> Part IV: German rights and interests outside of Europe
> Part V: Military, naval and air clauses

Part VI: Prisoners of war and graves
Part VII: Penalties
Part VIII: Reparation
Part IX: Financial clauses
Part X: Economic clauses
Part XI: Aerial navigation
Part XII: Ports, waterways and railways
Part XIII: Labour [International Labour Organization]
Part XIV: Guarantees (Western Europe, Eastern Europe)
Part XV: Miscellaneous provisions

By signing the treaty, each of the Central Powers was committing itself to the Covenant of the League of Nations. In the section on "frontiers" and related parts, each of the Central Powers' new borders was defined, typically with dramatic loss of territory at home and colonies abroad. The military clauses limited the size of the Central Powers' armed forces, often causing military materiel to be transferred to the victors. The reparations sections called for massive transfers of currency and other wealth from the vanquished to the victors over a period of years. For instance, the Treaty of Neuilly-sur-Seine stated, "Bulgaria, therefore, agrees to pay, and the Allied and Associated Powers agree to accept, as being such reparation as Bulgaria is able to make, the sum of 2,250,000,000 (two and a quarter milliards) francs gold."[7] In addition to direct financial payments, the Central Powers provided coal, machinery, and other goods. For instance, Germany was required to provide livestock to France and Belgium, where the land war was fought:

To the French Government.

500 stallions (3 to 7 years);
30,000 fillies and mares (18 months to 7 years), type: Ardennais, Boulonnais or Belgian;
2,000 bulls (18 months to 3 years);
90,000 mulch cows (2 to 6 years);
1,000 rams;
100,000 sheep;
10,000 goats.

To the Belgian Government.

200 stallions (3 to 7 years), large Belgian type;
5,000 mares (3 to 7 years), large Belgian type;
5,000 fillies (18 months to 3 years), large Belgian type;
2,000 bulls (18 months to 3 years);
50,000 mulch cows (2 to 6 years);
40,000 heifers;

> 200 rams;
> 20,000 sheep;
> 15,000 sows.

The animals delivered shall be of average health and condition.[8]

There were also various minor details in the treaties, such as the return of artworks, a Holy Quran to the Arab Hedjaz, and a skull to its original owner.[9] The precedents for the Allies' draconian reparation demands were victorious Germany's demands on Russia in 1917 and on France in 1871. Everyone at Versailles had a keen sense of what Germany might have demanded if Berlin had won the war.

Finally, each of these treaties included statements of war guilt and calls for war crimes tribunals. That general statement, which was less controversial in Sofia, Vienna, and Budapest but smoldered in the hearts of many Germans, stated,

> Bulgaria recognizes that, by joining in the war of aggression which Germany and Austria-Hungary waged against the Allied and Associated Powers, she has caused to the latter losses and sacrifices of all kinds, for which she ought to make complete reparation

What differentiated the German treaty from those of the other Central Powers was that in addition to the war guilt clause it pointedly named the German Emperor in Article 227 (Penalties):

> The Allied and Associated Powers publicly arraign William II of Hohenzollern, formerly German Emperor, for a supreme offence against international morality and the sanctity of treaties.
>
> A special tribunal will be constituted to try the accused, thereby assuring him the guarantees essential to the right of defense. It will be composed of five judges, one appointed by each of the following Powers: namely, the United States of America, Great Britain, France, Italy and Japan.
>
> In its decision the tribunal will be guided by the highest motives of international policy, with a view to vindicating the solemn obligations of international undertakings and the validity of international morality. It will be its duty to fix the punishment which it considers should be imposed.
>
> The Allied and Associated Powers will address a request to the Government of the Netherlands for the surrender to them of the ex-Emperor in order that he may be put on trial.

The Dutch government refused to hand over Kaiser Wilhelm II and he lived quietly in the Netherlands until his death in June 1941. However, a war crimes tribunal was set up in Leipzig and initially 900 defendants were named (ultimately, only twelve were brought to trial).[10]

In short, at the end of World War I the mighty Russian, Hapsburg, Ottoman, and German empires no longer existed.[11] Austria became a land-locked rump state, ceding Hungary and its Balkan territories (Slovenia, Croatia, Bosnia). Bulgaria was forced to relinquish lands captured during the war (Serbia, Macedonia) and after a near civil war transitioned to a quasi-democratic government. Hungary lost territory based on ethnic divisions, including Transylvania to Romania. The Ottoman Empire initially agreed to Allied occupation of Anatolia (modern-day Turkey) and lost its Palestinian and Mesopotamian territories. Germany lost all overseas territories and small but significant lands to France (Alsace-Lorraine, City of Danzig, Port of Memel). The question is, what made the leaders of the Entente decide on this dramatic, vengeful approach to the post-conflict international order?

Negotiating Versailles: Clemenceau, Lloyd George, and Wilson

France's Clemenceau: Make Germany suffer

The Paris Peace Conference, which resulted in the Versailles and related treaties, consisted of delegates from twenty-seven different countries, but was ostensibly led by the five major powers (U.S., U.K., France, Italy, Japan[12]). Japan was typically ignored, so scholars sometimes refer to a "Big Four" to mean the leaders of the U.S., U.K., France, and Italy, but in practice Italy was also sidelined from the decision-making,[13] meaning that the Big Three dominated the discussions. For our purposes, we will look at the primary negotiating positions of the Big Three—Clemenceau, Lloyd George, and Wilson—with an eye to whether their stated objectives for termination of the war and its aftermath advanced an enduring order, justice, and long-term conciliation. Although what follows is an imperfect summary of the complicated political milieu that Clemenceau, Lloyd George, and Wilson operated in, it nonetheless can give us an appreciation for the aspirations and realities available at war's end in 1919.

World War I's Western front was almost entirely fought in France and Belgium, and at war's end both Belgium and France wanted significant reparations from Germany. However, whereas Belgium's King Albert argued against draconian punishment of Germany (and the dethroning of so many Central European monarchs) as destabilizing, he had little impact on the treaty negotiations. In contrast, French Prime Minister Georges Clemenceau wanted not only vindication, but vengeance, and a new transcontinental political order that neutered the German people (Germany, Austria) and resulted not only in restitution but also new overseas territories for France.

Clemenceau's, and France's, memory was long. The French people were humiliated by the quick collapse of their armed forces in 1914 and over the course of the war lost 1.4 million troops and 4.3 million wounded. Parts of France were uninhabitable at war's end due to minefields and the decimation of artillery shelling. But France not only had the Great War in mind when it demanded German reparations. A generation earlier, in the Franco-Prussian War (1870–1871), Germany had humiliated the French Army, seized territory, marched victoriously through the streets of Paris, and forced the French to pay a 5-billion-franc indemnity.[14]

Consequently, the French citizenry were unified in demanding a pound of flesh from Germany and its allies, although riven at home by political intrigue and factionalization, from the French Right to surging communists enthused by events in Russia. Certainly, the French wanted some form of justice, but the typical French sentiments went far beyond justice to revenge. By revenge I mean that not only did the French want to see Germany and its allies take responsibility for and make amends for what had been done, but France wanted to hurt Germany: most French citizens wanted the satisfaction of seeing Germany, as a country, as set of leaders, and as a people expiate French losses through German pain and suffering. As French President Raymond Poincaré said in a 1922 speech,

> You who witnessed these horrors, you who saw your parents, wives, children fall under German bullets, how could you be expected to understand and stand idly by if today, after our victory, there were people sufficiently blind to advise you to leave unpunished the actions of such outrages, and to allow Germany to keep the indemnities she owes.[15]

What was galling was that the war actually never touched German soil: the German armies, however weak, marched home at war's end. This was in stark contrast to the wastelands of France and Belgium. So the French public and its leadership, as well as many of their allies among the publics of Belgium, the U.K., and elsewhere, wanted to crucify Germany. This was not vindication—it was vindictiveness of a very human kind.

In practice, this policy of revenge, as well as France's understanding of the strategic landscape, resulted in policies designed to weaken Germany and its closest allies so that a German state could never threaten France again. For example, not only was the Austro-Hungarian Empire dismembered, but independent, German-speaking Austria was left with only a small, land-locked territory and a legal prohibition from merging with Germany. A summary of German losses has already been provided. All of this was specifically designed to punish Germany and forestall its rising again as a threat to France and its allies. John Maynard Keynes observed:

> So far as possible, therefore, it was the policy of France to set the clock back and undo what, since 1870, the progress of Germany had accomplished. By loss of territory and other measures her population was to be curtailed; but chiefly the economic system, upon which she depended for her new strength, the vast fabric built upon iron, coal, and transport must be destroyed. If France could seize, even in part, what Germany was compelled to drop, the inequality of strength between the two rivals for European hegemony might be remedied for generations.[16]

In practice, Austria, Hungary, and Turkey paid virtually no direct monetary reparations due to their loss of territories and the collapse of their economies in the aftermath of the war. Bulgaria did pay reparations, as well as providing livestock and coal to its neighbors for a period of years. But it was Germany who bore the brunt of the reparations burden, with an interim payment due shortly after the war's end equivalent to $5 billion. A reparations commission was set up by the allies to determine what could reasonably be demanded. It is beyond the scope of this chapter to go into all the details of the reparations, except to examine the purpose of them. At the time, a distinction was made between paying for what had been destroyed and paying for the overall costs of the war. The latter clearly would be a far heavier burden for Germany to bear. This argument also says something about the notion of what reparations were considered to be by the parties. In some cases, reparations can be restitution for what was taken or destroyed and therefore are limited. But reparations can also be used as a tool for revenge, not only by grinding down one's adversary through almost unsurvivable burdens, but also because the wider notion of reparations—as paying for the entire costs of the war—is suggestive of war guilt. The French wanted Germany and its allies to accept sole guilt for causing the war and one way to not only hurt Germany but also exact payment for its aggression would be to saddle Germany with all of France's costs for the war.

When it came to colonial acquisitions, the French primarily asserted themselves over lands previously, and often loosely, belonging to the Ottoman Empire and nearby existing protectorates in North and West Africa. For instance, on League of Nations authority, France acquired the "mandate" for Syria and Lebanon (it had already tightened its grip on Morocco a few years earlier and administered much of North Africa), as well as German territories in Cameroon and Togoland. In Europe, what was most important to France—at the urging of Marshall Foch—was to recover Alsace-Lorraine (taken by Germany in 1871) and move the eastern border to the more defensible Rhine river. Foch bitterly forecast that the Versailles Treaty, by not breaking Germany up into smaller political units, set the stage for another war: "This is not peace; it is armistice for twenty years."[17] Although France wanted to occupy the Rhineland, Paris was disappointed that the final settlement called for the demilitarization of the Rhineland rather than its control by France and the allies. France and the U.K. did have a mandate, for fifteen years, over the coal-rich Saar Basin and later, when Germany could not pay its overwhelming reparations debt, the French and Belgian militaries occupied the industrial Ruhr Valley for two years. France was determined to make Germany pay and keep paying for what had been lost in the war.

In sum, Georges Clemenceau represented millions of wives, parents, orphans, and other French citizens who had endured an agonizing four years of war on their very doorstep. They deeply felt that the Franco–German, or better Teutonic–Gallic, rivalry extended back generations, and as feuding neighbors and strategic competitors it was hard to imagine a different form of relationship. Although not everyone in France agreed, the general approach to post-war settlement was to establish a new international order that scourged Germany for its aggression and substantively weakened Germany (and its allies) for the foreseeable future. The approach was vengeful in its desire not to simply hold the Central Powers accountable or require them to pay for some war costs, but to cause them additional pain and suffering. There were efforts at more targeted justice, such as war crimes tribunals, but these did not go far for practical reasons. And, although there were international voices, such as that of Woodrow Wilson, calling for steps toward some sort of international conciliation, this was not the position that France was operating from in 1919–1920.

Great Britain's David Lloyd George: Short-term politics and long-term statesmanship

David Lloyd George, the unconventional, brilliant parliamentarian from Wales, served in the Cabinet as President of the Board of Trade (1905–1908), Chancellor of the Exchequer (1908–1915), and then Minister of Munitions (1915–1916), turning around weak war production that had resulted in munitions shortages at the Front. He came to the prime ministership in 1916 and throughout argued for accountability for those he considered to be weak and ineffectual military leaders as well as for the aggressive prosecution of the war. He did not begin as a "hawk," arguing early on that war with Germany, if it could be averted, was not in Britain's interest because the two were major trading partners and such a war could have disastrous consequences. But, after the war began he insistently argued for novel, energetic action, such as attacks in the Balkans and efforts to bring Balkan and Mediterranean countries into the war on the side of the Entente.

But it is to war's end that we turn. David Lloyd George was a shrewd, bold elected official overseeing a coalition government. His own Liberal Party was fractured between his faction and that of Asquith, and Lloyd George consistently looked to the Conservative Party for support. Like many politicians, he gave hundreds of speeches, interviews, and commentaries, from Whitehall to newspaper interviews. Thus, on the one hand he was the leader of a powerful empire and on the other he had to be responsive to public opinion in a bruised and vengeful country.

Consequently, one finds many statements by Lloyd George about what should be done with regard to Germany, but for our purposes we will look at two. The first is a public statement of what should be done with Germany made while campaigning in November 1918. The second is a memo, marked "Secret," for internal use by the British delegation at the Paris Peace Conference in March 1919. In general it is noteworthy that Lloyd George's primary consideration is to balance justice with long-term European order, and focus sharpest attention narrowly on Germany's leaders while providing a path of targeted retributive justice that would ultimately restore Germany to the community of nations.

The armistice with Germany came into effect on November 11, 1918; a general parliamentary election followed on Saturday, November 14. In the run-up to the election, David Lloyd George was clearly seen as the man who had led Britain to victory despite many obstacles. His election speeches were in tune with a public weary of war and hungry for victory and vengeance. Shortly before the elections, he stated "that German industrial capacity 'will go a pretty long way'" and "We must have … the uttermost farthing," and "shall search their pockets for it." As the campaign closed, he summarized his program:

1. Trial of the exiled Kaiser Wilhelm II;
2. Punishment of those guilty of atrocities;
3. Fullest indemnity from Germany;
4. Britain for the British, socially and industrially;
5. Rehabilitation of those broken in the war; and
6. A happier country for all.[18]

This was Lloyd George's *public* position during an election cycle, and although it is tough on Germany and its allies, it is certainly not nearly as harsh as it could have been. Lloyd George calls for a juridical process for holding accountable the individual widely seen as responsible for orchestrating the war by goading Austria-Hungary into invading Serbia in the first place—Kaiser Wilhelm II. The Germans were also considered guilty of "atrocities," particularly in the early days of the war in what historians call the "rape of Belgium." These atrocities included the massacre of thousands of civilians,[19] the destruction of over 25,000 homes as well as public buildings, and the displacement of nearly one-fifth of Belgium's population in August–September 1914. For instance, German Chancellor Theobald Theodor Friedrich Alfred von Bethmann-Hollweg, who famously called the 1839 treaty guaranteeing Belgian neutrality just a "scrap of paper," was one of those who could have been called before a war crimes tribunal.[20]

In public pronouncements, Lloyd George also called for the "fullest indemnity" from Germany. Later we will look specifically at what the Versailles and other treaties demanded of Germany and its allies and what Britain was to receive. The key point, for the British electorate, was that Germany had started the war, and was responsible for the deaths of nearly a million men from the British Empire and over 2 million wounded. Germany (and its allies) should make atonement, and that payment should be for most or all of the cost of the war.[21] These funds would be necessary for the "rehabilitation of those broken in the war" and for Britain during a time of social, industrial, and economic upheaval.

In sum, David Lloyd George's public statements during the last days of the war and, not coincidentally, during a contested election focused on winning the war and holding Germany accountable. His public sentiments were clearly in harmony with the vengeance desired by much of the British public. However, when it came to strategizing a long-term agenda for advancing British interests and international security, his focus, as seen in the following dispatch to the British representatives at the Paris Peace Conference a few months later, remains tough while being realistic: he clearly understood the need to balance order, justice, and long-term conciliation.

But David Lloyd George had a different strategy for the private negotiations at Versailles. In a cable marked "Secret" he laid out some considerations for the negotiating position of the British government, and by extension, the allies. Lloyd

George recognized the tensions inherent in trying to actualize a new European political order in the face of spreading communism, widespread desolation, and calls for rough justice.

Lloyd George begins by suggesting that there are real yet ambiguous human elements that make any peace settlement tenuous. He recognizes that the vengeful demands of a victorious, wronged people may seem just in the present—with all of the horrors and bloodshed fresh in mind—but may be seen quite differently in the future. But, he opines, "what is difficult … is to draw up a peace which will not provoke a fresh struggle" in the future. In the real world of policy and policymaking, what should be the guiding principles? Here are Lloyd George's reflections and directions to the British negotiating team:

> When nations are exhausted by wars in which they have put forth all their strength and which leave them tired, bleeding and broken, it is not difficult to patch up a peace that may last until the generation which experienced the horrors of the war has passed away. Pictures of heroism and triumph only tempt those who know nothing of the sufferings and terrors of war. It is therefore comparatively easy to patch up a peace which will last for 30 years.
>
> What is difficult, however, is to draw up a peace which will not provoke a fresh struggle when those who have had practical experience of what war means have passed away. History has proved that a peace which has been hailed by a victorious nation as a triumph of diplomatic skill and statesmanship, even of moderation in the long run has proved itself to be shortsighted and charged with danger to the victor …
>
> You may strip Germany of her colonies, reduce her armaments to a mere police force and her navy to that of a fifth rate power; all the same in the end if she feels that she has been unjustly treated in the peace of 1919 she will find means of exacting retribution from her conquerors. The impression, the deep impression, made upon the human heart by four years of unexampled slaughter will disappear with the hearts upon which it has been marked by the terrible sword of the great war. The maintenance of peace will then depend upon there being no causes of exasperation constantly stirring up the spirit of patriotism, of justice or of fair play to achieve redress. Our terms may be severe, they may be stern and even ruthless but at the same time they can be so just that the country on which they are imposed will feel in its heart that it has no right to complain. But injustice, arrogance, displayed in the hour of triumph will never be forgotten or forgiven …
>
> If Germany goes over to the spartacists it is inevitable that she should throw in her lot with the Russian Bolshevists. Once that happens all Eastern Europe will be swept into the orbit of the Bolshevik revolution and within a year we may witness the spectacle of nearly three hundred million people organised into a vast red army under German instructors and German generals equipped with German cannon and German machine guns and prepared for a renewal of the attack on Western Europe. This is a prospect which no

one can face with equanimity. Yet the news which came from Hungary yesterday shows only too clearly that this danger is no fantasy …

If we are wise, we shall offer to Germany a peace, which while just, will be preferable for all sensible men to the alternative of Bolshevism. I would, therefore, put it in the forefront of the peace that once she accepts our terms, especially reparation, we will open to her the raw materials and markets of the world on equal terms with ourselves, and will do everything possible to enable the German people to get upon their legs again. We cannot both cripple her and expect her to pay.[22]

Lloyd George argued that efforts at justice should not undermine security (order), nor should punition make long-term conciliation impossible. He was writing with real-world events in mind, including the 1917 Bolshevik Revolution, and he cites communist agitation (the day before writing this memorandum) in Hungary. "If Germany goes over to the Spartacists" is a blunt assessment that there are already hundreds of thousands, if not millions, of Germans actively supportive of a Communist take-over.[23] The mutiny of the German Navy, parades of socialist workers, and partisan violence by communists were occurring across Germany. Indeed, it was this disorder that pushed the Germany High Command to tell Kaiser Wilhelm that he must bring the war to a close. Lloyd George recognized that the Paris Peace Conference needed to not push Germany's vast population and industrial strength into the hands of Lenin and his ilk.

So, Lloyd George summarizes that justice may be "severe," "stern," and even "ruthless, but at the same time [it] can be so just that the country on which [it is] imposed will feel in its heart that it has no right to complain." In many ways this language could have been written about Germany in March of 1946 rather than 1919. Today we know that what happened in the Versailles Treaty is precisely what Lloyd George forecast, and frankly, supported: "strip Germany of her colonies, reduce her armaments to a mere police force and her navy to that of a fifth rate power." Indeed, it is noteworthy that the British, like the French, did not just try to limit Germany's military strength but rather tried to profit as much as possible through a punitive victor's justice. For instance, Britain took over, under League of Nations mandates, today's Iraq and the region of Palestine while other colonies went to France. Germany's army, navy, and air force were dramatically reduced (the German fleet at the Scapa Flow was actually scuttled before Entente powers could take it over[24]).

David Lloyd George, thus, represented the positions of a wise statesman and a wily politician. He understood that there was tension between the vengeance demanded by many Western publics and the realities of the great game of high politics. He focused attention on punishing Germany, but did so in a way that made it unlikely that communists could take over the country, knowing at the same time that Germany required some economic success if it was to be able to pay its reparations bills to London and the other allies. His government realized that the aftermath of World War I was just one of the issues facing the British Empire, to include anti-colonial riots in India, the home rule question in Ireland, and the specter of workers' revolutions on the continent. Lloyd George recognized that punishment could not be open-ended and, just as he had argued before the war, it was in the best interests of the United Kingdom for its veritable trading partner, Germany, to return to the world stage as an active economic partner.

Woodrow Wilson: Idealism in transforming the world

"The moral climax of this, the culminating and final war for human liberty, has come." This is how Woodrow Wilson closed his famous Fourteen Points speech to a joint session of the U.S. Congress on January 8, 1918. This dramatic proclamation was not just an oratorical flourish in the moment; rather, it illustrates the transformational, moralistic, revolutionary nature of Woodrow Wilson's desired outcome for World War I. In short, President Wilson did not simply seek a return to the status quo ante bellum, nor even a revised international order that included some targeted punishment of aggression. Wilson sought a revolution of the global order, an end to the old institutional arrangements that had governed Europe and much of the globe for the preceding three centuries and a new system based on the self-determination of ethno-linguistic groups. Wilson's Fourteen Points attempted to end history.

The eminent just war philosopher Michael Walzer writes that in most cases a just war's end will be restrained, limited for the most part to the status quo ante bellum. The public desire for revenge at the end of World War I is an example of one of the reasons that Walzer suggests limits on war's end: a victor's justice may be so punitive as to sow the seeds of future wars. One can think of historical examples, such as Rome versus Carthage, or what at the time appeared to be the ongoing Teutonic–Gaullic competition that wended its way back from World War I to the Franco-Prussian War, the Napoleonic Wars, the wars of Frederick and Louis IV, and beyond. Past settlements can cause a seething resentment that results in future wars.

But Woodrow Wilson, like other Western leaders at the end of World War I, represented a populace that wanted retribution from Germany, in terms of not just an indemnity for the war, but a wider repayment for the costs and suffering of the war, in addition to some sort of punishment of the German nation and its leadership.

Wilson's speech does not speak in terms of vengeance or in terms of vindictive retribution. He envisions a break with the past, and the dawn of a revolutionary new era. Wilson proposes a peace that transcends historical realities by jettisoning the old political order and assuming that the establishment of a new liberal international regime will transform politics in such a way that the nitty-gritty of punitive justice simply vanishes.

When one reads Wilson's speech a century later, it does not seem revolutionary or transformational. All the talk of transparency, democracy, openness, the aspirations of ethnic and national groups, and a league of nations seems consonant with the spirit of our times and the goals of most citizens in most places since at least 1989, if not 1945. On the other hand, if one is suspicious about whether Wilson actually meant what he said, one could see it as the canny speech of a veteran politician in that it tries to bypass established centers of political power by speaking directly to the masses. Furthermore, Wilson rhetoricizes—with little practical detail—utopian but impractical goals.

But Wilson's goal really was a brave new world. First, Wilson distinguished not simply between the militarists and "the more liberal statesmen," but more importantly, between elites and the revolutionary spirit of the masses. He identifies the former as the old order, made up of that "military and imperialistic minority." In contrast, Wilson uses an almost Hegelian tone when speaking of the people that "liberal statesmen" in Europe represent: "to feel the force of their own peoples' thought and purpose …" Wilson asserts that there is a universal spirit of freedom advancing across the globe. This is a revolution. Today's reader is probably surprised that Wilson's exemplar is not the U.S. or any other Western power, nor even the unleashed energies in the collapsing empires of Central Europe, but rather the populace of Russia that was at the time going through the Communist Revolution. He says that the "voice of the Russian people" is calling for universal "definitions of principle and purpose," which to Wilson is "thrilling and compelling," because "their soul is not subservient" despite reverses on the battlefield. "They have refused to compound their ideals or desert others that they themselves may be safe." He concludes that the Russian people's "utmost hope" is not for vindication or vengeance, but for "liberty and ordered peace."

> It is that the world be made fit and safe to live in; and particularly that it be made safe for every peace-loving nation which, like our own, wishes to live its own life, determine its own institutions, be assured of justice and fair dealing by the other peoples of the world as against force and selfish aggression. All the peoples of the world are in effect partners in this interest, and for our own part we see very clearly that unless justice be done to others it will not be done to us. The program of the world's peace, therefore, is our program.[25]

In addition to Wilson's confidence in the spirit of a new age, he presents a dramatic reshaping of how politics should work. He derides the formal institutions, customs, and courtesies of yesteryear's political elites: that "is an age that is dead and gone." The practice of princes and generals, remote from the trenches, playing global chess in their ornate staterooms and making "secret covenants" that "upset the peace of the world," is over: "the day of conquest and aggrandizement is gone by." High politics should not be the domain of elites making secret bargains and competing for land and resources with little thought for the faceless everyman; it should be practiced in the light of day with the best interests of the global citizenry in mind.

Today's reader is typically familiar with the first four of Wilson's Fourteen Points, which outline what today we call a "liberal international order." In 2018 they do not sound revolutionary:

- Open covenants of peace, openly arrived at … Diplomacy shall proceed always frankly and in the public view.
- Absolute freedom of navigation upon the seas.
- The removal … of all economic barriers and the establishment of an equality of trade conditions among all the nations.
- Adequate guarantees given and taken that national armaments will be reduced to the lowest point consistent with <u>domestic</u> safety.[26]

In 1918, these goals sounded radical, and they struck at the old imperial order of not only America's enemies, but also her closest allies. Wilson called for "open" and "public" negotiations and peace treaties, whereas the high politics of Europe typically involved private diplomacy among elites. Professional diplomats and government officials asserted that such privacy is absolutely necessary in order for there to be the opportunities for negotiation and compromise; indeed, even the U.S. Continental Congress had to go into private sessions to complete its most important documents, such as the U.S. Constitution. But Wilson's argument struck at the motives of those in power. He was effectively arguing that the national interest was often out of touch with the interests of local people on the ground, and thus peace settlements typically just moved around pieces of geography between kings with little regard for the sentiments of the populace on the ground. A case in point during World War I was the sensitive Sykes–Picot Treaty between Britain and France. This May 1916 agreement secretly divided up Ottoman territory in the Near East between Paris and London, despite public assurances to some Arab leaders and the Balfour Declaration to Jews of independence should they join the Allied cause.[27]

The issues of "free navigation" and "free trade" also were a blow to most of the world's leading powers, including Britain and France. For the most part, the economics of Europe's imperial system was mercantilism. Colonies such as India and those in Africa provided raw materials to the imperial center as well as markets for finished goods, and these patterns of exchange were typically protected by a web of laws and policies that were well-known to American colonists in 1776: limitations on docking in foreign ports, limitations on trade with rival powers, various taxes and tariffs on imperial goods, government-sanctioned monopolies on certain industries, various subsidies, and the like. As the U.S. had virtually no colonies in 1918, Wilson was calling for a transformation of international markets and trade that would primarily affect his closest allies and their colonial dominions.

Wilson also called for dramatic disarmament: "Adequate guarantees given and taken that national armaments will be reduced to the lowest point consistent with <u>domestic</u> safety." Note that he does not call for national armaments reduced to the lowest point consistent with "international security" but rather with "domestic safety." Both in the early twentieth century and to this day, there has been a current of thought that blames World War I on arms manufacturers, particularly those in the United States. The logic is something like this: the strategic and colonial competition between the Central Powers and the West was exacerbated by the security dilemma—one country's legitimate defensive needs appeared threatening to its neighbors, and thus each technological improvement to weaponry made it more likely for war to break out and to go on longer. Clearly weapons do not cause a war, but a criticism of the arms industry is that the U.S., along with its allies, prolonged the war by profiting through wide-scale production of ammunition, weapons, and munitions. This ultimately came back to haunt the United States when it was forced to enter the war.

Consequently, Wilson articulates a future picture of a world governed by police, not national armies. Weapons are only needed for domestic security from criminal behavior, not to protect one country from its neighbors. This element of the Fourteen Points is utopian, but it is a layer buttressed by open diplomacy, freedom of the seas, and the collective security arrangements of the League of Nations charter. Wilson spent 1918 pushing toward a covenant of interdependent peace and security that ultimately became the charter of the League of Nations. The basic principle of the League of Nations was to maintain international security through a global, collective commitment to shared security: aggression by any state would be met by the power of a cooperating international community. The League would provide the forum for grievances to be worked out peacefully among governments, without resorting to violence. The League would trump the politics of nationalism, ideology, and the national interest in favor of mutual gains and restraint enforced by a vigilant international community.

Much more could be said about Wilson's Fourteen Points, but only one more point needs to be made. What is missing from the speech? Wilson has very little to say about justice. Indeed, it is clear that what was most important to Wilson was avoiding punition and seeking a form of global conciliation based on the creation of a new world order. In other words, Wilson was trying to leap through conciliation to a new, twentieth-century order without dealing with the elements of the nineteenth-century order that still existed and handling the justice issues present in the minds of Europeans, especially in Brussels, Rome, Paris, and London. Wilson was correct that 1919 was not just a new year but a new epoch, but many of his ideas would not become enshrined in such a charter until 1945, and it was not just his allies abroad that resisted him: the U.S. Congress and many Americans were suspicious of his grandiose plans as inviting risk and expense to the United States.

Conclusion

It is difficult not to rely on hindsight to say that the Versailles treaties ushered in Adolf Hitler, concentration camps, and World War II. Certainly many Germans felt wronged either by the admission of war guilt, or more widely by the sense that their lives and livelihoods were being unjustly ground to the bone throughout the 1920s. After the eleventh-hour, eleventh-day, eleventh-month armistice of 1918, no one could have predicted global events that would bring into conflict Stalin, Togo, Hitler, Churchill, and Franklin D. Roosevelt, nor the pace of industrial and technological advancement that would make the next great destructive on an entirely new scale.

Nonetheless, it is clear that some sort of middle approach that established order and limited justice would have been more likely to lead to long-term international stability than the long-term punishment of Germany and weakening of European institutions favored by Clemenceau, the French, and millions of other Europeans. David Lloyd George's preferred approach, in tune with both his long-term sense of global power shifts but also the day-to-day realities of elected office, blended elements of order and justice that could have, over time, led to conciliation among the Western adversaries. Woodrow Wilson's approach was never embraced by his own legislature, and the birth of new democracies in Central Europe often resulted in confusion rather than robust governance. It was to take many years before the practical elements of his Fourteen Points would be embraced in the UN Charter, and it may have been his messianic attitude that was responsible for so much failure at home and abroad after winning the war. Finding the right balance in post-conflict will continue to be a challenge for statesmen and their militaries at the end of each war.

Notes

1 See Mary McAuliffe, *Dawn of the Belle Epoque: The Paris of Monet, Zola, Bernhardt, Eiffel, Debussy, Clemenceau, and Their Friends* (New York: Rowman & Littlefield, 2011).

2 John Keegan, *The First World War* (London: Vintage, 2012); Margaret MacMillan, *Paris 1919: 6 Months That Changed the World* (New York: Random House, 2007).

3 The Russian Empire collapsed in 1917 and Moscow signed its own treaty with ascendant Germany at the time, the Treaty of Brest-Litvosk.

4 Milan Babik, "George D. Herron and the Eschatological Foundations of Woodrow Wilson's Foreign Policy, 1917–1919," *Diplomatic History*, vol. 35, no. 5 (November 2011), pp. 837–857, available at: www.jstor.org/stable/pdf/44254537.pdf?refreqid=excelsior%3Ab8602106a88ef4013fd43fe669139c6a. Lloyd Ambrosius, *Woodrow Wilson and American Internationalism* (Cambridge: Cambridge University Press, 2017), contains a useful section on George Herron and Wilson's messianism, starting on about p. 88. See also Cara Lea Burnidge, *A Peaceful Conquest: Woodrow Wilson, Religion, and the New World Order* (Chicago and London: University of Chicago Press, 2016); Barry Hankins, *Woodrow Wilson: Ruling Elder, Spiritual President* (Oxford: Oxford University Press, 2016); Malcolm D. Magee, *What the World Should Be: Woodrow Wilson and the Crafting of a Faith-Based Foreign Policy* (Waco, TX: Baylor University Press, 2008).

5 The Ottoman Empire lost huge amounts of territory; the rise of a nationalist faction in the military led by Kemal Attaturk revived Turkish fortunes, resulting in the birth of a modern Turkish state and the end of the sultanate a few years later. This resulted in the Treaty of Sevres becoming almost instantly obsolete and being superseded by the Treaty of Lausanne in 1923.

6 The names of the treaties typically derive from the suburb of Paris where they were signed.

7 "Treaty of Neuilly-sur-Seine, Section II—Part VII, Reparation, Articles 121–176," Brigham Young University Library WWI Document Archive, last modified August 27, 2007, available at: https://wwi.lib.byu.edu/index.php/Section_II_-_PART_VII,_REPARATION,_ARTICLES_121_-_176.

8 Michael Duffy, "Treaty of Versailles: Articles 231–247 and Annexes," FirstWorldWar.com, last modified August 22, 2009, available at: www.firstworldwar.com/source/versailles231-247.htm.

9 Jeanette Greenfield, *The Return of Cultural Treasures* (Cambridge: Cambridge University Press, 1996), pp. 280–281.

10 Gerd Hankel, "Lezpig War Crime Trials," *1914–1918 Online: International Encyclopedia of the First World War* (last modified October 21, 2016), available at: https://encyclopedia.1914-1918-online.net/article/leipzig_war_crimes_trials.

11 All of these losses are detailed in the treaties, but an easily accessible summary can be found here: www.worldology.com/Europe/world_war_1_effect.htm.

12 Japan had relatively little impact on the conference.

13 Italy left its alliance with the governments of the Central Powers and joined the Allied Powers; the secret Treaty of London spelled out Italian expectations of grabbing numerous colonies and strategic sites in the aftermath of the war. Italy did lose 700,000 personnel during the war and expected compensation, but received far less than it felt it was entitled to. Its leader, Prime Minister Vittorio Emanuele Orlando, operated from a weak position politically at home and abroad, and his inability to converse articulately in English hampered him at the peace conference. The Big Three, particularly Clemenceau (who labeled Orlando "The Weeper") treated him as inconsequential. Italy's inability to gain much at Paris became a point of contention used by Mussolini and his Fascists, calling it the "mutilated victory."

14 This amount was another example of tit for tat: it was based on the amount Napoleon had forced on Prussia in 1807.

15 Margaret MacMillan, *Paris 1919: 6 Months That Changed the World* (New York: Random House, 2007), p. 214.

16 John Maynard Keynes, *The Economic Consequences of Peace* (London: MacMillan, 1920), p. 32.

17 Corona Brezina, *The Treaty of Versailles, 1919: A Primary Source Examination of the Treaty That Ended World War I* (New York: The Rosen Publishing Group, 2006), p. 46.

18 Alfred F. Havighurst, *Britain In Transition: The Twentieth Century*, fourth ed. (Chicago: University of Chicago Press, 1962, 1985), p. 107.

19 The German military was responsible for well-documented atrocities against Belgium, including the destruction of civilian property and the killing of 6,000 civilians, plus an additional 17,700 who died during expulsion, deportation, imprisonment, or a death sentence by court; 25,000 homes and buildings in over 800 different municipalities were harmed or destroyed by the end of the first year of the war. Tragically, over a fifth of the Belgian population had to flee from the brutal German invasion. See www.worldology.com/Europe/world_war_1_effect.htm.

20 Apparently, Bethmann-Hollweg suggested that he, and not the Kaiser, be tried before a war crimes tribunal. Only about a dozen individuals were arraigned out of an initial list of 900.

21 U.K. statistics: about 700,000 British killed and another 250,000 from Australia, Canada, and other imperial dominions; 2.27 million; John Graham Royde-Smith, "World War I: Killed, Wounded, and Missing," *Encyclopaedia Britannica* (last modified October 25, 2017), available at: www.britannica.com/event/World-War-I/Killed-wounded-and-missing.

22 Lloyd Ambrosius, *Woodrow Wilson and American Internationalism* (Cambridge: Cambridge University Press, 2017), p. 88.

23 The Spartacists were a group of German radical socialists who wanted Germany to be run by the working classes. In January 1919, over 50,000 workers went strike and held a demonstration in Berlin.

24 The German fleet was self-scuttled at Scapa Flow, Scotland, on June 21, 1919. German Admiral Ludwig von Reuter became concerned that all of his ships would be rationed out to all of the Allied powers in the aftermath of WWI.

25 "President Woodrow Wilson's Fourteen Points (January, 8, 1918)," The Avalon Project, available at: http://avalon.law.yale.edu/20th_century/wilson14.asp (accessed September 8, 2016).

26 Ibid.

27 Prashant Koirala, "Sykes–Picot Agreement," *Encyclopaedia Britannica* (last Modified May 31, 2016), available at: www.britannica.com/event/Sykes-Picot-Agreement.

9

THE MORALITY OF VICTORY
IN CONTEMPORARY WARFARE

As the Allied forces neared victory over the Axis powers in 1945, there was no disagreement in Washington, London, and Moscow that victory—*winning*—was the
strategic objective. After nearly six years of war and the deaths of an estimated 60–
80 million combatants and civilians worldwide, the Allies agreed that victory must
be won. The losses were staggering and global: an estimated 3 percent of the world
population in 1940 had died on the battlefield or as the result of bombing, disease,
and famine.[1] Moreover, the nature of the warfare was so grotesque, including ethnic
cleansing, concentration camps, horrific medical experiments, and suicide missions,
that it defied common humanity. The Nazi threat impelled Churchill to trumpet,
"Victory at all costs, victory in spite of all terror, victory however long and hard the
road may be; for without victory, there is no survival."[2] In response to Pearl Harbor,
President Roosevelt asserted in his "Day of Infamy" speech, "No matter how long
it may take us to overcome this premeditated invasion, the American people in their
righteous might will win through to absolute victory."[3]

Winning mattered, but what then? Was there a moral component to victory?
The great debate at the time, at least among the Big Three who met at Tehran, Yalta,
and Potsdam[4] to sort out the war's aftermath, was about the quality of victory. Did
victory mean punishment of the evil Hun? Could victors extract a pound of flesh?
Where was the line between vindication and vengeance? What should be done differently than at Versailles twenty years earlier? What steps could be taken to ensure
that there would be no World War III? How would the Western democracies find
a *modus vivendi* with the Soviet Union in the post-war world? All of these matters
required debate and compromise, but there was no substitute for some sort of
unconditional surrender of the Axis powers. In 1945 anything else was unthinkable.

In contrast, today, Western governments and militaries often refrain from
discussions of victory. This is troubling. This chapter argues that the surrender
of victory as a political and ethical concept is a moral and strategic failure, both

for classical just war thinking and for broader political and military ethics today. Victory is a just war issue because just war thinking is concerned with the quality of peace: a satisfactory peace advances security and justice. Victory is a just war issue in that it links the reason a war is fought (*jus ad bellum*) with restraint in how a war is fought (*jus in bello*) and the construction of the post-war settlement (*jus post bellum*). This chapter is less a historical analysis than an examination of where we are at today when considering the morality of winning. In one sense, this chapter is a capstone chapter, linking the justification for going to war (e.g. the American War for Independence, War of 1812) with how war is fought (from Veracruz to Berlin), to the strategies and moral objectives that belligerents stand, fight, and die for. This chapter defines three notions of victory (defensive, offensive, moral), considers why victory has fallen out of vogue since World War II, discusses the linkage between war aims and winning, and argues that achieving victory can be a praiseworthy, necessary end such as in cases of self-defense, punishment of wrongdoing, restoration, and self-determination.

Defining victory in war

What is victory? Victory, in this context, is winning or success in war. Although there is a large literature and there are thousands of aphorisms, from Aristotle to Lombardi, about victory as mastery of self, this is not what is meant by victory in war. More specifically, victory in a specific contest can mean any one (or more) of three things:

1. Victory is not allowing an opponent to win.
2. Victory is defeating an opponent.
3. Victory is the vindication of values.

The strategist Basil Liddell-Hart contrasts *offensive* and *defensive* types of victory: "The acquisitive state, inherently unsatisfied, needs to gain victory in order to gain its object ... The conservative state can attain its object by foiling the other side's bid for victory."[5] Often, time and expense are the factors for a defensive victory. For instance one key element, though not the only one, of George Washington's long-term strategy was *not* to lose to the world's greatest navy and second-greatest army. Time was on the side of the Continentals if they could avoid major defeats. Historians typically call such a strategy "Fabian" after the Roman General and dictator Quintus Fabius Maximus Cunctator. The title "cunctator" ("lingerer") was added to his name first as an insult but became a badge of honor due to his strategy in opposing the Carthaginian military genius Hannibal in the Second Punic War. Rather than fight Hannibal openly and experience defeat like other Roman generals seeking decisive battlefield conquest and personal glory, Fabius employed a scorched-earth policy of retiring before Hannibal and at times harassing his supply lines, not allowing the Carthaginians to live off the land while on campaign. Similarly, the over-extension of ambitious leaders' armies, like those of Napoleon and Hitler in the vast Russian heartland, can result in defensive victory. As Leo Tolstoy, in *War and Peace*, described the disintegrating French Army of the Republic, "The strongest of all warriors are these two: Time and Patience."[6] Fierce defenders, from the Confederacy to the Viet Cong to the Afghan *mujaheddin*, exemplify how time and patience can be decisive by blocking victory, at least for a time, to one's adversary.

Not everyone agrees that defensive victory is satisfying or even possible. Field Marshall Haig, during World War I, observed how defensive stalemates can be costly for all involved: "The idea that a war can be won by standing on the defensive and waiting for the enemy to attack is a dangerous fallacy, which owes its inception to the desire to evade the price of victory." His French ally, Field Marshall Foch, came to a similar conclusion: "The will to conquer is the first condition of victory."[7] Thus, the second, more conventional definition of victory is outright defeat of one's opponent. This is the orthodox vision of victory: compelling one's opponent to submit to one's will, generally through offensive military action. Underlying this definition of victory is a notion that war is not an activity isolated unto itself; rather, it is an expression of politics and political will. As Clausewitz famously wrote,

> The political object is the goal, war is the means of reaching it, and the means can never be considered in isolation from their purposes …

and

> War is not merely a political act but a real political instrument, a continuation of political intercourse, a carrying out of the same by other means.[8]

The Fabian strategy was ultimately not sufficient to defeat Hannibal, who occupied a large swathe of Italy for fifteen years. Scipio Africanus ultimately beat Carthage by first besting Carthaginian armies in Spain and then taking the fight to Hannibal's homeland in North Africa, destroying Hannibal's ability to fight. This created a peace that lasted fifty years. So too, Wellington beat Napoleon, Grant beat Lee, Montgomery beat Rommel, and we remember momentous battles not just for the bloodshed but for their long-term political consequences: Tours, Gaugamela, Blenheim, Waterloo, Puthukkudiyirippu. Battlefield victories are important, but it is the strategic, political context that is of greater importance when a group or government capitulates to the demands of its enemy. Defeat need not mean "unconditional" surrender, but it does mean surrender and we often remember the political systems and leaders who won: Alexander, Lincoln, and Churchill. In this book, we have seen victors reflect both on victory and what might have been, from the outcome of the American War for Independence to Grant's reflections on the vicissitudes of Mexican politics.

This foreshadows a third form of winning: victory that has a *moral* dimension because the contestants represent utterly different views on what the world should look like. World War II was clearly this sort of war. Western Europe simply could no longer tolerate both the diabolical Aryan supremacy of National Socialism and the Christian and Enlightenment values embodied by the U.S. and its allies. Although some, such as Michael Walzer, see the Pacific theater differently, the clash between Washington and Tokyo was not simply conventional, but contrasted Western liberalism with the racial supremacy and associated barbarism of Japan.[9] World War II was a vindication of a set of Western liberal values, however imperfect, applied to the post-war environment. This became the basis for the Nuremberg and Tokyo trials, the Universal Declaration of Human Rights and United Nations Charter, and the Geneva Conventions of 1949 and similar standards such as the Genocide Convention and human rights laws, as well as a set of related institutions including the Marshall Plan and Bretton Woods system. This is order, justice, and the first steps toward conciliation.

Imagine the counterfactual: how an Axis victory would have resulted in a different set of opportunities and institutionalized values. Had the Nazis won, it still would have been "moral," but in a terrible, wicked sense. "Vindication" is not a moral judgment in retrospect about which values are superior—it is the recognition that at the end of some wars "victory" means more than going home with some material loss for the loser. "Vindication" means that the values of the victor become the worldview framing a new status quo. Tours confirmed continental Europe as Christian, setting the foundations of the Carolingian empire; Alexander's victories brought Hellenism to the Near East; Napoleon's victories and "Continental System" changed the role of church–state relations, legal codes, and many other elements of life across Europe; and the U.S. Civil War abolished slavery once and for all and dramatically altered the course of the country. So too, victors like Lenin, Mao, and the Khmer Rouge imposed a value system on their populaces and foes after winning. In each case, victory had far-reaching moral, social, and political consequences. Consequently, at the end of World War II, a liberal international order was re-established in the West; a Nazi victory would have established a contrasting moral order that privileged the Aryan race, the Nazi party and its ideology, and the personality cult of Adolf Hitler.

In sum, history is replete with examples of defensive, offensive, and moral victories. Yet today the virtue of victory is tarnished; winning is out of vogue. Indeed, those who argue for victory these days are portrayed as the doddering elderly or unsophisticated bullies. How this happened and why it must be reversed demands our attention.

The scandal of winning

What happened to victory? Why do today's Western statesmen and military leaders avoid, at least in public, talk of "winning"? As John David Lewis observes in his book *Nothing Less than Victory*, at the beginning of World War II, U.S. military doctrine asserted, "Decisive defeat in battle breaks the enemy's will to war and forces him to sue for peace which is the national aim."[10] But, as early as the 1950s, the U.S. military backed away from the value of victory, demurring, "Victory alone as an aim of war cannot be justified, since in itself victory does not always assure the realization of national objectives."[11]

Furthermore, despite the importance of the rule of law and the vindication of values in contemporary warfare, contemporary just war scholars have largely avoided the topic. With the exception of Michael Walzer's classic chapter, "War's End and the Importance of Winning," overt discussion of "winning" and "victory" is almost entirely absent from major works on just war theory and military ethics by Paul Ramsey, James Turner Johnson, Eric Patterson, Oliver O'Donovan, Nigel Biggar, J. Daryl Charles, Timothy Demy, and many others.[12]

What happened to victory? Victory is out of style for a variety of reasons, some compelling and others not.

First, *victory can be costly*. If World War I did not emphasize this point (see Chapter 8), World War II did. By the 1950s a lesson drawn from World War II seems to have been that the last country standing is going to be stuck with the costs of getting former enemies up and running again. The U.S. first "invested," to the tune of billions of dollars, its occupation forces in Germany and Japan to ensure that these defeated foes did not cause more war as well as to block the next enemy: energetic, expansionary Soviet Communism. Victory resulted in the costly Marshall Plan, which began as a response to the bankrupt British government and instability in Greece and Turkey. More recently, some such as Colin Powell have enunciated the so-called "Pottery Barn rule" to post-conflict: "if you broke it, you own [or fix] it."[13] Michael Walzer suggest that this is why China has been reluctant to support armed interventions of any kind abroad, because the intervening party takes on a set of costly obligations, whether it wants to or not.[14] The recent "reconstruction and stabilization" costs in Afghanistan and Iraq are cases in point. Despite the fact that many American and Coalition leaders eschewed the notion of "victory," they invested trillions of dollars after flushing al Qaeda and the Taliban out of their strongholds. The 1999 Kosovo intervention is a similar case: the West provided, to a tiny country of less than 2 million people, as many as 50,000 security personnel and on average over $1.5 billion per annum in the first seven years following the conflict.[15]

Second, *victory can be pyrrhic*. Pyrrhus of Epirus, after defeating Roman armies at tremendous cost, said that "one other such victory would utterly undo me" due to the loss of men, materiel, and commanders.[16] More recently, in the aftermath of World War II, many pragmatic thinkers came to see the pursuit of victory in the atomic age as suicidal. Reinhold Niebuhr, in *The Irony of American History*, noted that vast expenditures devoted to making the victorious U.S. safe resulted, ironically, in Americans feeling less safe:

> Meanwhile we are drawn into an historic situation in which the paradise of our domestic security is suspended in a hell of global insecurity; and the conviction of the perfect compatibility of virtue and prosperity which we have inherited from both our Calvinist and our Jeffersonian ancestors is challenged by the cruel facts of history. For our sense of responsibility to

a world community beyond our own borders is a virtue, even though it is partly derived from the prudent understanding of our own interests. But this virtue does not guarantee our ease, comfort, or prosperity. We are the poorer for the global responsibilities which we bear. And the fulfillments of our desires are mixed with frustrations and vexations.[17]

For the U.S., V-J and V-E days ushered in global commitments and a worldwide competition with a deadly, nuclear-armed rival. In other words, victory had not only bankrupted the British and French empires but may have set the Cold War world on the path of nuclear annihilation. Indeed, to speak of victory in the nuclear age seemed to many to be more Strangelovian than prudent. Likewise, over the past fifteen years many have wondered if the Global War on Terrorism, with its many tactical successes over terrorists in Afghanistan, Iraq, Yemen, and elsewhere, has been a pyrrhic victory at the strategic level; is victory even possible in complex cases?

A third view, *explicitly critical of victory, comes from revisionist scholars.* Since the 1950s, revisionist scholars like Gabriel Kolko have argued that America's victories in World War II (and subsequent foreign adventures) were not crusades to liberate Europe and better mankind, but rather the reactionary expressions of capitalist greed.[18] America won the war and immediately, according to Kolko, established a new world order based on cheap labor and access to natural resources, protected by U.S. military bases and fueling stations around the world. Such a view is rooted in charges of colonialism or neo-colonialism: any real effort at victory by the U.S. or other Western powers is simply an effort to maintain a world system of exclusionary capitalism, keeping down developing societies in a situation of economic and political peonage. For the past forty years, this view has been associated with world systems theory,[19] dependency theory,[20] and other neo-Marxist critiques.

Underlying the revisionist argument is the view that the patriotism that motivates many citizens and soldiers is really an opiate for the masses, a heady smokescreen orchestrated by elites as a way to deceive the masses into fighting capitalism's wars. Thus, victory benefits a global "core" of elites; the common person—regardless of race or nationality—is always the loser, a victim on the "periphery." The revisionist position often sounds conspiratorial: the U.S. invaded Afghanistan and Iraq at the behest of faceless corporations to access oil wealth,[21] global elites stoke the fires of war in the Congo to extract raw materials, etc. The result of these neo-Marxist critiques, trumpeted by Western media for a generation, is almost complete erosion of any belief in the value of victory in war.

Jean Bethke Elshtain, citing Nietzsche, identified an underlying assumption in the anti-victory viewpoint as *ressentiment* or "self-loathing."[22] She explicated and criticized the "liberal guilt" felt by many in the West that somehow they are responsible for all the problems of daily life in impoverished, war-torn countries. This self-loathing results in the denigration of Western values and codes of conduct, thus making the thought of a Western victory, even to liberate an oppressed group, smack of bigotry, racism, and exclusivity. This self-loathing about Western values and success plays into an interpersonal sense of injustice and unfairness: winners take advantage, winners are bullies, winning is something to be ashamed of.

Fourth, *victory has fallen out of vogue due to confusion over just war thinking and military ethics.* Today's quasi-pacifists, pretending to argue from a "just" or "justified" war perspective, claim that no war can really be accounted just until after it has been fought. The logic here is illogical: to decide whether or not the *casus belli* was just, one has to wait until after the war has been fought? This viewpoint disregards the fundamental just war criteria of *legitimate political authority, just cause,* and *right intention,* typically elevating "last resort" to preeminence and then saying that a war was unjust *ex post facto* based on the collateral damage and civilian casualties attendant to any war. This is really not a just war perspective because it erodes the privileged place of deontological criteria based on authority and morality into a cacophony of anti-military and anti-government protesting about development dollars, secrecy, and the like.[23] When unmasked, this critique is solely a utilitarian, cost–benefit argument rather than one rooted in the richer values of justice and peace that are at the heart of just war thinking.

Unfortunately, the demise of winning at the strategic level has been connected with the erosion of sentiment about the nobility of public service, particularly with regard to law enforcement (at home) and military service (abroad). Historically, the just war tradition (as well as the liberal-nationalist ideology of Western countries since Napoleon) saw soldiering as a noble activity. As James Turner Johnson has reported, the idea of chivalry is a critical influence on the development of just war thinking and is today an integral part of the war convention.[24] One did not necessarily have "dirty hands" if one defended the homeland: protecting the weak, punishing wrongdoers, and righting past wrongs, per Augustine, were elements of a noble calling and a key responsibility of government officials.[25] This was also true for citizen-soldiers who had to fight after their country was attacked, such as American GIs in World War I and World War II. Instead, as far back as the Spanish–American War but especially in recent decades, the profession of arms has been derided by some as, at best, a tragically dirty-hands profession, and at worst, immoral ("baby killers") at all times and in all places. This is a sad state of affairs when it comes to individuals facing harm on behalf of the commonweal. C.S. Lewis succinctly yet elegantly criticized such criticism during World War II: "It … robs lots of young Christians in the Services of something they have a right to, something which is the natural accompaniment of courage."[26]

Those who are deeply skeptical of military power and repelled by notions of victory have worked very hard, along with other well-meaning but naïve allies, to so shackle modern (usually Western) militaries that the "rules of engagement" make victory nearly impossible. This is also true for well-intentioned armed humanitarian interventions. Soldiers—like German military personnel in Afghanistan[27]—who are not allowed to carry a gun or shoot, who are not allowed to police certain civilian areas (like U.S. troops at times in Iraq and Afghanistan), who cannot hold a battle-field after dark but must retire behind distant fortifications (like the International Security Assistance Force in Afghanistan), who cannot impose curfews or disarm unlawful combatants … are in a situation that is a self-fulfilling prophecy of violence and failure.[28] At Srebrenica, the impotence of UN blue helmets resulted in over 7,000 civilian deaths. In each case, soldiers were simply not allowed to win.

Victory, at least in the West, has become financially and reputationally costly. Washington and its allies are gun-shy because they must constantly respond to charges of neo-colonialism, prejudice, and bullying in a world that remains insecure and violent. What is needed is a just war-informed, clear-headed approach to victory because winning continues to be crucial, even if it must be restrained and limited in some cases.

War aims, *jus ad bellum*, and victory

If it is just to go to war in the first place (*jus ad bellum*), then is it not just to win? Our focus here is on legitimate war aims: if the *casus belli* and stated goals of a belligerent meet the *jus ad bellum* criteria, then winning can be a moral enterprise. We will turn our focus to the connection between just war principles (*jus ad bellum*) and stated war aims—even in an evolving situation—with little focus on battlefield operations and *jus in bello* criteria. The link between *jus ad bellum* and victory in *jus post bellum* seems obvious. Strangely, however, there is not enough contemporary scholarship on this topic. Perhaps that is because it is taken for granted that just causes naturally should be consummated in victory.

Augustine famously wrote that wars are just to punish wrongdoers, right past wrongs, and prevent future wrongs.[29] This elegant phrase suggests at least four types of war aims that demand victory and are clearly moral: self-defense, punishment, national self-determination, and armed humanitarian intervention.

The first legitimate war aim where victory is morally appropriate is *self-defense*. Even for those who believe that "turn the other cheek" applies in international conflict, there is only one cheek to turn before statesmen must defend their populaces. Defending the lives, livelihoods, and way of life of one's citizenry is the fundamental *raison d'être* for the state: the essential social compact in domestic life is citizens subordinating themselves in some ways to government authority in return for a guarantee of security. Likewise, in international life the social compact in the society of states, and the cornerstone of international law, is the principle of sovereignty with its corollary of non-intervention. When this principle is violated, causing real harm to human life and property, it is the moral obligation of governments to defend themselves and their people. This was the argument made by American colonists in the Declaration of the United Colonies in Chapter 2.

Thus, in cases of self-defense, the war aim properly should be victory. This helps explain Winston Churchill's exhortation, after the fall of Poland, France, and much of Europe to Hitler's legions, that

> Even though large tracts of Europe and many old and famous States have fallen or may fall into the grip of the Gestapo and all the odious apparatus of Nazi rule, we shall not flag or fail. We shall go on to the end, we shall fight in

France, we shall fight on the seas and oceans, we shall fight with growing confidence and growing strength in the air, we shall defend our Island, whatever
the cost may be, we shall fight on the beaches, we shall fight on the landing
grounds, we shall fight in the fields and in the streets, we shall fight in the hills;
we shall never surrender, and even if, which I do not for a moment believe,
this Island or a large part of it were subjugated and starving, then our Empire
beyond the seas, armed and guarded by the British Fleet, would carry on the
struggle, until, in God's good time, the New World, with all its power and
might, steps forth to the rescue and the liberation of the old.[30]

When it came to fighting the Nazis, the alternative was most likely a notorious
defeat, a future that included Aryan supremacy, slavery, and concentration camps.

Self-defense is a moral war aim and its consummation in victory can be an ethical and noble end. It is the moral responsibility of the state to protect its people.
We may consider specific cases of self-defense to be noble, or even heroic, such
as the Finns fighting the Soviet colossus in 1941. At the time of this writing,
Ukraine is trying to maintain its sovereignty and equilibrium in an undeclared war
of aggression launched by neighboring Russia. Beginning in 2014 with an illegal
incursion into Crimea and subsequent annexation, Russian troops (in unmarked
uniforms) have intervened in, or invaded, Ukrainian territory in Donbass, Donetsk,
and Lugansk. The defense of its territory and people by Kiev—in other words,
victory—is moral.

A second case where the consummation of just war aims is a moral victory is
punishment. We often think about the Nuremberg or Tokyo trials as just, but at the
outset of World War II no one was thinking about punishment as a war aim. Usually
punishment is thought of as a secondary war aim, after a war has begun, or as a
war aim targeting a multiple offender. This is an important point: from Augustine
to today, the notion of punishment as a war aim has to do with punishing those
leaders who routinely violate international peace. Thus, individuals like Napoleon
and Serbia's Slobodan Milosevic become the targets of punishment for their
repeated violations of international order. Upon Napoleon's first defeat the Allied
forces agreed to a return to the status quo. But, following his unlawful hundred-
day return from exile to the battlefield and subsequent, final defeat at Waterloo,
France was punished: Napoleon's marshals were killed, France lost territory and
was forced to pay indemnities of 700 million francs, and was saddled with the
cost of supporting a 150,000-man army of occupation for up to five years.[31] In
the case of Milosevic, in the aftermath of the 1995 Dayton Accords he was more
or less let off the hook. However, in the context of the Kosovo crisis—where he
appeared once again to be responsible for war crimes—he was indicted on three
counts by the UN International Criminal Tribunal (May 1999) and subsequently
formally charged (November 2001).[32] The robust 1999 NATO intervention and
remanding him to the International Criminal Tribunal for the former Yugoslavia
(ICTY) were acts of punishment with a principled focus on Milosevic and his
regime's top supporters.

As Briand Orend, Eric Patterson, and others have written, the idea of punishment at war's end is complex, involving both punitive (who and how to punish) and reparative (to whom is something restored or vindicated) elements of justice.[33] Often the focus of punishment is on tactical-level violations of the laws of armed conflict (*jus in bello*), such as individual murder, rape, torture, or theft. But, at the strategic level, when one thinks about punishment as a *casus belli*, punition may be an important, expressly stated war aim to stop repeated violations of international order by someone like Saddam Hussein, Muammar Gaddafi, Charles Taylor, Osama bin Laden, and Joseph Kony. In these cases punishment is best focused on the senior-most leadership responsible for violations of international security, rather than making civilian populations on the losing side "pay," as happened to Germany after World War I. For instance, within the first six months of U.S. entry into World War II there were already people suggesting punishment of senior Axis leaders. There was a precedent for this: the failed Leipzig criminal tribunal following World War I, which was an attempt to hold senior German officials, such as Kaiser Wilhelm II, accountable for crimes of aggression. Punishment of leaders was on the minds of Europeans for years, including anti-Nazi Germans. For instance, theologian Dietrich Bonhoeffer's brother-in-law, Hans von Dohnányi, kept a secret file of Nazi crimes and atrocities for years with the goal of releasing the documents to prove the lawlessness and evil of the Nazis to the world.[34]

Furthermore, there are times when from the outset, armed action is clearly a case of just punishment, such as the immediate response to 9/11. It is important to note that the U.S. response following 9/11 was war, even if it was somewhat unconventional, with al Qaeda being a non-state actor aligned with a rogue regime in Kabul. The initial U.S. demand was to turn over the leadership of al Qaeda—Osama bin Laden—and the original war aim was not the reconstruction, or better, construction, of a twenty-first-century Afghanistan but rather to bring to justice those responsible for the 9/11 attacks. This was the argument made by President George W. Bush on September 20, 2001: "Our grief has turned to anger and anger to resolution. Whether we bring our enemies to justice or bring justice to our enemies, justice will be done."[35]

Note, Bush could have said, "our grief has turned to anger and our anger to hatred. We will revenge ourselves on our enemies. We will rain down wrath until we have destroyed them, their families ..." Yet he did not do so.

To this point we have established that self-defense and punishment of aggression are moral war aims that should result in victory. Third, and related to the notion of self-defense, victory as *self-determination* by national groups fighting oppression in the pursuit of self-government may be moral. National self-determination has been a fixture of modern international life since at least the nineteenth century, with the rise of ethno-nationalist claims to statehood across Europe and the consolidation, in at least two cases, of new, major ethno-national states (Italy and Germany). A subcurrent of World War I was national self-determination, which was seething below the surface in the Austro-Hungarian and Ottoman empires. With their loss at the hands of the Allies, both empires broke up. This "natural" process was accompanied by an ideology of self-determination in Woodrow Wilson's Fourteen Points and the Charter of the League of Nations. Wilson called for the "natural" and "absolutely unmolested opportunity of autonomous development" for ethno-national groups in the lands of these disintegrating empires.[36] The politics surrounding the writing and ratification of the League of Nations Charter took a different turn, with pressure from colonial powers like Great Britain and France to occupy former Ottoman lands while at the same time not jeopardizing their own colonies elsewhere. The Charter's language stated that it was a "sacred trust" for governments to "advance" colonial territories, under the mandate system, to political and economic development.[37] A new wave of post-colonial self-determination and independence movements ultimately helped cause the collapse of most European colonies in the decade following World War II. These were often justified under the language of the 1941 Atlantic Charter and especially the Charter of the United Nations (see Articles 55, 73, 77).[38] Indeed, the U.S. was sympathetic to indigenous, anti-colonial movements, leading to stances such as not supporting its close allies Britain and France during the 1956 Suez Crisis.

Self-determination as a legal concept in the context of war has been recognized in various covenants, most notably the recognition of non-state combatants fighting for national liberation (i.e. freedom fighters) in the First Protocol to the Geneva Convention of 1949. Such groups have a clear chain of command, distinguish themselves by some form of uniform or explicit marking, have declared themselves to be at "war" with an external governing power, and confine themselves to actions consonant with the law of armed conflict. It is beyond the scope of this chapter to discuss all of the controversies regarding these issues and potential cases from the American War for Independence to Bangsamoro groups in the Philippines today, but it is useful to note that the law of armed conflict does recognize the use of armed force in pursuit of national liberation by legitimate, representative groups. Clearly, if the cause of national liberation were to be just, then winning victory would, in theory, be a morally good end. To be clear, national self-determination as a war aim does not justify terrorism against civilians or other *jus in bello* violations: it is simply false that one man's terrorist is another man's freedom fighter. But, in terms of indigenous legitimate authority, right intention, and just cause, the objective of self-determination may be a moral end and victory may be a vindication of this end.

Fourth, victorious armed humanitarian intervention may meet the notion that victory is an appropriate war aim. There is an ever-growing literature on the morality of armed humanitarian intervention, but for the purpose of this chapter we will look at some of the most famous and enduring arguments that provide the foundation for much of the latest thinking on these issues. Hence, James Turner Johnson's *Morality and Contemporary Warfare* provides a thoughtful summary of the presuppositions and arguments justifying intervention made by Paul Ramsey, Michael Walzer, and the U.S. Council of Catholic Bishops.[39] All agree that, as a war aim, there are times that intervention is justified. Although the language is not that of victory, the conclusion is obvious: if intervention is justified, then surely winning is morally laudable?

From a *jus ad bellum* perspective, Johnson records Ramsey's argument that the right of intervention follows "not from the power, but from the responsibility, to intervene":

> States possess the right only insofar as they experience this responsibility as an obligation to act in the service of justice in the international arena ... With the overall context thus set for moral reasoning about intervention, Ramsey narrows his focus to define the allowable grounds for intervention, distinguishing two sorts: "ultimate," or "just war," grounds and "penultimate," or "secondary," ones. The former include "the requirements of justice, order ... the national and international common good, and domestic and international law." Ramsey also recognizes limits: "What needs morally to be done in the world always requires resources far greater than those available. The statesman ... is not called to office to aim at all the humanitarian good that can be aimed at in the world. Instead he must determine what he ought to do from out of the total humanitarian ought to be." Good statecraft involves careful choices among the possibilities for moral action. A justified intervention, then, is not one that serves this "ought to be" alone, any more than it would be one that served national interest alone.[40]

When it comes to Michael Walzer's exploration of intervention, Johnson cites a passage from Walzer's *Just and Unjust Wars*. Walzer argues that there are times when the principle of sovereignty may not

> seem to serve the purpose for which it was intended: (1) intervention in civil wars involving states in which there are two or more political communities, when one community resorts to force for the purpose of secession or "national liberation"; (2) counter-intervention in a conflict to offset a prior intervention by another power; and (3) intervention to counter extreme violations of human rights by fighters in the course of an armed conflict or by a government against its people. It is this latter that has been the most consistent focus of inquiry since the end of the Cold War.[41]

Johnson also references the U.S. Conference of Catholic Bishops, which has, on two occasions in the past generation, issued major letters on issues of war, peace, and peace-making: the 1983 *The Challenge of Peace*[42] and the 1993 *The Harvest of Justice*.[43] The former was largely written with nuclear annihilation in mind; the latter was written just as a new era of state disintegration and civil wars followed the collapse of the Soviet Union and its influence. As Johnson reports, in 1993 the bishops did support armed humanitarian intervention: "The forceful, direct intervention by one or more states or international organizations in the internal affairs of other states for essentially humanitarian purposes," including alleviating "internal chaos, repression and widespread loss of life." The aim of such intervention is "to protect human life and basic human rights" in such contexts.[44]

Such intervention, the statement continues, has been termed "obligatory" by Pope John Paul II "where the survival of populations and entire ethnic groups is seriously compromised." Under such circumstances, the Pope sees it as "a duty for nations and the international community." The argument here, like Ramsey's, is one of shared responsibility by governments to uphold human rights in international life. Johnson cites the bishops' letter:

> nevertheless, [considering] populations who are succumbing to the attacks of an unjust aggressor, states no longer have a "right to indifference." It seems clear that their duty is to disarm the aggressor if all other means have proved ineffective. The principles of sovereignty of states and of noninterference in their internal affairs cannot constitute a screen behind which torture and murder may be carried out.[45]

Ramsey, Walzer, and the Catholic Bishops' arguments have influenced succeeding scholars dealing with these issues, most notably the Responsibility to Protect (R2P) doctrine and reflections, as well as counterfactuals, considering Rwanda, Congo, Sudan, Afghanistan, Iraq, Kosovo, Bosnia, and Syria. Many of these cases are particularly tough because they move beyond the scope of *armed [humanitarian] intervention,* beyond the normal activities of war-fighting units: stabilization operations, reconstruction and rebuilding projects, law enforcement and rule-of-law activities (e.g. peace maintenance, constabulary services, courts), infrastructure construction and protection, the re-establishment of normal political institutions and procedures, and the like. In other words, it is one thing to call it victory when the killing is halted, as Vietnam did when it toppled Pol Pot in 1978 or UN peacekeepers, led by Australia, did in East Timor in 1999. Victory is going to be contextual in such cases, but that simply means that interveners should define it as clearly and early as possible, both in terms of objectives and in terms of investiture of resources. In short, few would argue—at least in principle—that there are not cases where armed humanitarian intervention is morally justified. Many point to the genocide in Rwanda and elsewhere as cases in point. In such instances, the war aim should be some clearly defined notion of victory.

Victory matters prudentially and morally

Victory matters. Like many other realms of human activity and relationships, inconclusive, doubtful, ambiguous pseudo-endings result in confusion and suffering. The just war tradition emphasizes prudence in real-world human affairs. This is especially true with regard to war.

There are at least four ways that victory is important. The first is that victory breaks cycles of tit for tat. Many wars, particularly in the developing world, are "low-intensity conflicts," civil wars, or other long-enduring, slowly simmering conflicts. This unending cycle of distrust, destruction, and occasional mass violence makes the idea of peace ephemeral, in part because no one can remember a time before war. Victory changes everything. Victory stops dead the cycle of interminable action, reaction, counter-reaction. This is an important point often missed by Americans because, with the exception of Vietnam, Americans typically experienced wars prior to 9/11 as tidy, short, and chronologically bounded: the War of 1812 (2.5 years), the Mexican–American War (22 months), the Spanish–American War (8 months), the U.S. Civil War (4 years), World War I (19 months), World War II (3 years, 8 months), the Korean Conflict (3 years), the first Persian Gulf War (7 months), and the 1999 Kosovo War (3 months).[46]

This is not how many people in the rest of the world have experienced wars. Thomas Hobbes, a native of persistently rainy England, satirically observed:

> For war consisteth not in battle only, or the act of fighting; but in a tract of time, wherein the will to contend by battle is sufficiently known: and therefore the notion of time, is to be considered in the nature of war; as it is in the nature of weather. For as the nature of foul weather, lieth not in a shower or two of rain; but in an inclination thereto of many days together: so the nature of war, consisteth not in actual fighting; but in the known disposition thereto, during all the time there is no assurance to the contrary. All other time is "peace."[47]

Individuals in today's greater Middle East or the Philippines or Afghanistan or Sudan have much in common with Europeans of previous centuries or the Greeks, Romans, Persians, and Carthaginians of antiquity. In Sudan, modern warfare erupted a year before independence in 1958[48] and lasted for a quarter-century, before a decade-long uncertain hiatus and then a second outbreak that burned an additional eighteen years, culminating in the Comprehensive Peace Agreement in 2005.[49] Today's two Sudans remains volatile and violent. So too, every Afghan child and parent knows nothing but war; even most grandparents do not remember a time of peace. The same is true for many in the Great Lakes and western (Atlantic) stretches of Africa and in a myriad of other locales, from Jerusalem to Karachi, and from the jungles of the Philippines to the rain forests of Colombia. These wars drain treasuries, denude the environment, destroy already-weak infrastructure, and make the trust necessary for peace seem impossible. Decisive victory can break the cycle and provide an opportunity for a more secure and enduring order.

Second, victory can establish the basis for a new status quo, one that is more secure than the previous conditions of instability and/or injustice. We are reminded of Augustine's argument that the end of war is a "better state of peace."[50] This suggests that the environment before the outbreak of some hot wars was unstable and perhaps unjust. Just warriors and just political leaders should, assuming a moral *casus belli* and ethical restraint in how war is fought, fight to win and thereby establish a better peace. It is hard to imagine how defeat or long-term stalemate, again assuming just beginnings, will result in such a "better" state. Certainly many victories that we venerate, such as those that established the Concert of Vienna or the post–World War II liberal order, are treasured not just for the sacrifice entailed but also for resolving of security and moral paradoxes of the past, however imperfectly.

Third, victory roots the present in the future. Indeed, winning is the first invest-ment in the future. Victory lays the first stones in a new foundation of political order and may set societies on a path to justice and perhaps conciliation. Winning, and how winning is achieved, is not divorced from post-conflict, but it is a critical step in establishing the post-war order. A just victory is often expensive, but victors should not immediately shy away from investing in peace. Rather, some of the investment of revenue and energy that went into war can be redirected to establishing the conditions and institution of an orderly peace and conditions of justice, perhaps even conciliation. Victory makes this possible. Victory allows for some remediation or reversal of the causes of the war as well as space for justice claims stemming from how the war was fought. Wars that do not end conclusively lack these opportunities. Unfortunately, winning works both ways: victory for an oppressive regime, like the Nazis in 1939 or the Soviets in 1945, can establish an unjust order.

Fourth, victory may allow good to triumph over evil. I realize that we are speaking both in ideal and relative terms: ideal because few wars have the heinous evil of Nazism so clearly exposed, and relative because we live in an imperfect world with limitations, errors, and wrongdoing on all sides that may have to be addressed. The Allies understood this and court-martialed some of their own for wrongdoing, such as theft and rape, at the end of World War II. Nonetheless, victory is important in beating aggressors, torturers, despoilers, rapists, and enslavers because it calls to account wrongdoers and publicly declares those activities as wrong. Victory provides the opportunity to vindicate values. It is one thing to claim that the Japanese concentration camps were wrong from the sidelines; it is a far different and morally important enterprise to defeat those governments, liberate the slaves, re-establish human rights, and promote national and international security.

Conclusion

Victory may take a variety of forms: a Fabian posture of defense, offensive war that overcomes a battlefield and political adversary, or the vindication of a political worldview. Until recently the moral and prudential value of victory was assumed, but changes in the destructive power of humanity's weapons as well as changing values in the West have made victory a concept under strain. Just war scholars, including this author, have either assumed too much or said too little about the eth-ical imperative of victory and its links to war aims, *jus ad bellum* criteria, and *jus post bellum*. Moreover, the disjuncture between citizens and academics seems even more pronounced, with the former investing their children and tax dollars in the national security enterprise, only to often be scolded by members of the intelligentsia that national sacrifice is meaningless, wars cannot or should not be won, and winners are bullies, colonizers, and warmongers.

More work needs to be done. This chapter has focused on an under-appreciated issue in contemporary military and political ethics: the moral intersection of war aims and victory. An additional important step, but one which has received greater recent attention, is to consider how the way that war is fought is intertwined with realizing victory. The just war tradition has quite a bit to say about the boundaries of proportionality and discrimination when it comes to self-defense and survival (i.e. supreme emergency), but more is needed on how the evolution of combat realities on actual battlefields over a period of time correspondingly changes notions of victory. For instance, as Chapter 4 discusses, U.S. involvement in Vietnam in 1962 was not the same as its involvement with the Vietnamese in 1972; British involvement in Afghanistan in 2013 was not the same as British involvement a decade (or a century) earlier. In short, notions of responsibility for what one has done change, and this needs greater explanation in a subsequent chapter. The next generation needs to proceed toward victory, when necessary, with these debates in mind so that they can act with both thoughtful restraint and appropriate boldness.

Notes

1 I.C.B. Dear and M.R.D. Foot, *Oxford Companion to World War II* (Oxford: Oxford University Press, 2005), p. 290; John W. Dower, *War Without Mercy* (New York Pantheon, 1986), p. 11.

2 Winston Churchill, "Blood, Toil, Tears and Sweat," Speech delivered to the House of Commons (May 13, 1940), available at: www.winstonchurchill.org/resources/speeches/1940-the-finest-hour/blood-toil-tears-and-sweat.

3 Franklin D. Roosevelt, "Pearl Harbor Speech: Day of Infamy," Digital History, ID 1082, available at: www.digitalhistory.uh.edu/disp_textbook.cfm?smtID=3&psid=1082 (accessed December 1, 2017).

4 At Potsdam, President Harry S. Truman led the U.S. delegation due to the recent death of his predecessor.

5 Quoted in Michael Walzer, *Just and Unjust Wars*, third ed. (New York: Basic Books, 2000), p. 118.

6 Leo Tolstoy, *War and Peace* (Oxford: Oxford University Press, 2000), p. 524.

7 Haig's quote is from his "final dispatch," dated March 21, 1919. Foch's dispatch in complete primary textual forms is available at: www.firstworldwar.com/source (accessed September 5, 2016). Foch's quote has been widely replayed, and can be found in *Littell's Living Age*, vol. 298 (E. Littell & Company, 1918), p. 264, available at: https://play.google.com/store/books/details?id=9wY4AQAAIAAJ&rdid=book-9wY4AQAAIAAJ&rdot=1 (accessed September 5, 2016).

8 Michael Howard and Peter Paret, *Clausewitz: On War* (Princeton, NJ: Princeton University Press, 1994).

9 Walzer, *Just and Unjust Wars*. See his argument in chapter 7, "War's Ends, and the Importance of Winning Well."

10 John David Lewis, *Nothing Less Than Victory: Decisive Wars and the Lessons of History* (Princeton, NJ: Princeton University Press, 2013), p. 1.

11 Ibid.

12 Nigel Biggar, *In Defense of War* (Oxford: Oxford University Press, 2015); J. Daryl Charles, *Between Pacifism and Jihad: The Christian and the Just War* (Colorado Springs, CO: Intervarsity Press); James Turner Johnson, *Morality and Contemporary Warfare* (New Haven, CT: Yale University Press, 1999); Oliver O'Donovan, *The Just War Revisited* (Cambridge: Cambridge University Press).

13 For a recent application to Syria, see "The Pottery Barn Rule: Syria Edition," *The Atlantic* (September 30, 2015), available at: www.theatlantic.com/international/archive/2015/09/the-pottery-barn-rule-syria-edition/408193/.

14 Michael Walzer, *Arguing About War* (New Haven, CT: Yale University Press, 2009). See his arguments in chapter 5 on "The Politics of Rescue" and the final sub-chapter on "Just and Unjust Occupations."

15 Eric Patterson and Roger C. Mason. "Why Kosovo Doesn't Matter—And How It Should," *International Politics*, vol. 47, no. 1 (2010).

16 John Dryden and Arthur Hugh, *Plutarch's Lives*, English translation (New York: Modern Library, 2001).

17 Reinhold Niebuhr, *The Irony of American History* (New York: Scribner's, 1952), p. 4.

18 Gabriel Kolko, *Confronting the Third World: United States Foreign Policy 1945–1980* (New York: Pantheon, 1988).

19 Immanuel Wallerstein, *The Modern World-System I: Capitalist Agriculture and the Origins of the European World-Economy in the Sixteenth Century* (New York: Academic Press, 1978).

20 F.H. Cardoso and E. Faletto, *Dependency and Development in Latin America*, transl. M.M. Urquidi (Berkley and Los Angeles: University of California Press, 1979); Paul James, "Post-Dependency: The Third World in an Era of Globalism and Late Capitalism," *Alternatives: Social Transformation and Human Governance*, vol. 2, no. 22 (1997).

21 It is noteworthy that Afghanistan does not have oil wealth, yet I've been told many times that the 2001 Afghanistan invasion was to gain access to oil.

22 Jean Bethke Elshtain, *Just War against Terror* (New York: Basic Books, 2003).

23 This is discussed at length in Eric Patterson, *Just War Thinking: Pragmatism and Morality in the Struggle against Contemporary Threats* (Lanham, MD: Lexington Books, 2007).

24 James Turner Johnson, *The Just War Tradition and the Restraint of War: A Moral and Historical Inquiry* (Princeton, NJ: Princeton University Press, 1981).

25 J. Daryl Charles and Timothy Demy, *War, Peace, and Christianity: Questions and Answers from a Just War Perspective* (Wheaton, IL: Crossway, 2010).

26 Ibid., p. 68.

27 Stefan Theil, "German Soldiers Can't Shoot," *The Daily Beast* (June 26, 2011), available at: www.thedailybeast.com/articles/2011/06/26/german-soldiers-can-t-shoot.html (accessed September 5, 2016).

28 Jessica Donati and Habib Khan Totakhil, "U.S. Military Rules of Engagement in Afghanistan Questioned," *Wall Street Journal* (February 1, 2016), available at: www.wsj.com/articles/u-s-military-rules-of-engagement-in-afghanistan-questioned-1454349100 (accessed September 5, 2016); Edwin Mora, "Top US Commander in Afghanistan: I Do Not Have the Authority to Attack Taliban Just Because They Are Taliban," *Breitbart* (February 2, 2016), available at: www.breitbart.com/national-security/2016/02/02/top-u-s-commander-in-afghanistan-i-do-not-have-authority-to-attack-taliban-just-because-theyre-taliban/ (accessed September 5, 2016); Rowan Scarborough, "Rules of engagement limit the actions of U.S. troops and drones in Afghanistan," *The Washington Times* (November 26, 2013), available at: www.washingtontimes.com/news/2013/nov/26/rules-of-engagement-bind-us-troops-actions-in-afgh/ (accessed September 5, 2016).

29 Charles and Demy.

30 Churchill.

31 See David Cordingly, *The Billy Ruffian: The Bellerophon and the Downfall of Napoleon* (New York: Bloomsbury USA, 2003); Philip Dwyer, *The French Revolution and Napoleon: A Sourcebook* (London: Routledge, 2002.); Alan Schom, *One Hundred Days: Napoleon's Road to Waterloo* (San Francisco: Harper-Collins, 1998).

32 "Milosevic Charged with Bosnian Genocide," BBC News (November 23, 2001), available at: http://news.bbc.co.uk/2/hi/europe/1672414.stm. Note, Milosevic was ultimately arrested locally for election fraud and then turned over to the international community.

33 Brian Orend, *War and International Justice* (Ontario: Wilfred Laurier University Press, 2000); Eric Patterson, *Ending Wars Well: Just War Theory in Post-Conflict* (New Haven, CT: Yale University Press, 2012); Nigel Biggar, "Making Peace or Doing Justice: Must We Choose?" and Jean Bethke Elshtain, "Politics and Forgiveness," in *Burying the Past: Making Peace and Doing Justice after Civil Conflict*, ed. Nigel Biggar (Washington, DC: Georgetown University Press, 2003); Mohamed Othman, "Justice and Reconciliation," and Howard Adelman, "Rule-Based Reconciliation," in *Roads to Reconciliation*, ed. Elin Skaar, Siri Gloppen, and Astri Suhrke (Lanham, MD: Lexington Books, 2005).

34 Fritz Stern and Elisabeth Sifton, *No Ordinary Men: Dietrich Bonhoeffer and Hans von Dohnanyi: Resisters against Hitler in Church and State* (New York: New York Review Books Collections, 2013).

35 George W. Bush, National Address (2001), available at: www.washingtonpost.com/wp-srv/nation/specials/attacked/transcripts/bushaddress_092001.html.

36 "President Woodrow Wilson's Fourteen Points, 8 January, 1918," The Avalon Project, available at: http://avalon.law.yale.edu/20th_century/wilson14.asp (accessed September 8, 2016).

37 "The Covenant of the League of Nations," The Avalon Project, available at: http://avalon.law.yale.edu/20th_century/leagcov.asp (accessed September 8, 2016).

38 In practice, self-determination was a major component of what Huntington identified as the first two "waves" of democratization, with popular sovereignty (a domestic analogue of self-determination) driving the third and ostensible fourth waves. See Samuel P. Huntington, *The Third Wave: Democratization in the Late Twentieth Century* (Oklahoma City: University of Oklahoma Press, 1993).

39 Johnson, *Morality and Contemporary Warfare*.

40 Ibid., pp. 77–78.

41 Johnson is quoting directly from Walzer, *Just and Unjust Wars*, second ed. (New York: Basic Books, 1992), p. 90.

42 Johnson, *Morality and Contemporary Warfare*, p. 91.

43 Ibid.

44 Ibid., pp. 92–93.

45 Ibid., pp. 95–96.

46 Zoltan Grossman, "From Wounded Knee to Syria: A Century of U.S. Military Interventions," Evergreen State College (2014), available at: http://academic.evergreen.edu/g/grossmaz/interventions.html.

47 Thomas Hobbes, *Leviathan*, ed. Edwin Curley (Indianapolis, IN: Hackett, 1994), ch. 13, par. 8.

48 Helen Chapin Metz, *Sudan: Country Study* (Washington, DC: Library of Congress, 1994), available at: https://cdn.loc.gov/master/frd/frdcstdy/su/sudancountrystud00metz/sudancountrystud00metz.pdf.

49 Eric Patterson and John Lango, "South Sudan Independence: International Contingency Planning and Just War Theory," *International Journal of Applied Philosophy* (Fall 2010).

50 Augustine, *The City of God*, ed. David Knowles (New York: Penguin Classics, 2000).

10

CONCLUSION

Just war dilemmas since 9/11

For at least the last half-century it has been said that there is an "American way of war." It has also been said that the U.S. military is characterized by leading successive "next generations of warfare" and/or the next "revolution in military affairs." I agree that there is an American way of war. I disagree that the only way to understand the U.S. way of war, and American leadership, is in terms of technology and material resources.

Historians have been using the idea of an American way of war since the U.S. Civil War. The Union army, woefully unprepared for war, had to steadily build up, over time, its manpower and technological resources. Eventually, the North marshaled overwhelming financial resources, manpower, and military strength to crush its adversary. This incremental, industrial American way of war supported the Allies during World War I and was "the arsenal of democracy" in World War II. Max Boot, citing historian Russell Weigley's famous book, writes, "[America] won not by tactical or strategic brilliance but by the sheer weight of numbers—the awesome destructive power that only a fully mobilized and highly industrialized democracy can bring to bear. In all these conflicts, U.S. armies composed of citizen-soldiers suffered and inflicted massive casualties."[1] The concept assumes that the United States is slow to wrath, and chooses not to maintain a large standing military force. This was true at least until the 1950s. Nevertheless, dormancy followed by mobilizing and deploying awesome resources is not the best way to think about an American way of war. A second, related American-way-of-war literature emphasizes the role of superior technology and innovation, with the U.S. being uniquely suited both to adapt and to innovate. This is true from the Gatling gun to the era of Rosie the Riveter to the real-world legacy of Ronald Reagan's Strategic Defense Initiative. Often this writing looks back to historical innovations, such as the advent of gunpowder, and then observes contemporary "next-gen" warfare and various "revolutions in military affairs," which the U.S. military helpfully abbreviates to RMA.[2] True, the United States has an amazing capacity for techno-logical innovation, especially in the battle space: stealth aircraft, precision-guided munitions and drones, the Defense Advanced Research Projects Agency (DARPA) and the internet and GPS, and autonomous vehicles. But again, this is not what best characterizes the American way of war.

What makes the U.S. distinct, and characterizes the American way of war all the way back to colonial times, is *ideas*: the widespread discussion and debate about the ethics of war among citizens and leaders. Just war historians realize that this is true, but those moral discussions are largely left to the footnotes of American history. In fact, during every U.S. conflict there has been robust public debate about whether or not to go to war in the first place, and after the decision has been made, debate continued on the ethics of how the war was fought. Moreover, the U.S. is unique in the fact that even when it's victorious, it prosecutes some of its own military per-sonnel who have violated the laws of armed conflict. This simply was not the case in most polities in the past.

Thus, a major dimension of an American way of war, and the chief focus of this book, is a concern with the intersection of politics, military force, and morality. Francis Lieber agreed that this is fundamental. The fifteenth article of his Code states, "Men who take up arms against one another in public war do not cease on this account to be moral beings, responsible to one another and to God." This comports with U.S. history. As a democracy with intellectual and moral roots in Christianity and the Enlightenment, the American public and its institutions have long engaged in contentious deliberation about the morality of warfare.

This concluding chapter looks at some, though not all, of the challenges that Western just war thinking faces today. It begins with reflection on how much the context of just war writing has changed since 9/11 and then advances to some issues about responsibility and authority in a democratic world, technological change, and justice. In part, I am reinforcing arguments that I have made elsewhere about the need for coherent just war thinking applied to contemporary international security. At the same time I am suggesting a research agenda for the next generation of just war thinkers to advance. The most pressing issues for today's, and tomorrow's, just war thinking are not about tactics and tools such as bombs, guns, and drones. Rather, the true challenges come from the dilution and distortion of fundamental just war principles involving authority, just cause, intentions, responsibility, order, and justice. We need moral, practical statesmanship rooted in just war thinking to make the tough, often imperfect, decisions about when to act, when to refrain from action, and how to behave with both boldness and restraint. We also need to think through the implications of democratic processes and procedures, whether nation-ally or internationally, for just war decision-making.

The changing context since 9/11

When the terrorists attacked New York City and Washington, DC, on September 11, 2001, the context and content of just war scholarship was quite different in a number of ways from today, and those differences are important when we think about just war thinking for the 2020s.

Traditional international relations and security studies were still heavily influenced by Cold War thinking, including deterrence, power balancing, the ethics of nuclear weapons, and the like. The Soviet Union and Warsaw Pact had collapsed only a few years earlier and many were justifiably concerned about a new Cold War, characterized by a revanchist Russia (recall Russian troops landing at the same airfield as NATO troops in Kosovo in 1999[3]) and the rise of China (e.g. the F-4 incident in early 2001). However, a different set of themes were also on the rise, with an emphasis on global economic redistribution, transitional justice, prevention of genocide, and empowering international institutions.

These latter issues were typically framed in terms of idealistic, moralistic, views of Western obligation and opportunity. Idealists expected increasing international cooperation through international law and institutions. Some wondered if traditional collective security organizations, like NATO, would follow the Warsaw Pact into extinction; others had an eye on the increasingly assertive UN General Assembly and perhaps drastic reform of the UN Security Council, to make the latter more inclusive of weak states and dilute the power of the Big Five). This idealism was perhaps best stated by those who called the West's intervention in Kosovo "illegal" because it lacked UN Security Council authorization. In other words, the idealists were so convinced of the rightness of process and rules in their brave new world that saving civilians from Slobodan Milosevic's ethnic cleansing was secondary.

We can see this idealistic ideology at work in many ways when it comes to conflict and its resolution. An example is the "Responsibility to Protect" (R2P). R2P is idealistic because it goes far beyond stopping the killing by envisioning the transformation of post-conflict societies at the expense of international norms like sovereignty.

The *Responsibility to Protect* document derived from a Canadian-sponsored initiative to galvanize international support for a robust intervention mandate in grotesque cases of human suffering. Canada is keenly aware of this issue: it was a Canadian General who oversaw the failed UN mission in Rwanda during the 1994 genocide. Between Rwanda, Bosnia, and other terrible wars, R2P's proponents asserted a moral responsibility to intervene on behalf of human life and a related "responsibility to rebuild in the three most immediately crucial areas of security, justice and economic development." To summarize, the "responsibility to rebuild" is to impose security, install juridical and law enforcement mechanisms, and deeply invest in economic development.[4]

At first glance, the International Commission on Intervention and State Sovereignty's "responsibility to rebuild" sounds akin to this book's approach to *jus post bellum*. In part, this is due to R2P's rehearsal of just war tenets (proportionality, discrimination) and its emphasis on decisively stopping the killing and on basic security. Nonetheless, the "responsibility to rebuild" says nothing about the deeper context-specific philosophical questions about the nature of political order and the implementation of post-conflict justice. Strangely, it calls only for the apprehension of intervening troops who violate the laws of armed conflict, remaining mute on punishing those who initiated the conflict or locals who violate the war convention. On domestic justice it offers the following cookie-cutter approach: "A number of non-governmental bodies have developed 'justice packages,' which can be adapted to the specific conditions of a wide variety of operations"[5] In short, the "responsibility to rebuild" puts zero responsibility on the host nation while imposing huge obligations on interveners, assuming that a "package" of Western institutions and monies will somehow make everything turn out alright. Hence, whereas R2P begins with a noble aspiration—to save human life—the "responsibility to rebuild" shows its true colors: it is a grand scheme for nation-building, financial transfers from Western donors, and political transformation; it is not, on paper at least, characterized by restraint. Ironically, R2P's heyday was short-lived. When the Iraq and Afghanistan wars spiraled out of control, the developing world realized that it really did not welcome Western armed intervention.

The second, related idealistic trend in ethics-of-war scholarship was pre- and post-conflict redistribution of wealth. At the heart of this was the view that the "root cause" of war is individual poverty and societal resource scarcity. This notion, rooted in modernization and secularization theories, argued that the ethno-nationalist and religio-cultural wars of the 1980s (Bosnia, Sudan, Iraq–Iran, Pakistan–India, Sri Lanka) were not caused by clashes between civilizations or wars of ideas, but simply by the power politics that resulted from economic injustice. This myth was popular among Western elites until Islamic State (ISIS) shattered it, proving that it and its predecessors (e.g. al Qaeda, Hezbollah, Hamas) were motivated by their understanding of their religious obligations and/or had religiously determined legitimations for violence. This view is idealistic because it relies on a belief that simply raising the standard of living for people around the globe will overcome chauvinism and violence, and especially because prejudice is informed by ideational, rather than solely material, elements.

A third idealistic trend in writing on the ethics of war and international affairs just before 9/11 was the effort to create an International Criminal Court (ICC). This was founded in 1999 under the Rome Statute. The idea was to go beyond past international law criminalizing aggression and establish a new institution with the mandate to do so. This occurred at the same time that the UN-sponsored international tribunals for Rwanda and the former Yugoslavia were just finding their footing. Those interested in justice, as I am, welcome efforts at international justice, but what makes the ICC idealistic is that the justification for its establishment was not to punish wrongdoers, but that it would be a deterrent to future aggression. It is hard to imagine that there is any national leader or senior military officer in the world who worries about a future trial before the ICC, and the Court has come under fire because its first cases have all been against Africans. What also makes it idealistic is that it erodes state sovereignty in favor of so-called international "norms."

What is worrying is that these grand flourishes may erode established political compacts and order. For example, in the 1980s, long-term autocrats could accept a deal, leave office peacefully, and retire to a private life somewhere at home (as many Latin American Generals did) or abroad (Idi Amin, Ferdinand Marcos). As political scientists Daniel Kemaric and Abel Escribà-Folch have found, the last decade has seen the abrogation of this arrangement, most notably in the hounding of Chile's Augusto Pinochet.[6] This makes it increasingly likely that authoritarians will double down and repress public movements toward democratic transition.

Thus far I have argued that much of the thinking on the nexus of ethics, security, and post-conflict circa 2000 was idealistically critical of the assumptions of the past, such as state sovereignty and non-intervention, favoring idealistic mechanisms to transcend the past through armed humanitarian intervention, wealth transfers and rebuilding, and global justice mechanisms. When it comes to operational just war thinking, similar trends emerged at this time. The first was the privileging of last resort over all other *jus ad bellum* criteria. Here is a university ethicist reflecting on the U.S. intervention in Afghanistan in the autumn of 2001:

> I don't think we can know that it really is a just war until it's over and done with and all of the information has surfaced about what actually happened. At this point in time, I find it very premature to say that this is a just war, particularly considering the reports that residential areas in Afghanistan have in fact been bombed ... One of the foundations of the church's tradition of just-war theory is that it begins with the fundamental assumption that war is *not* justified ... It's true that the common good of the international community is threatened by terrorism. So it is an issue of defending the common good, but even after you look at that "cause," you have to make sure that a violent response that takes human lives is really a "last resort."[7]

The basic idea seemed to be that if armchair experts and philosophers could second-guess the expertise of diplomats and public officials long enough, it would forestall a "rush" to an unjust war. Related to this, and to R2P, was the muddling of the deontological concepts of legitimate authority, just cause, and right intention. Idealists criticized the national interest, arguing that in the twenty-first century only the UN had the legitimate authority to sanction military force. Just cause was limited to those military actions in which the U.S. and its allies could demonstrate that no national interests were involved. Thus, the only appropriate use of the U.S. military was as a humanitarian "force for good"[8] providing global public goods such as search and rescue, counter-piracy, humanitarian relief, logistic and operational capacities, and the like, particularly in the wake of earthquakes, famine, and tsunamis. In its most critical form, this arguments asserted that the global West owes the rest of the world assistance thanks to historical colonialism, imperialism, and other forms of white man's injustice.

This criticism from ethicists and others continues to occur as NATO, and especially the United States, rely more and more on smart weapons to limit collateral damage. Indeed, the past fifteen years can be characterized as a period of almost

Vietnam-like media fascination with civilian casualties, at the hands of Coalition (rather than terrorist) forces in Afghanistan and Iraq. At the same time, the Pentagon expanded, in both its troop training and its public relations, the expansive, expensive effort to limit the loss of human life and private property, to the point of putting U.S. troops at significant additional risk in many instances. But, no matter how precise and limited the work of unmanned aerial vehicles (UAVs), precision-guided munitions, and other "smart" technologies, not to mention how much risk U.S. troops take on, the U.S. military was damned for being too rough, too heavy-handed, and too destructive.

What has been most problematic for recent international relations is the double double-cross that President Obama and his European allies pulled in Libya in 2011. The first double-cross was that the West reneged on the explicit deal of 2003: Libya gave up its nuclear weapons program following robust U.S. intervention in Iraq, in exchange for which the U.S. was not to advance regime change in Libya.[9] Gaddafi did give up his WMD program, which was dismantled and shipped to the U.S. This was a huge international security victory for the George W. Bush administration and for international order more generally. But less than a decade later Gaddafi was deposed by the West, causing regional instability that continues to this day. What lessons did this double-cross send to despots the world over, such as Zimbabwe's Robert Mugabe? Perhaps that it is best to arm oneself and never accommodate the West.

The second double-cross concerns Russia. The West persuaded Russia to endorse a no-fly zone over Libya on the explicit promise of no regime change. That is not what happened, and to this day Russia seethes over what appears to have been deliberate deception. We can see evidence of this not simply in Moscow's rhetoric but in the hardening of the Kremlin's policy in support of Bashar al Assad in Syria. Again, the point has to do with an over-emphasis on idealized justice that works to the practical unraveling of international order.

In sum, a lot has changed in world politics since the early 2000s, and in general, scholars and observers of the ethics of warfare should feel chastened by reality. From the ruthless Taliban to the diabolical ISIS, it is clear that there are motivations for hatred and violence that go far beyond mere poverty. After almost twenty years, the ineffectual war crimes tribunals in the former Yugoslavia and Rwanda finally finished their business in 2018. The results were so modest, and were achieved at so great an expense, that they had to be justified as "recording history" rather than punishing wrongdoers and providing restitution to victims on any scale. The developing world backtracked on R2P within just a few years of trumpeting it as a landmark. The failures of two Arab Springs, the crafty geopolitics of authoritarian China, the reassertion of Russian power, and global Islamist terrorism suggest a return to history, not its end. Fortunately, just war thinking, with enduring roots in the realities of human anthropology, prudence, and justice, provides an organized framework for addressing the ethics of warfare and statecraft, and thus remains well-suited to tackling the evolving challenges of national and international security in the twenty-first century.

Just war thinking and technology

Our technology has caught up with science fiction. Today's computers, networks, robots, and virtual capabilities would have been considered mere fantasy just a generation ago. One would think that after a century of moral quandaries presented, with startling sophistication, by writers like Jules Verne, H.G. Welles, Robert C. Clark, and especially Isaac Asimov, not to mention the writers of *Star Trek* and other cinema, we would be better prepared for the ethics of drones, smart weapons, artificial intelligence, and the like. At the same time, it is ironic that our fiercest adversaries in the past two decades have relied on old-fashioned tactics and savagery that would have been easily recognizable to the Goths and Mongols.

As we think about how just war thinking can and should engage the fantastic present and coming future, the good news is that just war thinking has inherent resources to deal with twenty-first century threats, weapons, and ways of war. That is because just war thinking focuses on issues of legitimacy, political responsibility, and political order first and foremost, and these issues remain rather stable, whether one is facing the Carthaginians or the Klingons. To achieve this engagement, emergent just war thinking needs to focus its attention on the fundamentals, with specific focus on the multi-dimensionality of political authority and how to end wars well.

Unfortunately, much just war thinking of the past half-century has been stuck in a bizarre state of *noblesse oblige*. Western technologies made it increasingly possible to punch from afar, and this felt unsportsmanlike. From aerial bombing of those who could not take to the skies to a host of other technologies that gave the U.K., U.S., and other industrialized powers the technological upper hand, there has been much handwringing among some ethicists that all of this is somehow unfair. The just war tradition does have some roots in the medieval code of chivalry and the tradition of staged individual combat (e.g. jousting, dueling) in which opponents were, at least in theory, evenly matched. It is an unrealistic, romantic image of war that clouds the real issues at hand, such as how inequalities of technology, when restrained by proper authorities or policy, can actually limit the destructiveness of conflict.

Lest just war thinking get stranded in a quagmire of mediocrity, a robust research agenda is needed. There are many areas to consider, but for our purposes three trends should be considered. They are: widening the analysis of threat and what is threatening, carefully examining agency and responsibility, and addressing the blurring of domestic and international realms of activity. Later in the chapter we will also look at the intersection of democracy and just war thinking with a focus on the issues of citizenship, morality, and political responsibility.

Fifteen years ago I argued that just war thinking needed to move beyond simply responding to aggression to action based on threat analysis:

> The twenty-first century security dilemma is that we live in an uncertain environment even if war is not being actively waged on a battlefield. Consequently, in an era of multiple, often undeclared threats to national security, states must take responsibility for preparing for and at times

prosecuting a war against those threats to their security. This means that states need to think about a robust, multi-dimensional security agenda that includes defensive and offensive operations in terms of finance, diplomacy, covert operations, propaganda, and at times military force. Such calculation in the face of threats may resemble the Cold War policy of containment. In other contexts, it may justify preemptive or preventive war as well as military humanitarian intervention. In short, it is irresponsible, an abdication of responsibility, for states to not act.[10]

It is even truer today that governments should focus on threats. The ubiquitous attempts to violate our electronic systems in every domain—government, military, economic, personal—suggest that the cyber-world is indeed Hobbesian. We are in a never-ending low-intensity conflict that is being waged all around us. Add to the cyber realm the issues of terrorism, WMDs, and organized crime and one recognizes that governments must be on a constant war-footing against the forces of lawlessness and violence. Just war thinking should not get bogged down in the micro-elements of a given technology. Instead, we should focus attention on the responsibility that legitimate political authorities have to defend the lives, livelihoods, and way of life of their citizens. This includes thoughtfully considering preventive and preemptive action in the context of the instantaneity of the digital world, where the capacity of nefarious actors to do significant harm may be unconstrained by the types of chronological and geographical barriers to destructive power that we took for granted in the past.

A related point, in terms of threats, is the democratization of weaponry that has exponentially elevated the destructive potential of individuals and small, non-state actors. The worst that an individual could have done in the past was assassination of a head of state. However, it is possible today for an individual or small group to wreak havoc on their adversaries, whether through a cyber-attack, a dirty bomb, or a weapon of mass effect such as an electromagnetic pulse (EMP) device. These tools were not available outside of state hands until very recently, but they could be devastating today in an increasingly networked, energy-reliant world. Hollywood has made millions of dollars forecasting the chaos that would follow an EMP blast in Shanghai, London, or New York, but just war thinkers have done little to address how calculations of risk and threat should be a part of the responsibilities for reflection and action incumbent upon national political leaders.

There is some intelligent, nuanced thinking occurring that explores issues of moral agency and moral responsibility when it comes to technology, usually with a focus on artificial intelligence (AI) and unmanned force-employing technologies.[11] The science fiction concern about AI had to do with limiting the possibilities of technology's independence, such as via Asimov's Three Laws of Robotics, lest a robot such as Skynet awaken and decide, in a Darwinian twist, that humans are the problem and should be eliminated.[12] Whether or not such is really a long-term problem, at present there are some pressing, overlapping considerations that require more just war thinking.

The first has to do with inhuman speeds of decision-making. The U.S. Air Force trains its pilots to Observe, Orient, Decide, and Act and then do it again: the famous OODA loop. The goal for American strategists since the first Gulf War in 1991 has been to disrupt the enemy's OODA loop, such as by the cutting of command, control, and communications functions, while at the same time the U.S. OODA loop is moving quickly and reliably based on real-time data, superior preparation, and computerized forecasting.[13] The U.S. can therefore decide and respond more quickly and flexibly than its enemies. However, with increasingly complex technological systems that are moving at light speed, it is increasingly difficult for the human overseers of technology to respond with prudence. During the Cold War, there were famous cases of near nuclear war due to minor errors, usually checked by a courageous junior officer somewhere in a remote missile silo. At today's high speeds, will there be time to think before automatic action? This is particularly true as cyber-systems are constructed to respond immediately and dynamically to probes and attacks. Clearly there are multiple technical, logistical, and ethical issues embedded in this discussion, such as how software safeguards to prevent intrusion by nefarious actors may make it difficult to exercise friendly control over malfunctions or unintended actions.

Second, fast, powerful, semi-autonomous technology operates at the edge of (though not beyond) human accountability and the speed of dynamic solutions, which means that it may be impossible to retrieve mistakes or change course when new information is received. Moreover, in the case of malfunction, again the speed and complexity of systems may make it impossible for humans to stop or modify the automatic nature of some weapons. Who then is "responsible?" And is it even appropriate to hold "someone" responsible for an unseen technical glitch or error, or even worse, for the unexpected action of a technology that is logically following its inherent protocols?

Finally, and worryingly, the technicians who build and maintain these weapon are unlikely to be schooled in just war thinking. Just like arms manufacturers of the past, they are typically utilitarians. They are not, however, elected leaders, experienced field officers, or just war experts. This means that both in coding and in application it is likely that the types of parameters and safeguards that just war thinking would want may never be considered as essential in the writing of the code's DNA.

One of the things that we should be reminded of by the past quarter-century is the disconnect between policy, positive international law, and technological abilities. The capabilities of technology move so fast as to leave international lawyers dithering at the negotiating table even when the technology being debated has been surpassed.

This is not the case for ethics. The deontological nature of the primary just war criteria, as well as the prudential nature of the secondary criteria, means that thoughtful reflection can be applied to a variety of novel weapons, tactics, and technologies. This is going to be increasingly important as change continues apace in technological warfare. But the focus, again, should be on forcing political authorities to take responsibility for thoughtful ethical analysis and not simply rely on utilitarianism.

Related to the law/ethics dilemma is the increasing overlap, or better, loss of distinction, between domestic and international uses of force. In the U.S., in particular, our political and legal tradition sharply delineates the domestic (local and state law enforcement, the FBI) from national security and international law enforcement (e.g. Department of Defense, CIA, etc.). We do this for reasons going back to colonial times when British troops systematically violated the rights of average citizens. Nevertheless, the past two decades have seen the steady erosion of the difference, for reasons both mundane (e.g. better disaster coordination after Hurricane Katrina) and strategic (global terrorism after 9/11). Hence, just war thinking will continue to be consulted on a wide range of use-of-force scenarios, to include those of intrusive surveillance, law enforcement's application of deadly force, non-lethal weaponry, and the like.

The good news is, again, that just war thinking has a rich history of such analysis. Historically there was little difference between the domestic and international uses of force: all who wielded the sword legitimately were deputized as agents of the state, and thus just war thinking applied to the decision-makers as well as to the concrete activities of their subordinates. Indeed, it may be helpful for the current generation of just war thinkers to worry less about the distinction between soldiers and police and focus more on issues of how force is utilized, and restrained, appropriately. An obvious application of this is to international peacekeeping troops operating under the auspices of the United Nations, but the application is clearly far wider as well.

Just war and GI Joe

For the majority of Western just war history, the focus has been on the decisions that elites, in or out of uniform, made. The basic justness of war rested on the shoulders of Scipio Africanus, Charlemagne, Wellington, Lincoln, Churchill, and their subordinate commanders. This was true at the strategic as well as the operational and tactical levels: the troops were to follow orders.

This facelessness and namelessness of the *hoi polloi* does not sit well with the American national spirit for a number of reasons, from the volunteer ethos that has characterized America's warriors since the seventeenth century to the social mobility of American society. For our purposes, there are two contemporary issues that require further consideration. Both have to do with the moral value of the average Joe in uniform.

The first issue is theoretical: the concept of military necessity needs to be reintroduced to just war thinking. Every military manual explicates the importance of the principle of military necessity, which was defined earlier as the idea that battlefield commanders may take actions on the battlefield that meet battlefield objectives—even if there is some harm to civilians or private property—if those actions do not otherwise violate the laws of war.[14] Throughout history, military necessity was taken for granted because it implies stewardship of men and materiel. Military ethicists such as Francis Lieber and the regulations of Western national militaries rely on the historical, prudential principle of military necessity because it is central to victory and troop protection. In contrast, today's just war scholars almost never talk about military necessity, particularly since the Vietnam era. This is true of both secular and religiously informed just war writing. Sadly, the idealistic orientation of academic and religious just war writing attempts to impose so many limits on military operations as to make those operations impossible to even launch. Often there is an anti-military sentiment lurking in that literature. In other words, to many such writers, the destructiveness of war is illegitimate, unlawful, and criminal and so are its agents.

Interwoven with the loss of military necessity is the presupposition, obvious in much of the contemporary philosophical literature on just war, that soldiers' lives are worth less, far less, than the lives of civilians. We see evidence of this in the call for dramatic limitations on how force can be employed by the good guys (not just the bad guys). The assumption seems to be that once an individual puts on the uniform, their life is worth significantly less than the lives of civilians. This is a trade-off: the authorization to kill makes someone less morally valuable than someone else who does not have that authorization. This line of thinking suggests that the troops should go to extraordinary lengths to save and protect private property and individual, civilian lives.

I am not disputing the importance of proper discrimination and proportionality, but it is important to rethink some of our presuppositions about the moral worth of citizen-soldiers. In a democracy, every citizen matters. Soldiers are not second-class citizens. This just as true when Socrates served as a hoplite as when John Rawls was a GI in the Pacific during World War II. Indeed, in the case of Rawls and his fellow GIs, they were unwilling participants in a war started by Imperial Japan. On December 7, 1941, only about 300,000 Americans were serving in the military. Pearl Harbor compelled students, bakers, farmers, merchants, mechanics, teachers, and many others to become warriors. Why should their lives count for less, when one is doing the cost–benefit analyses, than the lives of Japanese civilians? Both when it comes to the local battlefield (military necessity) and when it comes to the strategic decisions made by presidents (such as ending the war quickly via atomic weapons), the lives of these individual men in uniform matter. Their lives matter as citizens, the backbone of democracy. Just war thinking needs to develop a more sophisticated approach to the worth of average soldiers when considering how to balance troop protection and military necessity with discrimination and proportionality. Some of these issues were raised earlier in this book in considering presidential responsibility during World War II to protect the troops and bring war to conclusion, as well as society's responsibility to the wounded, orphans, and veterans after the Vietnam War. In the democratic twenty-first century, we need more sophisticated consideration not just of the duties, but also of the rights, of our service personnel and the claims they should be able to make on their political leaders regarding their security. We also need thoughtful consideration about what we expect from civilian leaders when it comes to making decisions about sending soldiers, even if they are volunteers, into harm's way. Armed humanitarian intervention is a case in point: volunteers sign up to defend their own country and its national interests. Most do not think they are giving Turtle Bay *carte blanche* to send them into harm's way in Somalia, Rwanda, Bosnia, East Timor, Congo, and other dangerous places. In sum, we need more just war thinking on various aspects of citizenship and warfare.

Just war and democracy

Just war thinking predates contemporary forms of representative government by centuries. The political milieu of the original Roman and later scholastic just war theorists was hierarchical and monarchical. Thus, *jus ad bellum* considerations were the domain of a single sovereign, in practice a king and his advisors. *Jus in bello* norms were also the domain of an exclusive group in the feudal and early modern eras. In the age of chivalry, knights had a code of fair play to which they subscribed in battle. Often the average foot soldier was in actuality a tenant farmer or townsman recruited for a short time to battle on behalf of his lord or to protect the village. They had no training on the laws of war or the chivalric code. In sum, *jus ad bellum* and *jus in bello* considerations were largely the writ of elites for centuries.

The past two centuries have seen numerous innovations in the structure and behavior of Western polities. Perhaps the most important developments that affect this discussion are the rise of the mass army and the accompanying mobilization of the entire nation for total war, as well as the simultaneous introduction of mass politics in the form of parliamentary and presidential forms of republican government.[15] Thus, one should ask how just war thinking—a doctrine from another historical era—interacts with representative government.[16]

Democracy and public opinion

Is democracy equipped to handle the reflective nature of just war thinking? The answer may be "no." Democracy-in-practice today has several shortcomings which may weaken its ability to engage in the moral discourse necessary for just war thinking. The first and most obvious failing is the nature of public opinion itself. Oliver O'Donovan suggests, "The opinionated public constitutes a positive obstacle to deliberation about the praxis of judgment."[17] Republics are structured so that politicians must respond to public opinion in some measure or they will no longer have a job. Recent history provides us with many examples of politicians who charted a course that they felt was dictated by public opinion but was not necessarily in the national interest nor attuned to justice.

Unfortunately, popular democratic theory trumpets "majority rule" without appreciating how often majorities, or mobs, get it wrong. In other words, public opinion is not necessarily virtuous simply because it represents the will of the majority. Although public opinion may be wise and moral, when it comes to foreign and military policy it is just as likely to be misinformed, uninformed, or wrong—not to mention cowardly or malicious. As de Tocqueville noted almost two centuries ago, it is possible that public opinion represents something far from the best in the citizenry because it may reflect the lowest common denominator—what we can all agree upon or what the polls say a plurality can live with.[18]

Public opinion is complex and often not the best guide to policy, but it is the very heart of contemporary representative government.[19] Public opinion in the American South goaded the country to civil war, and war "fever" was responsible in large part for the early revolutionary wars of France, the Spanish–American War, and World War I. Public opinion has supported questionable means such as the internment of Japanese-Americans, and supported the war effort in Vietnam well into the early 1970s, but the American public was against helping the Poles, British, and French in 1939–1940 and opposed intervention in Korea a decade later. However, more often than not it seems that a characteristic of democracy is deliberate stupor when confronted with legitimate opportunities for the use of force. For example, Neville Chamberlain's appeasement of Hitler was dictated by the public's unwillingness to confront the Nazi threat. The reluctance of the Roosevelt administration to engage in the wars in Europe and Asia was likewise caused by overreliance on public opinion.[20]

At times the unwillingness to act is a direct contravention of the principle of responsibility adumbrated earlier in this work. This is not to say that the U.S. should or should not have engaged its military in specific instances like Bosnia, Somalia, Rwanda, or elsewhere. Rather, the question is a more subtle one: was the decision to use force (Haiti, Iraq) or not use force (Rwanda, North Korea) based on clear considerations of the responsibilities of the U.S. government to defend and enhance the security of its public and the international system? Can uninterested public opinion be counted on to provide ethical guidance about the appropriate means to counter insecurity and genocide, even if it means a massive introduction of foreign troops, martial law, and robust rules of engagement including "shoot to kill" authorization? A real discussion of responsibility is where contemporary just war thinking should begin, and such analysis should be applied on a case-by-case basis to the real conflicts of the world today. The decision might be to employ force, or it might be to not engage the military. Regardless of the ultimate decision, the obvious dilemma of public-opinion-based foreign policies is that they may result in inaction that is detrimental to promoting security and preserving human life.

In sum, public opinion can be too militaristic, dragging its leaders into total wars without regard for the wisdom or virtue of conflict. Or, public opinion can drag its feet resulting in temerity and inaction. Majoritarian politics are not necessarily moral politics. What makes the moral content of applying public opinion to such questions even more problematic is that contemporary publics are increasingly unlikely to share a common moral basis, making it a doubly problematic foundation from which to derive policies about life and death.

Moral pluralism

The increasing import of public opinion is not simply a structural component of representative governance, nor is it just a political reality in the calculus of those campaigning for public office. There is a deeper philosophical trend, a democratization of values, apparent in Western society as well. One author has pointed to some of the symptoms of what he calls "radical individualism" ("Don't tell me what to do!") and "radical egalitarianism" ("No one is better than me!").[21] This results in a loss of hierarchies, of shared meaning, and of collective truth because no one's ideas are superior to my own. The Left has noticed this and criticizes the lack of moral restraint of individuals in the marketplace; the Right has likewise observed this trend and condemns the lack of moral restraint in Hollywood.

This heterodoxy of values is symptomatic of the normative pluralism associated with ethical relativism and postmodernity. The key feature of these trends is moral pluralism: the loss of or emancipation from (depending on one's point of view) a single, shared basis for morality within Western culture. Postmodernity is the notion that the rationalist and universalistic paradigm associated with the Enlightenment and its antecedents is best understood as simply one narrative of human experience among many. The postmodern project is to strip all meta-narratives—the accepted ways of viewing the world—of their emperor's clothing and reveal how such discourses are really myths designed to protect the power of some and disenfranchise others. Consequently, any statement of universal morality, such as those associated with Christianity, the natural law tradition, and Western civilization, is anathema to postmodern intelligentsia.

It is possible that there are positive features to the postmodern critique. For instance, it may shine a light on past abuses and lack of toleration in Western society. It may also help us develop a sense of humility with regard to the contributions and values of non-Western civilizations.

That being said, humility and introspection are not a sufficient basis for developing a political ethic of responsibility or for evaluating the just application of military force. In theory, the moral pluralism of postmodernity asserts that the values of each tribe may be useful within their context, but that there are no universal moral norms. Furthermore, in practice postmodernism advocates an ethical relativism which robs society of the moral tools necessary for reflection, restraint, and the pursuit of security and justice.

How can a postmodern public debate *jus ad bellum*? Is there a moral basis for a postmodern *jus in bello*? It is beyond the scope of this work to offer an in-depth critique of the ethical relativism explicit in postmodernism, but suffice it to say that such a view is diametrically opposed to the value system of traditional and contemporary just war thinking. Historical just war theory was tied to a religious understanding of the structure of the world order: the value of politics, the need for political authorities to fight evil and punish evil-doers, the right of self-defense, the legitimate justice of some causes, and a useful moral order that could distinguish between unfortunate but lawful warfare and cold-blooded murder.

Contemporary just war thinking in any of its forms, sacred or secular, has an explicit moral position—it values human life and international security. The tenets of just war thinking privilege human life and the conditions which make for moral living in society.

In contrast, the postmodern relativism popular in the academy and some of the press for the past thirty years provides no basis, other than perhaps mob rule or elite guidance, for a comprehensive understanding of justice and consistent policies dedicated to the preservation of human life and international security. Unfortunately, as Western civilization succumbs to the meaninglessness of postmodern philosophy, it erodes the foundations for thinking about justice and war.

Just war thinking's progeny, international law and the war convention, are entirely secular in nature. Nonetheless, postmodernism challenges even the secular legal paradigm regarding justice and war. First, international law is based in part on a set of historical and philosophical assumptions that predate contemporary post-modernity. The state system and legal authority, the notion of sovereignty and non-intervention, the war convention which grants or observes legal rights to enemy combatants even when they are from a different civilization—these are ideas based on Western philosophical notions of the rule of law, authority, and the value of individual human life. One has to wonder how postmodernism's project to deconstruct political life, theoretically and practically, complements the existing state system. Indeed, the deconstructionist project may be a threat to the norms of Western international politics.

Of course, one could make the positivist case that contemporary international law is simply the sum of agreements signed among states such as laws, treaties, and conventions. This strips the law of nations of its normative and historical context and allows us to entertain the postmodern project of deconstructing such covenants in order to display the power relations inherent in them. It is unclear what practical political value such efforts would have, and even then the questions remain: on what basis is law created? What should be the philosophical foundation for considerations of human life, conflict, and war? Indeed, what is the postmodern rationale for protecting individual human life anyway?

Postmodernism renders a potent challenge to just war thinking. Postmodernism is skeptical of ethical norms, is ambivalent about a philosophical basis for right and wrong, and disdains the claims of universal morality. It lacks any rationale for restraint in war—it does not have a moral organizing center like Augustine's *caritas*, Aquinas' justice, Grotius' customary law, Elshtain's "equal regard," or this work's focus on responsibility and security. Moreover, without universal values of some sort the normative content of the American Declaration of Independence, the French Declaration of the Rights of Man, and the Universal Declaration of Human Rights are meaningless, as are all attempts at mitigating war for moral reasons based on distaste for destruction and regard for human life.

In sum, proponents of just war thinking must engage the postmodern challenge in the twenty-first century. Just war thinking must demonstrate not only its utility in real-world politics, but also the superiority of its philosophical foundations in comparison with the deconstructionist and relativistic claims of postmodernism. This is a debate that is happening at a practical level in international politics. The trial of Slobodan Milosevic before the International Criminal Tribunal for Yugoslavia was such an exercise. Milosevic represented the postmodern position: he challenged the very existence and authority of the court as well as any universal standards of accountability to which he was responsible. It was not surprising that same charges of victor's justice and ethical relativism were made in the trial of Iraqi dictator Saddam Hussein.

However, the other arena of conflict between the claims of justice and post-modernism is in the academy. Just war thinkers must assert their case for just war thinking before the university elites of the Western world and persuade future generations that the philosophy which sees claims of order and justice as universal is superior to the relativism of postmodernism.

Just war thinking and the changing international system

One of just war thinking's greatest achievements is to be adaptable enough to wea-ther the changes in international life. This flexibility is challenged today by the evo-lution of domestic and international political systems. The issue of *right authority* in traditional just war theory is the most problematic criterion, as forms of governance change. The *responsibility* emphasized in this work shares many of the features of right authority and is likewise affected by changes in the structure of international politics.

Historical just war doctrine located authority in a single person. That person was sovereign in his or her realm and made the ultimate decisions about war and peace. During the medieval period that person existed in the web of social obligations characteristic of feudalism, but nonetheless was the final authority when it came to decisions about the use of force. With the rise of the "new monarchies" in the early modern period the sovereign individual became inextricably linked to the state, hence Louis XIV's famous "l'etat c'est moi."[22] In the nineteenth century the state began to de-link itself from an individual monarch by instituting constitutional provisions and national parliaments, but again the seat of sovereignty remained in the state. Interestingly, the doctrine of democracy is a radical departure from such views of sovereignty, because in its classical form sovereignty rests in the people and is delegated to the state. Nevertheless, in the practice of twentieth-century inter-national politics states remained the preeminent sovereign actors in world politics.

We may be at a new crossroads in international affairs that problematizes the notions of authority and responsibility when it comes to war. The "democratiza-tion" of firepower to non-state actors, the rise of military humanitarian interven-tion in failing states, and the increasing respect accorded supranational institutions, notably the United Nations, bespeak a changing world. In this world the notion of political responsibility at the heart of any discussion of justice and war is fluid.

On the one hand, international life now has units smaller than states utilizing the weapons once reserved for government arsenals in their assault on states. This is true of guerrilla and insurgent campaigns, drug cartels, and private security firms, as well as legitimate revolutionary movements. When it comes to the question of authority there is little disagreement that in general these types of movements are illegitimate and have no proper authority. In other words, the perpetrators of violence via terrorism or insurgency such as Colombia's drug cartels, Afghanistan's rural warlords, Iraqi Sunni suicide bombers, or the shock troops of al Qaeda and Hezbollah have no legitimacy, no real political authority, and no responsibility for or to their intended constituencies. Hence their reliance on terror rather than the voting booth.

Although many developing states find their sovereignty challenged by sub-state movements, just war thinking's larger focus on state responsibility faces little challenge from sub-state movements because the illegitimacy of such groups and their methods actually reifies the sovereign state system. On the other hand, it is the augmentation of authority at the supranational level that most challenges just war thinking today. Numerous dilemmas suggest themselves, such as: when states fail and other states intervene via supranational agencies, who is morally responsible? When states fail and their neighbors refuse to intervene, who is morally responsible? When states turn to international agencies, notably the UN, NATO, or the African Union (AU), to act where individual states have refused to act, who is morally responsible?

The UN is the most interesting case because it is not a politico-military alliance like NATO. In theory it is an agency at the mercy of states, because in theory it derives its authority from the authority delegated to it by states. But the UN is more than the sum of its parts. It has established programs such as UNICEF and UNESCO and thousands of employees spread around the world. The UN is an enduring institution that has outlived many countries (e.g. Zaire, the Soviet Union, Yugoslavia, Rhodesia) and has taken on a life of its own. Many states cannot challenge its power, at least not if they are poor, backward, and not members of the Security Council.

Numerous contemporary just war quasi-pacifists no longer trust individual states to make the decision to go to war. The most famous recent case, that of the U.S. invasion of Iraq, is telling in the just war debates that surrounded the six months of controversy leading to armed conflict in March 2003. Many critics misused the just war tenet of *right authority* by claiming that only the UN has the authority to declare war in the twenty-first century.

This argument is novel. It claims that states are no longer ultimately responsible for international security and that such authority resides in the UN. This is not simply a practical political argument: it is one with moral content. The idea that a supranational entity, the harbinger of a world government, should be the guarantor of world peace is not new—plans for "perpetual peace" and world government are old hat. But it foreshadows a radical shift in sovereignty away from states to centralized governance.

The questions multiply. If the UN is the only legitimate forum for deciding to utilize force, then is it the sole sovereign authority in international relations? How does one implement *jus ad bellum* at the Security Council, or worse, at the General Assembly? Should UN constituents have voted on each criterion to determine whether or not to halt Saddam Hussein's advance into Kuwait? What of the *jus in bello* criteria? Who is responsible for the behavior of UN blue helmets? Currently it is up to individual states to train their troops and loan them to the UN. Is the UN morally accountable for the misdeeds of its peacekeepers, such as the rapes of African women by African blue helmets under UN auspices? UN Secretariats are notorious for dodging any question of responsibility for the actions of their functionaries and family members. Can we realistically expect more in the context of war?

Just war by committee is likely to achieve little that is just or effective in fighting wars, punishing evil-doers, and halting aggression. Indeed, a problem shared by the EU, the African Union, and the UN is the tendency toward inaction when action is called for. The hallmark of such collectives is dithering when responsible action is required. Why is this the case? Supranational organizations, especially the UN, tend to require consensus among members to act. Because the UN is not a unified whole with a single set of interests, it is often paralyzed because its constituents cannot agree on action. This is certainly the case for any of the murderous wars of the 1990s in Europe, Asia, and Africa. If military humanitarian intervention did finally occur, it was generally undermanned and poorly supported. This raises the question of whether states can pawn off their responsibility for security onto international organizations.

A second, deeper flaw of supranational organizations serving as the twenty-first-century locus of responsibility for international security is their inability to make right distinctions. This is especially true of the UN. The first rule of the UN is that all states are equal and, except in extreme cases, sovereignty and non-intervention are inviolable rights. It certainly seems absurd that tiny Equatorial Guinea has a vote in the General Assembly but that the world's seventh-largest economy, California, does not. It is absurd that authoritarian regimes like Angola and the Democratic Republic of Congo sit on the UN Human Rights Commission (their terms end in 2020). In short, the UN is simply not representative of the realities of global politics today due to its very constitution.

This moral confusion results in the UN refusing to take sides in a given conflict. This has been a boon to dictators, thugs, and murderers particularly in the age of genocide. The UN's position consistently is to not take sides in an interstate war but to treat with the "legitimate" representatives of all sides in the conflict. This effort at neutral arbitration emasculates the UN as a real force for security and justice. Moreover, the statist nature of the UN often predisposes it to value the reigning government in intrastate conflicts, regardless of its actual legitimacy or the cruelty of its policies, rather than the popular representatives of challengers. If the UN does engage both sides in peace talks to end a long-term civil war, or deals with multiple governments in an interstate war, its policy is to deal with each equally, not casting blame or aspersions on any party. In sum, just war thinking emphasizes the responsibility of states to protect their populaces first and then promote international security outside their borders. In contrast, the UN does not have the inherent resources to meet the demands of international security.

Conclusion

Just war thinking is not a dying art. We live in a complex, dangerous world that needs moral leadership and moral action, galvanized by intellectuals, citizens, and public servants who ask tough questions about the ethics of employing force. The changing nature of our institutions, legal systems, and threats suggests many opportunities for just war scholarship in the days ahead. When we look back on many of the security judgments made by the U.S. in the past three centuries, we can see the import of moral reasoning in decisions to go to war and decisions about how force is used. Part of the American way of war is this emphasis on moral interrogation of just cause and right intention when it comes to a specific conflict. This is in our very DNA as citizens, because our Founding Fathers provided such an example before resolving to defend themselves against British, and mercenary, forces. This is not exclusive to the U.S., and we see similar arguments made in Western capitals due to our shared philosophical and historical roots. But the wellspring of just war thinking must be applied, and refreshed, by each generation as it meets the security challenges of its own time and place.

Notes

1 Max Boot, "The New American Way of War," *Foreign Affairs* (July/August 2003), available at: www.foreignaffairs.com/articles/united-states/2003-07-01/new-american-way-war. The *magnum opus* of this tradition is Russell Weigley's *The American Way of War: A History of United States Military and Policy* (New York: Macmillan, 1973).

2 See MacGregor Knox and Williamson Murray, *The Dynamics of Military Revolution: 1300–2050* (New York: Cambridge University Press, 2001); Williamson Murray and Allan Millett, *Military Innovation in the Interwar Period* (New York: Cambridge University Press, 1996); Colin Gray, *Strategy for Chaos: Revolutions in Military Affairs and the Evidence of History* (London: Frank Cass, 2002); Frederick Kagan, *Finding the Target: The Transformation of American Military Policy* (New York: Encounter Books, 2006).

3 See the memoir by James Blunt and subsequent new stories, including. "How James Blunt saved us from World War 3," *The Independent* (November 15, 2010), available at: www.independent.co.uk/news/people/news/how-james-blunt-saved-us-from-world-war-3-2134203.html.

4 The International Commission on Intervention and State Sovereignty, *The Responsibility to Protect* (2004), p. 43.

5 Ibid., p. 42.

6 Daniel Kemaric and Abel Escribà-Folch, "Where Do Ousted Dictators Go? Fewer Countries Now Offer a Warm Welcome," *The Washington Post* (January 30, 3017), available at: www.washingtonpost.com/news/monkey-cage/wp/2017/01/30/where-do-ousted-dictators-go-fewer-countries-now-offer-a-warm-welcome/?utm_term=.837955d2502b.

7 Interview with Lisa Sowles Cahill, Boston College ethicist, *US Catholic* (December 2001), available at www.uscatholic.org/2001/12/cov0112.htm.

8 "Why the Navy Abandoned Its Latest Slogan," NPR: *All Things Considered* (June 13, 2015), available at: www.npr.org/2015/06/13/414239773/why-the-navy-abandoned-its-latest-slogan.

9 At the same time, the Libyans desperately wanted out from under draconian sanctions and finally provided compensation, due to strong U.S. and British pressure, to families victimized by the downing of Pan Am 103.

10 Eric Patterson, *Just War Thinking: Morality and Pragmatism in the Struggle against Contemporary Threats* (Lanham, MD: Lexington Books, 2007), p. 42.

11 See for instance Michael Gross, *Soft War: The Ethics of Unarmed Conflict* (Cambridge: Cambridge University Press, 2017), and Mary Manjikian, *Cybersecurity Ethics: An Introduction* (New York: Routledge, 2017).

12 Isaac Asimov's Three Laws of Robotics have had wide-ranging impact in discussions of robotics and AI beyond their original statements in his science fiction books. They are: (1) A robot may not injure a human being or, through inaction, allow a human being to come to harm. (2) A robot must obey orders given it by human beings except where such orders would conflict with the First Law. (3) A robot must protect its own existence as long as such protection does not conflict with the First or Second Law. The Skynet reference is to the *Terminator* movie franchise.

13 Col. Phillip S. Meilinger, ed., *The Evolution of Airpower Theory* (Maxwell Air Force Base, AL: Air University Press, 1997).

14 Articles 14–16 of Lieber's Code deal with military necessity.

15 An interesting introduction to norms of civilized warfare among the first standing armies of modern Europe is Robert A. Kann, "The Law of Nations and the Conduct of War in the Early Times of the Standing Army," *The Journal of Politics*, vol. 6, no. 1 (February 1944).

16 "Democracy" is used here to mean forms of contemporary representative government such as those we have in the West. At a minimum, democracy in practice today is characterized by two things. The first is free, fair, and contested *elections* which provide the opportunity for citizens to have a voice in the direction of their country and the circulation of elites. The second is the rule of law, most notably the enshrinement of individual *civil liberties* including freedoms of speech, press, assembly, worship, and so forth. No country meets the minimum qualifications of democracy without some form of elections and the protection of individual civil liberties by law.

17 Oliver O'Donovan, *The Just War Revisited* (Cambridge: Cambridge University Press, 2003), p. 17.

18 Reinhold Niebuhr understood the difference between the morality of individuals and the character of collectives. In his famous *Moral Man and Immoral Society* (Chicago: Scribner's, 1934), he asserted that individuals may choose altruistic behavior at times in accord with the best aspirations of the human race. Individuals may act selflessly to provide services and benefits to others even if it is not in the benefactor's best "interest." However, Niebuhr observed that this was generally not true of collectives. Instead, he argued that societies, whether democratic or not, usually fail to live up to idealistic expectations because they act on the collective impulses of the majority in ways that protect and promote the interests of what sociologists would call the "in-group" in competition with other societies.

19 Democratic peace theorists argue that the reluctance of democracies to go to war is a good thing and exactly why the spread of democracy around the globe is imperative. The expansive form of democratic peace theory (DPT) suggests that democracies are more pacific than other types of regimes. In its more limited form, DPT asserts that

democracies are unlikely to go to war against one another and therefore herald an era of democratic peace. Why is this the case? DPT advocates suggest two major lines of reasoning. The first has to do with political structure. The structure of democratic government is slow and conflictual. It takes time for citizens and public officials to debate the merits of using force, and it often takes considerable effort for the government to be in the position to act. A second school of DPT suggests that democratic culture deserves the credit for the absence of war between democracies in the twentieth century. Democracies are characterized by openness, tolerance, the opportunity for debate, and peaceful conflict resolution. DPT argues that these traits characterize not only domestic politics but also the interactions between democratic governments. In other words, it is the nature of democracy to resolve conflict peacefully, both at home and abroad. However, it is unclear what role DPT has when it comes to the need for decisive action, such as to stand up to Hitler or live up to commitments under the Genocide Convention.

20 Kathleen M. McGraw provides a very different analysis—politicians use moral justifications to shape public perception and opinion on some issues. The dilemma is the near impossibility of discerning veritable versus deceitful moral justifications by leaders. "Manipulating Public Opinion with Moral Justification," *Annals of the American Academy of Political and Social Science*, vol. 560, "The Future of Fact," (November 1998).

21 Robert Bork, *Slouching toward Gomorrah: Modern Liberalism and American Decline* (New York: Reganbooks, 1996).

22 "I am the state" or, better, "The state is me."

SELECT BIBLIOGRAPHY

Aquinas, Thomas. *On Law, Morality, and Politics*, ed. William P. Baumgarth and Richard J. Regan (Indianapolis, IN: Hackett, 1988).

Aristotle. *The Nicomachean Ethics*, trans. David Ross (Oxford: Oxford University Press, 1980).

Aristotle. *Politics*, trans. Benjamin Jowett (Chicago: University of Chicago Press, 1984).

Augustine. *The City of God*, ed. David Knowles (New York: Penguin Classics, 1984).

Bainton, Roland. *Christian Attitudes toward War and Peace* (New York: Abingdon, 1960).

Biggar, Nigel. *Burying the Past: Making Peace and Doing Justice after Civil Conflict* (Washington D.C.: Georgetown University Press, 2003).

Biggar, Nigel. *In Defence of War* (Oxford: Oxford University Press, 2013).

Burleigh, Michael. *Moral Combat: Good and Evil in World War II* (New York: HarperCollins Publishers, 2011).

Caldwell, Dan, and Williams, Robert, Jr. *Seeking Security in an Insecure World* (Oxford: Rowman & Littlefield, 2006).

Charles, J. Daryl. *Between Pacifism and Jihad: The Christian and the Just War* (Colorado Springs, CO: Intervarsity Press, 2005).

Charles, J. Daryl. "Presumption against War or Presumption against Injustice? The Just War Tradition Reconsidered," *Journal of Church and State*, vol. 48, no. 3 (2005).

Charles, J. Daryl, and Demy, Timothy J. *War, Peace, and Christianity: Questions and Answers from a Just-War Perspective* (Wheaton, IL: Crossway Publishing, 2010).

Clausewitz, Carl von. *On War*, ed. Michael Howard and Peter Paret (Princeton, NJ: Princeton University Press, 1976; first ed. 1832).

Cook, Martin L. "The Role of the Military in the Decision to Use Armed Force." In *The Ashgate Research Companion to Military Ethics*, ed. James Turner Johnson and Eric D. Patterson (Burlington, VT: Ashgate Publishing Company, 2016).

Elshtain, Jean Bethke. *Augustine and the Limits of Politics* (South Bend, IN: University of Notre Dame Press, 1993).

Elshtain, Jean Bethke. *Just War against Terror* (New York: Basic Books, 2003).

Elshtain, Jean Bethke, ed. *Just War Theory* (New York: New York University Press, 1992).

Grotius, Hugo. *The Rights of War and Peace*, ed. Richard Tuck (Oxford: Oxford University Press, 2001).

Hillenbrand, Laura. *Unbroken: A World War II Story of Survival, Resilience, and Redemption* (New York: Random House, 2010).

Hobbes, Thomas. *Leviathan*, ed. Richard Tuck (New York: Penguin Classics, 1982).

Johnson, James Turner. *Morality and Contemporary Warfare* (New Haven, CT: Yale University Press, 1999).

Johnson, James Turner, and Patterson, Eric D., eds. *The Ashgate Research Companion to Military Ethics* (Burlington, VT: Ashgate Publishing Company, 2016).

Miller, Frances Trevelyan. *History of World War II* (Philadelphia: Universal Book and Bible House, 1945).

O'Donovan, Oliver. *In Pursuit of a Christian View of War*. Grove Booklet on Ethics No. 15 (Cambridge: Grove Books Publishing, 1995).

O'Donovan, Oliver. *The Just War Revisited* (Cambridge: Cambridge University Press, 2003).

Orend, Brian. *War and International Justice* (Ontario: Wilfred Laurier University Press, 2000).

Patterson, Eric. *Ending Wars Well: Order, Justice, and Conciliation in Contemporary Post-Conflict* (New Haven, CT: Yale University Press, 2012).

Patterson, Eric. *Just War Thinking: Morality and Pragmatism in the Struggle against Contemporary Threats* (Lanham, MD: Lexington Books, 2007).

Patterson, Eric, ed. *Ethics beyond War's End* (Washington, DC: Georgetown University Press, 2012).

Ramsey, Paul. *The Just War: Force and Political Responsibility*, rev. ed. (Lanham, MD: Rowman & Littlefield, 2002).

Ramsey, Paul. *War and the Christian Conscience/How Shall Modern War Be Conducted Justly?* (Durham, NC: Duke University Press, 1961, 1985).

Rodin, David, and Shue, Henry. *Just and Unjust Warriors: The Moral and Legal Status of Soldiers* (New York: Oxford University Press, 2008).

Russell, Frederick H. *The Just War in the Middle Ages* (Cambridge: Cambridge University Press, 1975).

Scott, James B. *The Spanish Origins of International Law: Lectures of Francisco de Vitoria (1480–1546) and Francisco Suarez (1548–1617)* (Washington, DC: Georgetown University Press, 1929).

Vitoria, Francisco de. "On the Law of War." In Political Writings, ed. Anthony Pagden and Jeremy Lawrance (Cambridge: Cambridge University Press, 1991; first ed. 1557).

Vitoria, Francisco de. *De Indis et de Iure Belli Reflectiones*, ed. Ernest Nys, trans. J.P. Bate (New York: Oceana/Wildy and Sons, 1964).

Walzer, Michael. *Just and Unjust Wars*, third ed. (New York: Basic Books, 2000).

INDEX